"A concrete and visionary book . . . wonderfully practical, lays down goals and guidelines, offers examples and warns of obstacles."

—*Publishers Weekly*

"A joy to read! George Wood takes us right along with him into schools that have a lot to teach all Americans. His discoveries suggest a coherent yet dynamic philosophy of education, as well as a wealth of practical steps."

—Frances Moore Lappe, co-founder, Institute for the Arts of Democracy

"Wood's book will encourage those concerned about future generations to feel that solutions to our declining schools can be found and that the means are within our grasp."

—*Modern Maturity*

GEORGE H. WOOD, Ph.D., is a founding member of the Institute for Democracy in Education at Ohio University and a professor of Education at Ohio University. He is married and has two sons.

SCHOOLS THAT WORK

America's
Most
Innovative
Public
Education
Programs

George H. Wood, Ph.D.

A PLUME BOOK

PLUME
Published by the Penguin Group
Penguin Books USA Inc., 375 Hudson Street,
New York, New York 10014, U.S.A.
Penguin Books Ltd, 27 Wrights Lane,
London W8 5TZ, England
Penguin Books Australia Ltd, Ringwood,
Victoria, Australia
Penguin Books Canada Ltd, 10 Alcorn Avenue,
Toronto, Ontario, Canada M4V 3B2
Penguin Books (N.Z.) Ltd, 182–190 Wairau Road,
Auckland 10, New Zealand

Penguin Books Ltd, Registered Offices:
Harmondsworth, Middlesex, England

Published by Plume, an imprint of New American Library, a division of
Penguin Books USA Inc. Previously published in a Dutton edition.

First Plume Printing, April, 1993
10 9 8 7 6 5 4 3 2 1

Ⓟ REGISTERED TRADEMARK—MARCA REGISTRADA

LIBRARY OF CONGRESS CATALOGING-IN-PUBLICATION DATA
Wood, George H.
   Schools that work : America's most innovative public education
programs / George H. Wood.
         p.   cm.
   Includes bibliographical references and index.
   ISBN 0-452-26959-8
   1. Public schools—United States.   2. Educational change—United
States.   I. Title.
[LA217.2.W66   1993]
371'.00973—dc20   92-35766
                                                       CIP

Original hardcover design by Eve L. Kirch
Printed in the United States of America

For the members of the Institute for Democracy in Education
and the thousands of other educators who make a difference
in the daily lives of America's children

Contents

Acknowledgments

In the following pages you will meet some of the most extraordinary educators in the United States today. Through the five years that it has taken to pull this book together, I have relied on them for more than just the chance to observe their schools. I have also benefitted from their advice, their insights into what is important and what is not, and often from a warm meal and comfortable bed in their homes. I do not have the space to name all of them; and besides, you will meet them soon enough. But every single one is a hero in my mind and in the lives of the students with whom they work every day. First and foremost, credit must go to them for making this book possible.

In each location, particular individuals went out of their way to make sure my work succeeded. In Athens County, Ohio, Joette Weber, Joyce Hannenberg, Charlotte Newman, Mick Cummings, Marcia Burchby, and Bill Elasky were not only willing to be part of this study but allowed me to practice on them first. Before I went further afield, I started with this group of teachers, close to home, in order to learn how to observe in a classroom without getting in the way. Fortunately for me, they wanted me in the way and helped me learn to work with their students while taking notes, always suggesting some activity that would not allow me to sit quietly in the corner. Their principals, Clyde Jarvis at Chauncey Elementary and Cindy Hartman at Amesville Elementary, were willing to cooperate by giving me the free run of each school, and I am grateful to them for making me feel welcome.

In Chicago I have to thank my good friend Bill Ayers for putting me in touch with Dick Streedain at Hubbard Woods Elementary. Dick and his wife Ann Shimojima were always willing hosts, and a meal there was almost like being back at home. While in Chicago, I also made my home with John and Pat Duffy, along with all five of their kids. For as long as I live, I'll be telling the story of how John and the kids, led by Timmy (age four at the time), went searching for me the night I lost my way getting off of the El.

In Wisconsin, Bob Peterson was my contact and guide. No matter how busy he was, no matter what the latest emergency seemed to be, he always had time for yet another question. I am sure I often tried his patience, but he never let it show. My sister-in-law, Kathleen Burchby, her husband Dennis Christensen, and friends Jim, Sally, Erin, and Ryan Gorman were my hosts in Milwaukee, and were reliable sources of information on the evolving politics of education in that city.

Heather Lewis with the Center for Collaborative Education coordinated all my visits to Central Park East Secondary School in New York. With dozens of other concerns demanding her attention, including her own election to a community board of education, she never forgot that I was coming, or to pick up an extra coffee for me from the deli across the street. And, as with so many others, Debbie Meier found a spare bed in her house for me and taught me how to order New York carry-out from a maze of menus.

Up in New Hampshire, Don Weisberger took me, a total stranger, in tow, allowing me to spend a week in his home while I visited Thayer Junior and Senior High School. Dennis Littky was similarly hospitable, although I'm not sure I want to spend too much more time living without running water or electricity. I have a standing invitation to return to his cabin on the mountain, but I'll wait for a few more modern conveniences.

Margie Bennett, who has since left the Foxfire staff, was my first contact with the folks in Rabun Gap. She found me waiting for a contact that had forgotten I was coming and immediately put me up in her home. Her openness and trust symbolized all that the Foxfire program stands for. Since her departure, Hilton Smith has kept me in close contact with all that goes on in those Georgia hills, and Joyce Colburn takes care of all the logistical arrangements for each visit.

All of these visits were made possible by the generous support of the Ohio University College of Education. My colleagues supported this effort, read drafts of this work, and were willing to excuse my absences from faculty meetings for the year I was on sabbatical in order to visit these schools. Without this support, both financial and intellectual, I would not have been able to complete this work.

After the writing was done, I was to find out how hard it is to sell a book on what is good about American schools. Two people, however, never gave up and kept my spirits high throughout the process of finding a suitable publisher. My agent, Denise Marcil, not only taught me the ins and outs of the publishing world, but kept me from ever losing faith that we would find a publisher. Her assistant, Jane Penn, held my hand over the phone, promised me she really liked the book, and let me know that every author gets rejected on occasion.

Once the book went to Dutton I was fortunate to end up in the hands of Alexia Dorsyzinski. She is everything an author hopes for in an editor, someone who convinces you that every change she wants you to make was really your idea in the first place.

My writing is also better for the careful attention it received from Sandra Hoyt. More than a typist, she was an insightful critic with an eye for trite phrases, misused words, and my multiple grammatical errors. Her patience under pressure made all the difference.

Since this book is about good teaching, I should note that I've had my share of good teachers as well. It began with my mother, Eldora Wood, who gave up teaching in a one room schoolhouse in Iowa to teach my brothers and sisters and myself about patience, justice, compassion, and truth. These vital lessons were followed up by Bill Geer, a professor at the University of North Carolina who opened my young eyes to new worlds, just by asking the right questions—I've not been the same since. Then there was Pearl Johnson, my first department chairperson at Lake Orion Junior High School, and her husband Bill. They both gently reminded me that I was, after all, a first-year teacher who was expected to make mistakes and *learn* from them. Mike Woods picked up where Pearl left off, helping me to learn the power of a good question, and the importance of suspending judgment. Somewhere in all this figures in my father, Fred, who didn't live long enough to see my work in print, but did make sure I never forgot the value of hard work at every task.

Finally, there is no denying the price that my family had to pay for this project to be carried out. My wife, Marcia, had to juggle a teaching career and the raising of two children by herself while I was on the road. And my sons, Michael and John, didn't see much of their father for weeks at a time. When I was finally home, they often wished I would leave again, because putting all that I had learned into print proved to be a trying and difficult task. I can only hope that now that they see this in print, they are half as proud of me as I am of them.

Introduction:
Can We Have Schools
That Work?

There are schools and classrooms in the United States today that you know are special the moment you step into them. The first clues are visual. It might be that the halls are full of student projects and art work, covering what are usually drab, industrial-strength green cinder blocks. Or it might be the absence of posted rules carefully outlining what one can or cannot do. Then there are the materials—not merely textbooks—that spill out of every corner of the building. Primary classrooms brimming with children's books, blocks, string, cardboard scraps, plants, animals, rocks, paints, and assorted theater props; for older children, hands-on equipment such as tape-recorders, cameras, science apparatus, novels, charts and graphs, and objects of art.

Walk down the halls and notice the physical set-up of these rooms. It's hard to find one with desks lined up in straight rows, presided over by a lectern and a chalkboard full of notes. Instead, desks, or just as likely tables, are arranged in small groups throughout the room. Work spaces for different tasks have been created, with an easy chair or two for reading, a table with materials for writing, a darkroom built in a spare corner, or just plain open space for gatherings.

There is a delightful sense of purposeful clutter to these class-rooms and schools. They are places to do things in, not places to sit and watch. Real work goes on here, and real products (not end-less streams of blue dittos) go home.

Then there are the individuals who populate the building. First you notice the kids. Moments after you enter the school they want you to know this is someplace special. One child takes you by the hand to show you her painting on the wall. Another offers to read to you from his journal. A high school boy, decked out in a T-shirt proclaiming his favorite heavy metal band, shares an interview he's just finished with an eighty-year-old bluegrass musician. First graders offer to read you a book, and they bring their favorite, the one they just wrote and illustrated as a class project. A shy sixteen-year-old explains her science project, which involves an inventory of plant and animal species in the forest next to the school. Her not-so-shy friend then whisks you out the door so you can see for yourself the rare specimen they found the day before.

And the teachers. They have never met a stranger. You seldom need an appointment to visit; they are happy to have you join in. They are so proud of their students, so enamored with learning, so happy to be there that you catch yourself wanting to sign up for the next term. Listen to them talk about their charges, as they demonstrate an understanding of their students' personal as well as intellectual needs. They also know the value of hooking the stu-dents, of making the subject real, of giving kids a reason to learn. A child rarely asks these teachers, "why do we have to know this?" because virtually everything they learn relates to a real job at hand. These teachers are folks with a mission, of which each child is a part.

No closed-door office manager principal works here. You walk down the hall with him or her only to be stopped dozens of times by kids, teachers, or parents. The principal greets each child by name and asks questions about his or her specific problems or tri-umphs. To the teachers, this principal is a partner. Constantly pro-viding the staff with new ideas, finding ways to make projects work rather than reasons why they shouldn't take place: cheerleading, instructing, leading, coaching, all these things and more. To parents, this principal is the one out front, listening, finding ways to make the school more responsive to the community and to the needs of kids.

Observe the work going on. It is seldom quiet, and not often teacher-centered either. Children are doing things, not just watching someone else. These are schools where learning is not a spectator sport. You will find class meetings going on, with kids planning the next class project or working out class rules. They are more likely to be working in groups than alone, collaborating to solve a difficult math problem or gathering historical information for a presentation. They are busy writing their own books, newsletters, and newspapers, or producing their own videotapes. Or they are very carefully putting the finishing touches on the next display for public consumption of what they have learned about houses, trees, the solar system, Steinbeck, geometric equations, or the Constitution.

These schools and classrooms are the ones that make learning come alive. Kids can't wait to get in them, often arriving well before school to begin project work or to seek out help from a teacher. And they are places that no one is in a hurry to leave at the end of the day. More than one child occasionally misses the bus home in order to finish a project, and classrooms are occupied by teachers long after the last child has left.

For the past several years I have been the guest of the young people and adults who work in such schools. I have made it my business to try to see these schools from the viewpoint of students and teachers. Along the way I have found myself watching these schools as a parent as well, wondering how I would feel if my children attended one of them. I have taken notes and pictures, interviewed students, teachers, administrators, and parents, followed students from class to class, sat in on faculty, administrative, and parent meetings. I have stayed in the homes of educators who work in these schools, shared meals with them, and talked long into the night about their work, their students, and their future.

In visiting these schools, whose stories you will read in the pages that follow, I was after the answer to just one question: Could every American school work so well for every child? After years of observing, talking, and participating I am persuaded that the answer to that question is yes. But only if we redirect our focus in the quest for good schools. The focus, to date, has been primarily on schools that fail and reforms that will do nothing to alter that failure. This focus will make it harder for children to find classrooms like these to learn in.

Almost daily, since the release of Ronald Reagan's 1983 Commission on Educational Excellence report entitled *A Nation At Risk*, we have been told how bad our schools are. Report after report has sounded the alarm that America is at risk from a "rising tide of mediocrity" in our schools that threatens "our very future as a nation and as a people." Local papers offer up front page headlines blaring "Schools Get An F" or "Johnny Still Can't Read." But as a former teacher and now a teacher of teachers I know of excellent teaching going on in schools all over the country, in all types of communities. I was troubled that these schools did not figure in the national debate over the future of American education. In fact, we seem to be much more interested in poor schools, schools that are failing, than we are in schools that are succeeding.

So I set out in search of the stories good schools have to tell us. Believing that we are more likely to learn from success than failure, I wanted to find out how and why so many schools do so well in spite of the odds stacked against them. Why, for example, in Appalachian Ohio, where over one third of the population is poor (and seventy-five percent of the poor are children) are there classrooms where every child succeeds and virtually every parent is involved? Or why, in the mean streets of Harlem, is there a high school with no dropouts and of whose graduates virtually all go on to college? These success stories are worth more than dozens of reports from committees of so-called educational experts. From these schools, we can learn how to fulfill public education's most fundamental purpose—the development in our children of the habits of heart and mind that make democratic life possible.

Today we seem to hear little about the democratic purpose of public education. Perhaps we should remind ourselves that this was the reason for establishing free public education. In 1782, Thomas Jefferson, the father of American public schooling, made it clear that democracy could not survive without "those talents which nature has sown as liberally among the poor as well as the rich, but which perish without use, if not sought for and cultivated. Every government degenerates where trusted to the rulers of the people alone. The people themselves therefore are its only safe depositories. And to render even them safe, their minds must be improved."

Education was to be the tool that made self-government possible. It was to develop in all citizens the characteristics, skills, wisdom, and virtues necessary for public life. Thus, intoned the Massachusetts Constitution of 1780, as "Wisdom and knowledge, as well as virtue, [is] diffused generally among the body of the people, being necessary for the preservation of their rights and liberties [it is necessary for the government to spread] the opportunities and advantages of education in the various parts of the country, and among different orders of people."

What does democratic life require of us? What of those things can we affect in the schools? Fundamentally, democracy requires citizens who participate broadly in informed public decision-making with an eye toward the common good. Citizens must thus be literate, able not only to master the rudiments of reading, writing, and computing, but able to use these tools as ways of understanding the world and making their voices heard in it. We must also know how to find and evaluate information, how to sift through the items that bombard us daily, to sort the useful from the superfluous, the clearly propagandistic from the approximate truths.

Members of the republic must also have an ongoing sense of community, an obligation to the common good. Citizens should see themselves as members of a community that makes their individuality possible, and they should value and nurture that community. Democracy also requires that we each have courage, that we believe our actions are important and valued, and that we have not only a right, but an obligation to participate publicly. The democratic citizen is, in sum, the individual who has the intellectual skills and conviction necessary to participate publicly in making the many choices that confront us, in ways that will promote the common good.

Many commentators lament the loss of such citizens. We have become fragmented into mutually exclusive and warring interest groups, groups that we quickly abandon as the issues change or as our perceived self-interests relocate. There seems to be no community interest, no public voice which speaks with authority for the good of all. Such a condition results from numerous factors, not the least of which is the abandonment of politics by common citizens, leaving the experts in charge. But as Jefferson pointed out, when the governed abandon the public sphere and turn over governing to the politicians, the politicians prey on the public in their own self-interest, utilizing apathy, mistrust, and divisiveness as their most valued tools.

Mission This deterioration is precisely why recovery of the democratic mission of public education is so vital today. While schools are not the only places where democratic virtues should be nourished, they form one of the few experiences all Americans hold in common. As such, schools should be the primary place where all citizens engage in using and developing common sense, that is, the sense to live in common.

The educators that you will meet in the pages that follow have not forgotten this central mission of schools. As we shall see, they work hard to insure that every child is a member of the school community, that what their students learn is connected with the world at large and has a genuine purpose, and that students see how to make a difference in their neighborhoods and cities. These teachers are the hope for America's schools. They are also gravely at risk due to many of the official school reforms we hear put forward today.

As noted earlier, proposals for reforming schools today are plentiful. What is amazing is how similar they are in focus and how much damage they would do to schools that work well. We are witnessing a "legislated excellence" movement throughout America that, while perhaps well-intentioned, will make excellence in education even more difficult to attain.

The legislated excellence movement is primarily concerned with the American economy, not with the lives of our children. Its agenda is driven by a preoccupation with the box scores of international economic competition: the GNP and balance of trade figures are read like a doctor reads a patient's vital signs. Our apparent inability

School reform is tied to economic productivity

to continue consuming at the world's highest standard of living is blamed on the schools. Rather than solving or preventing the greed that led to the savings and loan crisis, the lack of will and wasteful spending that led to the national debt, or tax policies that encourage leveraged buy-outs instead of capital investment, we turn to schools to solve the crisis in our own economy.[1]

The school reform reports issued daily are very clear about this agenda. They argue that schools are not providing adequate training for future workers, leading to a decline in manufacturing abilities, culminating in our international economic decline. Even the "Education President," George Bush, and the nation's governors are caught up in the emotion of the moment. In the report from their summit meeting on education they declared that "The President and the nation's governors agree that a better educated citizenry is the key to the continued growth and prosperity of the United States . . . as a nation, we must have an educated work force, second to none, in order to succeed in an increasingly competitive world economy."[2] And while in the governors' 1990 document prominence is given to the school's role in preparing citizens to "participate in our democracy" and "function effectively in increasingly diverse communities," most of their recommendations are tied to economic productivity, the ability to enter the job market, and our ability to keep pace in the world market. Harold Howe, a former U.S. Commissioner of Education, has summarized the trend thusly:

> [Economic advancement] is the engine that is driving the present school reform movement. It demands that schools produce excellence among the children of the poor for the sake of the nation's economic health. It wastes little time with concepts of equity or of our nation's need for independent-minded citizens to make a democracy and a complex society workable. Lip service is paid to these latter concepts, but after appropriate rhetoric has been supplied, school reform is back to the serious business of rescuing our corporations from Japanese competition.[3]

Of course, tampering with the schools will not solve our economic problems. At no time in the history of this, or any other industrialized nation, has increasing school achievement led to greater economic productivity. It is precisely the other way around—increases in economic productivity led to increases in school attainment and achievement. Furthermore, it is difficult to believe that the most crucial problem facing American industry is a lack of an educated work force. Try convincing any 10th grade English teacher of that as she desperately tries to coax a student to stay in school (so he can get a job upon graduation) as the local industry packs its bags and moves to Mexico, South Korea, or the Caribbean. One doubts that such moves are due to a search for more high school graduates to work the shop floor.

Were these reform reports merely cases of poor arithmetic they could be easily dismissed. However, their strident tone and well-financed public reception, along with the simplistic answers they offer, have generated a great number of attempts at reforming the schools. Parents, justifiably concerned with the quality of their children's education, find just enough truth in these reports to ignore much of what is wrong with them and call for some action on their recommendations. State legislatures, which hold the ultimate responsibility for public schools, have rushed to mandate these recommendations.

What is interesting is how mundane most of these recommendations are. The much-touted legislated-excellence agenda can be boiled down to one word: MORE. The list is simple—more core subjects (the five basics—English, math, science, social science, computer science), more testing of students, and more time in school. Virtually every report on schools recites the same litany of recommendations meant to apply to all children, kindergarten through twelfth grade.

Simplistic as these reforms sound, when they become legislative mandates they put at risk the schools described in the opening pages of this book. They are turned into reform programs like Georgia's, where the state government has gone so far as to specify objectives for all students in all subjects, the methods of teacher evaluation, and a standardized testing sequence all the way down to kindergarten. Or they show up as they did in one Ohio school, where teachers are confronted with over 230 "pupil performance objectives" in the area of reading alone, and not one of these mentions that children might learn to love books. State after state has joined the parade of mandate and test. The 1970s and 1980s witnessed a campaign of excellence through testing in schools. To make matters worse, the 1990s have opened with legislation from The White House calling for a nation-wide standardized test to measure every student's achievement.

The unfortunate consequence of this campaign will be to simply swallow up the school day with drill-and-kill exercises designed to prepare students for the onslaught of tests. Already teachers are reporting that the state-mandated curriculum requirements make projects that go beyond the textbooks more difficult. In fact, anything that doesn't come directly from a textbook, or appear on the state-mandated tests, is actively discouraged. Here is how several teachers put it:

The tests the students have to take are geared to the textbooks, the textbooks are boring, below the kids' abilities, and geared to workbook sheets and dittos. My administrator wants high test scores because they make the school—him, really—look good. Any space I can find to really get kids involved in class, to really cut loose on a project, shrinks almost every day. And I have to fight for every minute of it. (An elementary school teacher.)

As part of the recent educational reforms in my county, every single school in the county teaches the same basic curriculum. Everybody is basically doing the same thing at the same time in the same way. And since no one else has an English class producing a journal, that means we can't either. (A middle school English teacher.)

We're not allowed field trips anymore. The state requires so many minutes in each subject for each student. Since a field trip would spill over from my history class into the time currently scheduled for other areas, they just don't allow them. (A high school history teacher.)[4]

These frustrations, faced by good teachers everywhere, are the direct result of the current excellence-through-testing school reform movement. They are making it harder, daily, for the educators you will meet in this book to prepare students for democracy.

Why is this happening? Why do we rush to impose uniform solutions to non-uniform schoolhouses? Why do we put some of the best teachers and schools at risk, take away from students some of the most exciting school experiences they will have, and spend millions on testing programs (money desperately needed by so many schools) that will do little, if anything, to improve public education? I believe there are two answers to these questions.

First, we have been preoccupied with school pathology. Reports of bad schools, schools that fail, schools that seem utterly hopeless dominate the news. William Bennett, Secretary of Education for the Reagan Administration, is more responsible than any other individual for this preoccupation. He used his position to loudly criticize and attack education in general, teachers and schools in particular (calling the Chicago schools, for example, the nation's worst). Bennett has often been applauded for bringing much needed attention to the ills of schools. It has been a hollow victory. Such attention has, for nearly ten years, done little to improve the quality of the daily lives of children in schools. What such attention has done is demoralize teachers and mislead the American public into believing the majority of schools are similarly sick.

Most American schools are, in fact, simply average. And most Americans, according to Gallup poll results, are generally satisfied with their neighborhood school. In the vast majority of schools kids are safe and a curriculum that represents the reforms cited above is in place. In fact, to implement most of the changes the reports call for would change schooling very little, if at all, for the majority of American students. They might find themselves complaining about a longer school year or day, they might be taking home more homework, and they definitely would be taking more standardized tests, but they would not find their daily tasks any more educational.

This does not mean that average schooling is good enough. It only means that reforms that focus on teaching for tests and memorization rather than application and imagination, on coverage of content rather than commitment to learning, on skills rather than wisdom, will not change what is currently going on in schools. Of course schools should be better. But by concentrating only on the weakest of schools, reforms are generated that at best apply only to a narrow band of schools and at worst hamper or destroy the excellent work being done by many teachers.

Aside from an overemphasis on what is wrong with schools, the current legislated excellence movement also, as pointed out above, overemphasizes the vocational aspect of public schooling. The push is on for better training of workers. But there is an alternative way to think about our schools that will generate a very different school reform agenda. The centerpiece of that alternative vision is seeing schools as sites where we prepare active, participatory, democratic citizens.

most + premise for this book

This task of public education, the education of democratic citizens, is most at risk in our schools. Looking inside schools, and not just at test scores, our best reporters on school life indicate that schools are not currently places where the characteristics of participatory, democratic citizenship can be nourished. Traits such as a commitment to community and a desire to participate, values such as a sense of justice, equality, or liberty, skills of interpretation, debate, and compromise, habits of reflection, study, examining multiple perspectives, form the basics of democratic citizenship. These are the basics that make our fondest images of ourselves come to life. And these are the basics that are being shoved out of the classrooms and schoolhouses in this country to make room for state-mandated tests, work sheets, and objectives.

In the pages that follow you will meet teachers, administrators, parents, and students who are engaged in educating for the basics of democratic citizenship. They work in the type of schools described in the opening pages, in schools that work. They work in spite of, and sometimes in open defiance of, current legislated-excellence mandates and reforms. And they are the types of teachers and schools that we should watch, listen to, and learn from if we want our just average schools to become good ones.

PART ONE

The Schools

Rural southeastern Ohio, tucked in the foothills of the Appalachian Mountains, abounding in scenic vistas with explosions of color that attract tourists every fall and spring—the same colors that hide the poverty of homes without running water, an intractable unemployment rate, and an adult illiteracy rate of one in four. New York City's Harlem neighborhood, historically known as the national center of black culture, today blighted by overcrowded tenements, trash piled high on the streets, and armies of the homeless, drug pushers, and the simply unconnected. New Hampshire, picture-postcard state that attracts sightseers, hikers, skiers, and hunters to its villages and mountains—yet manages to spend less per child for education than virtually any other state. And, north of Chicago, the suburb of Winnetka, where the *average* family income approaches $100,000 per year, where children of the well-to-do take advantage of all the American dream has to offer, and where, in the sanctity of their own school, one child lost his life and others lost parts of their childhood to the bullets from the gun of a crazed assassin. All of these settings have something very special in common. They hold in their midst a national treasure, the keys to our future as a democratic republic: public schools that are schools for democracy.

These are schools and teachers that we must pay attention to if we are to improve the schools we have.

Pathological schools, sick schools, tell us little but that something is wrong, yet so much of our attention is directed toward them. We seem obsessed as a nation with school failure, with horror stories, with ridicule. In the press, at public forums, at backyard barbecues, the national pastime seems to have become trading stories about bad teaching. And why not? It's so much easier to complain than to construct, to shame than support.

Some of this rising tide of discontent is justified. Poor schools and poor teachers ought to be exposed, and they should be replaced if they refuse to improve. However, every good teacher knows that ridicule and criticism do not motivate learners. Too much of either of these is more likely to cause a person to shun learning, to avoid a task at which he or she has failed, to look for other places to put his or her energies. This is precisely what has happened in the teaching profession. Teacher morale is at its lowest point in years. Teachers feel abused and ignored; they feel as if the public they have tried to serve has turned on them.

If we want schools to improve, we need to look at healthy schools. These schools will give us the vision, the food for our dreams, that is necessary if we are to improve the daily lives of children and adults in America's schools. Healthy schools—healthy in body, mind, and spirit—do more than just raise test scores; they give us ideas about how we can improve our children's workplaces, and they provide the inspiration to get it done.

Healthy schools and classrooms exist today, in our cities, suburbs, and rural areas. They are located in both wealthy and poor areas, serving white, black, Hispanic, Asian, Native American—all different types of children—in all areas of the country. Sometimes in just one classroom inside a school; other times it's a group of teachers, and once in a while an entire school breaks free and genuinely works in the best interests of our kids and our communities. From these sites we can learn what makes their success possible. We can locate common threads that run through all of them, that make them go; we can see the passions that are present every day in their work. The search for those themes makes up the body of this work.

Before we visit some of these successful schools, several provisos are added here at the insistence of the educators who are discussed in the following pages. Often, when I talk about their work, they have stopped me short and cautioned me not to get carried away. "You just see it when it works," one first-grade teacher said. "There are days when I don't like myself as a teacher." Thus, proviso number one: The successes of these educators are the focus here. By their own admission, however, nothing always works perfectly, and there are days that you might not find the folks you read about in these pages if you visited their classrooms or schools. To put it most clearly, in the words of another first-grade teacher: "I am as democratic as I can stand to be, and that changes on some days."

Proviso two was put forth by one of the principals you will meet: "I don't give advice." The classrooms and schools described in these pages are not meant to be recipes to be copied in every school. Rather, they are models from which we can learn, each one offering educators something different. The worst way to look at them is the way one teacher did after listening to a presentation on a new approach to teaching reading. "This is great," she commented afterward. "I'm going to start this system in my classroom tomorrow. And if the kids don't like it, it's back to the workbooks." Unfortunately, her kids probably didn't like it, because it wasn't her approach. It was just another prepackaged step-by-step approach that ignored who those students and that teacher were together. Each of the educators and programs in these pages developed over countless hours of experimentation and trial and error. All of the educators freely admit that they are continually evolving, always learning, visiting other schools, trying out different things. The point is not to try to copy what you find here, but to use these ideas as they make sense in your own community.

Proviso number three: This book represents only a sampling of what is out there. These are not the only successful teachers and schools in the country. They are the ones I know the best, the ones I have had the most contact with over the years. Certainly there are many more schools and teachers that could have been, should have been, included in these pages. Many of them are in the private or alternative sector, an area not discussed in this work. My goal has not been to find all of these; rather, it has been to get to know a few schools very well. With that in mind you should not scan these pages looking for your neighborhood school, but rather read this book looking for characteristics of your school reflected in the work of others.

Proviso four: I have made a point of using the real names of the teachers and schools involved in this work. My reasoning is that I believe these educators are heroic individuals, as are all good teachers, and they deserve the credit due them. Many of them felt otherwise—they felt that in using their names I might be suggesting that in some way they were better than their peers, to whom they feel a close bond of collegiality. To this I can only say that their names do deserve to be in print, not as icons to be praised, but as testaments to the good work of so many good educators.

CHAPTER 1

Not So Elementary Schools

In the back corner of Joette Weber's second-grade classroom in Chauncey, Ohio, Tony, Annette, and Crystal are gathered around an orange-colored mass sitting on a scale. Crystal is the only one willing to touch it, placing it so that the other two can weigh, measure, and draw sketches of it.

Drawing nearer, I encounter an odor that certainly isn't typical of most classrooms. Liquid oozes from the mass, and is quickly collected by Tony for "future study."

It's February, which explains the mess when Annette informs us, "This is our pumpkin project." "Where did you get the pumpkin?" I ask. "Oh, we carved it for Halloween." Now I understand, as I back away, claiming to need a better angle from which to take a picture.

Joette, never one for passive visitors, has soon arranged my visits to coincide with the weekly pumpkin observations. As I join each team of three students, we record a series of measurements (height, weight, circumference), make several observations about color, appearance, and changes since our last visit, and then draw pictures of the rapidly deteriorating jack-o'-lantern.

Each team member keeps a log, and each has a job; fortunately for me someone else is always willing to move the pumpkin. The students' discussions have echoes of lab work—repeating observations so everyone agrees, calculating changes, making inferences about why things are happening. Lately, tracking a growing green fungus (or is it a mold?) has been the topic of conversation. Someone brings a microscope to class, and a new world of investigation opens up.

The class gathers weekly to share observations and discuss what they are finding. And plans are made to turn the project into the class exhibit in the school science fair. "This way we all win, not just the kids whose parents help them at home," Joette says. "Think of all they get from this," she reflects over a cup of tea after school. "They are *doing* science, not just reading about it. They use math skills, writing skills, reading skills, and they produce a real product— something they are proud of. Plus they learn to work together and build on one another's strengths. You won't find anything like this in a curriculum guide, but you tell me whether or not they are learning."

Of course they are, as is so clear at their weekly discussions.

"The pumpkin weighs less because the water in it is going away," chirps Annette.

"Where does it go?" asks Joette.

"In the air."

"It hides."

"No." Billy waits for the class to become quiet, and then goes on. "It evaporates."

"That's it, it evaporates! Good. So what is left?" Joette takes them further.

"Orange stuff."

"Pulp."

"Rotten pumpkin pie." We all laugh.

"OK," Joette continues, "so where will that stuff go?"

"The green stuff will eat it," Jamey adds this time.

"Well, let's watch that," Joette starts to wrap up.

"Yeah, it will turn into compost, like in our backyard," Rory adds. "And then it's good for the garden."

With this comment they are off on a discussion of soil, nutrients, and then are back to making good guesses about what will happen.

"You know, this happens to everything alive," says Shawna, who hasn't said a word for the past twenty-five minutes and now speaks up so softly we all strain to hear her. "Everything gets born, grows, dies, and just rottens away. Even us, I think."

What we learn in elementary school sets the foundation for a life of learning. With this in mind, many school reformers see this period as a time to cram kids' heads full of facts, figures, and rules. Dictionaries of children's cultural literacy are published, and even babies and toddlers may face a barrage of academic drills rather than parental hugs.

But there is another way. Elementary school can be a place where, in addition to and beyond the mere memorization of facts, children learn to think, to cooperate, and to be actively engaged. It is the place where we can lay the foundation upon which democracy is built. A foundation of insightful, creative, compassionate, happy, and wise young people. In elementary schools that work, the building of such a foundation is job one. I invite you to visit a few more of these schools and classrooms with me.

Athens County, Ohio: One Classroom at a Time

The foothills of the Appalachian Mountains have historically been a hiding place. When Native Americans were being driven to the west, many of them disappeared into the region's thick woods and steep hillsides, taking the untillable land that no one else wanted. During the Civil War, hundreds of runaway slaves found this same terrain to be a welcome stop on the Underground Railroad, helped by Native Americans and whites alike. The lack of transportation and communication in the area later helped hide the violence against working people during the coal wars and the poverty of the Depression from the national spotlight. Today the bucolic beauty of the region hides a deeply entrenched and long-standing poverty. Also hidden here, from the sights of the almighty report writers, are some of the best teachers in the United States today. In fact, so many good teachers work in this area that it was difficult to choose just a few with whom to spend time.

In 1985, a group of Appalachian teachers in Ohio decided they had had enough. They were tired of the endless stream of reports that not only ignored teachers' input about schooling but called for reforms that were antiteacher, antistudent, and antidemocratic. They knew that children learn by doing, that schools should be child-centered places, and that the ultimate aim of education is to develop citizens, not just workers. As one teacher put it, "The list of reforms was the most antistudent list we could imagine. More tests, more homework, more drill, more hours, more days. It's as if we are to just do more of what isn't working now. And the outcome of all this was to go back to the basics. Well, I've been teaching for sixteen years and I don't ever remember leaving the basics. What we feel these reforms really mean is to take control away from us and to turn the kids into little assembly-line products—none of us thinking or engaging, just doing what we are told."

These teachers and others like them throughout the area decided to fight back. One way of doing that was to organize outside of their schools, which they did by forming the Institute for Democracy in Education. (For information about this and other progressive educational reform groups throughout the country, see the Appendix, "Resources for Change.") The Institute is devoted to promoting school practices that give students an experience with democracy and to supporting teachers who are involved in such work. A direct consequence of organizing the Institute outside of the schools has been that it is easier for these teachers to fight the legislated-excellence movement in a more personal way—by making their classrooms islands of democracy.

Walking into the main entrance of Amesville (Ohio) Elementary's "upper building," you are greeted by a feast for the eyes.[1] There, in the hall, is the current exhibit produced by Marcia Burchby's first-grade students. It could be a collection of miniature houses (tree houses, apartment buildings, log cabins) accompanied by a chart portraying the results of their survey of housing types in the community. Or maybe it's a painstakingly constructed gingerbread house, accompanied by other items from the class fairy-tale museum. Or a carousel, complete with photos of each child riding a horse and gracing a table full of books, charts, stories, and graphs about transportation. Just in case you missed the display, several hands take yours at once, guiding you back into the hall to make sure you see their handiwork, the detail that went into it, the care with which it was prepared.

The reason these six-year-olds are so insistent that you pay close attention to their work is simple: it's theirs. From choosing the topic to choosing the materials, these kids have a say. "I want them not only to learn to read and write and compute," says Marcia, "I also want them to begin to learn how to choose what to read or write, to work together, and to have some control over their lives . . . I guess I mean I want them to be empowered." That's why the walls in this room are covered with real art, not twenty look-alike cut-out-color Mickey Mouse characters. Again from Marcia: "We have to respect the child's work as his or her work. It may not be perfect, and it may not even be like anything we have seen before. But it is that child's and we should respect it as that."

This respect for the child as a learner, as a collaborator, shows up again on the sheet of poster board that displays the class rules. At first glance, a list that begins with "No Smoking" and proceeds to "No Throwing Books at the Lights" seems a bit unusual for a first-grade room. "Well, they made all the rules themselves as a group," I'm informed. "It's their space as much as mine. Besides, we all agree that the rules boil down to taking care of each other and our stuff."

To understand how all this works, it helps to know that Marcia's teaching is primarily thematic. "I choose a theme by paying attention to the kids. I know what they are interested in; I try and think about what interests we might develop together. Then I use that theme to organize our activities." An ever-popular theme is the environment, with the children's interest piqued by the yearly schoolwide recycling day. Book displays are continually changed so that the room is filled with literature about the environment. Dr. Seuss's *The Lorax*, a tale of environmental woe ending with a child holding the key to potential salvation, becomes the theme book for the group; a recycling project or similar effort is chosen by the class; a hall display on what can or cannot be reused is set up; field trips are taken through the village to pick up litter; kids write their own versions of the Lorax story and illustrate them in their own books; and a "dump," filled with dirt and various objects, is set up so they can all watch what decomposes and what doesn't. The entire curriculum—reading, writing, science, social studies, art, math (carefully figuring how much for each aluminum can they will get at the recycling center), and even music—is brought to bear on this one issue.

"I'm trying to get at several things at once," Marcia explains. "First I want the kids to be doing something real, to know that what they learn here is useful and that it matters. Second, I want them to see that they can make a difference. Finally, I want us all to have a lot of fun." All of these efforts are apparent in Marcia's room, from the determination with which the children approach their work to the obvious pleasure they take in showing off the finished product.

It's the middle of the morning, and Dustin, a child who is struggling a bit more with writing and reading than others, approaches Marcia. He holds out yet another book that he is writing, filled with drawings of trucks, and this time something new—letters, literally dozens of letters, piled up on one another so that even Marcia, who encourages inventive spelling, can't sort them out. Getting it perfect isn't the issue. Usually she can get enough of the words to make sense of the writing, and then she can coax the students to write more, which they gladly do in order to have their voices heard. But Dustin's letters, as welcome as they are, mean nothing to Marcia, and Dustin doesn't remember what they were meant to say either. No big deal; the little figure, whose pants rise a full three inches off his shoes but are always too big around the waist, just walks up to a group of his fellow students and asks: "Any you kids can read?" After enough tries, sure enough, Dustin can read it with Billy's help and soon he is back to Marcia with a complete and illustrated book. These are indeed empowered children.

In the "lower building" at Amesville, Mick Cummings and his fourth graders take apart the science book, looking for topics that interest them. They choose carefully, slow to discard anything that might hold hidden interest, quick to indicate their desire to find out more about the chapter on "Reproduction," human and otherwise. Having chosen a list of topics, they now abandon the text, using the topics selected and their own backgrounds to build units of study. The possibilities for each topic, bounded only by the students' imagination, seem limitless.

In order to focus the class effort, Mick has the group choose the first topic for investigation. It doesn't seem to surprise him that "Reproduction" is the overwhelming favorite. The topic chosen, the class begins building a learning "web." Placing the general theme in the center of the board, the class develops a list of subtopics that might be explored. These include plant and animal reproduction, birth, DNA, genetics, and the all-encompassing "other." Groups are formed to investigate each topic and come up with a list of questions to be answered. Before the day is over every child has an assignment from the first topic of study—as you might guess, "Reproduction"— and is taking home a list of things to find, build, or ask his or her parents about. Within days the room is filled with photos, displays, and posters. And the students have long since surpassed the limited bits of information in the text.

In virtually every area of the curriculum Mick follows the same pattern: sorting through what is possible, helping students choose the areas to pursue, and then developing a plan to cover it. The key questions are simple; what do we already know, what more do we want to learn, and how can we find out? And the end products are always memorable, from the times the school playground is turned into a giant launching pad for student-built rockets to the beautifully illustrated and bound books written by the kids.

But what of the chapters that aren't covered, the texts that aren't opened? "I never worry about covering everything in the book . . . racing through a textbook is not the way kids learn," explains Mick, sharing his insights with other teachers. "What is important is that we do a few things very well, and that the kids really get into it and take charge. We learn *how* to learn, how to find out, what the general concepts are. The children score just as well or better on the standardized test scores when we do it this way, but that's not the point. The point is that they are taking control of what they learn." The hope is that they will have learned this lesson for the rest of their lives.

Most schools are quiet on Saturday morning, especially after a new snow. But as on many weekend days and weekday evenings, Bill Elasky's sixth-grade room at Amesville is alive with activity. It centers on the Amesville Water Chemists (the name that Bill's 1987/ 88 twelve- and thirteen-year-olds have given themselves), busily mapping out area streams and creeks, developing film and printing photos, testing water samples, and just trying to get warm after an early morning foray collecting test tubes full of water from the local watershed. What started as a simple question from Bill at the beginning of the year—"What would you guys like to study?"—has exploded into a project that covers almost all of the sixth-grade curriculum.

It started simply enough with a chemical spill in the nearby creek, the natural curiosity of young people about what is going on around them, and a teacher willing to help them find out. Before they finished, the group had become one of the area's most reliable sources of information on water quality both in homes and in the wild. The students sought out and received instruction on how to sample and test water, researched and ordered testing kits, raised funds for their work, performed tests, and developed a variety of reports. Their work was featured in local papers and they were and continue to be in demand as guest speakers at educational conferences (including Ohio 2,000, the state task force on improving public education).

The room in which all this takes place is woefully small and ill-equipped. But scrounging supplies and space and creatively arranging the room are second nature to a good teacher. Bill visits public libraries on weekends, converts an underutilized closet into a darkroom, borrows refrigerator space to hold samples. And, as we will continue to see in good classrooms, the walls are covered with indicators of the work going on: job lists, ways to facilitate group work, "Things We've Learned," a sample of a business letter requesting funds, maps, photos—every inch is covered.

"We cover the curriculum by choosing real things that the kids and I are interested in," explained Bill Elasky about his teaching philosophy. "We get so involved in it that I sometimes hate for the weekend to come, or snow days; I used to look forward to them—now I go to school anyway and often several kids show up, too." In Bill's class every student has a job, something he or she masters and teaches others, and every student counts. "I think they realize that they can work together. That they each have strengths to share and weaknesses that need help . . . And they also know they are making a difference in this community."

And what did the kids learn, besides how cold creek water can be on a winter morning? Listen: "We learned how to do something, not just learned about something." "We learned about how things really work." "We learned more than we ever learn in the textbooks. All they do is start over every year and cover the same stuff." "We learned how to use what we know. In the [text] books we never do anything real. I mean, how often are you going to copy down sentences and fill in the commas in a real job?" "We learned what we needed to know to get the job done. Teachers shouldn't keep teaching us things we already know. They should have us do projects like this and then teach us things we need to get it done." After a thoughtful pause, one last comment is offered. "Other teachers should teach the way Mr. E does. It's more fun for us kids and I think the teachers would like it better too."

Joyce Hanenberg, Charlotte Newman, and Joette Weber are seldom thought of as individual teachers. Between the three of them they have amassed over forty years of teaching experience, the last six spent together in the primary wing of Chauncey Elementary School. This primary wing, with its crowd of ninety or so first and second graders, usually catches a visitor's attention first when he or she enters the school.

The primary wing is at the end of the first corridor to your left as you enter Chauncey Elementary. To really understand what goes on here you need to arrive about an hour or so before school. A quick check of the walls in the wing will clue you in to the theme currently guiding most of the classroom work. The "humor" theme featured two large cut-out figures dominating the hallway, each with a speech bubble to be filled in by kids with their favorite jokes. You are just as likely to be swooped down on by birds or fish, tangled in a giant spider web, warmed by a glowing sunrise, repulsed by decaying jack-o'-lanterns, or caught up in a story, song, or poem that is retold and illustrated in expansive wall displays or dioramas. You will find the three teachers together, sharing ideas, trading notes on the day, laughing over stories about the children. And they know the children well, as they follow them for two years, teaching them both first and then second grade before returning to pick up another group of first graders.

When the first children drift in, they select the place at one of the tables they will occupy today, then dash off. The entire end of the hall hums like a beehive. All of the rooms are open for students to move around in, showing friends their latest artistic endeavor, working in groups on a play, finding out what resources one of the other rooms might have to help with a project. There is an indescribable sense of community here. All the space in this wing is common property; teachers, students, and parents alike share it.

If you visit on Monday you will be expected to join all the students at "Primary Forum." Gathered together in the multipurpose room, the group begins with an activity that either students or teachers have organized. It could be something having to do with the theme the classes are studying: a presentation by two first graders on the art of Georgia O'Keeffe, a newfound favorite of theirs; a game in which all blue-eyed blondes are told to stay in the back of the room, experiencing in a small way the segregation that Martin Luther King, Jr., fought against (his birthday is celebrated this week); or a guest speaker complete with his bicycle and the equipment that accompanied him on his recent cross-country trip. After the presentation, there is an open forum, when any teacher or student can bring up an issue that concerns him or her. Again, the topics are varied—running out of paper in the bathroom, pushing on the slide, or helping one seven-year-old who had just "lost" his best friend to a new kid in town. The grand finale is a celebration. Outstanding

lack of teacher-centered activities

effort or achievement in any area is recognized and all those with birthdays during the week are sung to. Every child is recognized, all teachers know all children, and the sense of community is contagious. Kids walk out the door arm in arm, hand in hand, laughing, singing, smiling—even the ones whose day didn't start so well.

Back in the classrooms, the work of the day begins. Children rapidly scramble to all types of activities and ongoing projects. It's not long before you realize that something is missing in these rooms. It's hard for the uninitiated to put a finger on it, but if you've been around elementary classrooms long enough the absences are striking. The first one is the lack of what is called, in educational jargon, teacher-centered activities—most of us know it as just lecture. Instead, kids and teachers meet in small groups or one-on-one to go over activities and then disperse to take on the project at hand.

Soon you realize that the ever-present worksheets, or dittos, which occupy so much of an elementary student's time, are not being used.[2] And the traditional tool for dumbing-down instruction and pressing flowers, the textbook, is nowhere in sight. That's because in these classrooms the time is consumed by reading *real* children's literature, not weak, watered-down stories in readers. Writing flows naturally from the classroom themes and fills student journals, annotates displays, and even takes the form of a letter to the superintendent of schools requesting a map for the classroom. Science experiments linked to the class theme—water, food, and other materials left out to freeze, the decomposing pumpkin, or the plants growing in the room—occupy every available space.

As all this work and motion go on, each teacher from time to time invites groups of students to join her in reading. Finally, something we are accustomed to, a reading group. These, however, are not reading groups in the traditional sense, with children grouped by perceived reading ability, each group using a different reader. Instead, children read the same books in mixed-ability groups, with the groups changing in makeup all the time. This simple difference strikes right at the heart of one of the most antidemocratic aspects of American public education: in most schools children are segregated by ability, either within a classroom or in academic tracks. Once children are placed in these tracks or ability groups, they are labeled for life, and those who are labeled as slow or deficient fall further and further behind. This problem need not occur, and Joette, Joyce, and Charlotte prove it every day. "In my classroom," Joyce says, "we all just read. We don't divide up by ability, we just read together whatever books fit the theme. The children are not only learning to read this way, but they feel better about themselves as well. And I feel better about myself as a teacher."

After a particularly intense morning, where Joette and her students have been working hard on editing their most recent writings, Joette makes a decision. Noticing students starting to drift, and feeling that she herself is worn out, she raises a question with the class. "Need a break?" Most heads nod in assent; one or two want to keep on with their writing. Simply enough, she decides it's time for recess, and with that decision you notice something else that is missing—outside control of the school day. With the exception of the start and end of the day and the lunch period, the staff at Chauncey choose what their day looks like. "It's really quite simple," says Joette. "There is no reason why everyone in a school has to do everything at the same time. Our principal [Clyde Jarvis] trusts us to make the right decisions about our students and their needs. I think that makes it easier for us to trust our students to make their own decisions as well." Real decisions made in the context of a real community: that's what Chauncey Elementary is all about.

Milwaukee, Wisconsin: The Struggle for a Decent School

On Fratney Street, in the Riverwest neighborhood of Milwaukee, sits a tan, three-story school building that seems literally to emerge from the asphalt that surrounds it. This building is the home of La Escuela Fratney, or, in English, Fratney School: a multicultural, two-way bilingual elementary school that has been hailed as the future of education in the city. For the struggle it took just to open Fratney in the fall of 1988, you would not have imagined that such a future lay in store for its three hundred-plus students and staff.

Fratney had been slated to be closed and reopened as what was to be called an Exemplary Teaching Center. Sounding idyllic, it was in fact a nightmare to parents who were told that their children would be the guinea pigs for weak teachers who would be imported to the school for two-and-a-half-week fix-up sessions. Parents logically asked if it really made sense for their kids to be taught by a series of struggling teachers. They had another vision for the school, a vision of a "school that would provide the highest-quality education for all of our children, black, white, and Hispanic," according to Marty Horning, an area parent.

The work for the school began with the dream of a group of parents and teachers. Bob Peterson, who teaches at Fratney, says the group ("Neighbors for a New Fratney") dreamed of "a decent school that children want to attend, based in an integrated neighborhood, teaching children to be bilingual in Spanish and English, using cooperative and innovative methods, governed by a council of parents and teachers." The proposal that emerged called for a school that would celebrate the diversity and strength of the integrated Riverwest neighborhood. The school would be a two-way bilingual, multicultural, whole-language, site-based-managed building. (More about each of these later.)

A neighborhood-based campaign for the school culminated in the presentation of the Fratney plan to the city school board at a January 19, 1988, meeting. In spite of a snow-and-sleet storm that shut down much of the city, seventy-five parents, teachers, and community members attended in a show of support that shocked the board and administration. By February 10, under growing community pressure, the plan was approved by the board, and Fratney was scheduled to open in the fall as one of Milwaukee's most progressive open-enrollment schools.

What is exciting about the Fratney project is not that it did open, it's what the teachers and staff have been able to build in terms of the school program, classroom atmosphere, and school management. How the Riverwest community's dream has come to life is what interests us most.

The summer prior to the opening of Fratney School, a draft of a curriculum was put together by a team of five teachers. If they were not going to rely on textbooks for the school program, they would have to rely on their own experiences as teachers, experiences students bring with them to school, general areas of knowledge that society considers important for children to learn, and current social issues. There is very little in the way of school materials that would meet the standards of two-way bilingual, whole-language, multicultural, and gender-equal education, so the teachers had to start from scratch. The curriculum that these staff members outlined was discussed, modified, and finally endorsed by the school community, and it now guides the Fratney family.

First, a few definitions. *Two-way bilingual* means a program in which instruction is given in both English and another language, in this case Spanish, with students learning to read first in their mother language and by grade five being bilingual and biliterate. *Whole language* means that students learn to read and write by reading and writing, not performing endless drill exercises. Through reading real books rather than programmed readers, writing self-initiated stories, and sharing language experiences, children learn that language is for making meaning, for accomplishing something both public and private. The *multicultural* aspect of the curriculum stresses the history and culture of several nationalities and ethnic groups in addition to the traditional norms. *Gender-equal* means that the curriculum reflects the achievements of both women and men throughout history as well as teaching children that both racism and sexism are unhealthy, unscientific, and unacceptable. Most of the schools we are visiting encompass some components of each of these efforts; at La Escuela Fratney these very themes were the reasons for starting the school in the first place.

To bring together these keys to the curriculum, the school year is organized around themes. Drawing from the diversity of the Riverwest neighborhood itself, a series of six themes, each lasting six weeks, made up the first school year.[3] They were the following:

- Our Roots in the School and Community
- The Native American Experience
- The African-American Experience
- The Hispanic Experience

- The Asian-American/Pacific American Experience
- We Are a Multicultural Nation

Traditional school subjects—math, science, social studies, art, and all the rest—are woven into each theme. Further, within each theme students help select potential activities. With each theme, teachers try to teach one entire segment, for example, insect life on the river (part of the fourth-grade science curriculum linked to the first theme on the local community), entirely in Spanish.

In practice, the entire school comes alive with each theme. Field trips take children into the community to explore the roots and strengths of their ethnic heritage. School assemblies feature performances or presentations related to the theme. The library features books and materials linked to the theme for students, teachers, and parents. Hall displays, brightly colored and often prepared by students, let everyone in on the topics at hand.

But the real action is in the classrooms. For example, during the African-American theme, Rita Tenorio's students listen to her read *Follow the Drinking Gourd,* a story of slaves escaping to freedom via the Underground Railroad. Finishing the story, Rita pulls out large sheets of newsprint on which she has pasted pictures from the story. Each student takes a turn naming something in the picture, in either Spanish or English, and the words become the class vocabulary list for this theme. During the Hispanic-American theme Becky Trayser's fifth graders have a wide range of choices they can make to explore this element of the curriculum. Activities include an interview with a community member about his or her life in the United States, an art project involving native Spanish style, a mapping exercise, a retelling of a historical event from a Hispanic perspective, or researching a current affairs issue of concern to the Hispanic population. In virtually every classroom the curriculum weaves back and forth through the thematic approach taken by the school.

Not all classroom work is tightly tied to a specific theme, but everything is connected to the overall principles that guide the school. For example, when dealing with fairy tales in a reading anthology, teacher Becky Trayser makes sure traditional male/female roles are reversed in rewrites of the stories. In Rita Tenorio's kindergarten room, the five-year-olds are in the process of writing yet another book together about something they have done—this time making butter. In Bob Peterson's resource room children are busy putting their latest piece of writing into a word processor so that they can print, laminate, and bind another book—former non-readers now proud of their ability as authors.

It's 11:15 A.M. in Becky's room on the third floor. The room is quiet, as every child sits hunched over a piece of writing. A timer goes off and the children effortlessly find partners with whom to share the day's writing. Stories, poems, and the rest are retold with great dramatics, and the kids show off what they have done. Next, Becky calls for nominations for readers—students who, in the judgment of their peers, have written something worth sharing with the entire group. Several students read, and these nine- and ten-year-olds share stories that are often funny, filled with good dialogue, and reflecting of a multicultural theme, with males and females in all sorts of nonstereotypical roles. After each reading, Becky raises the question of where their work might find an outlet, who might want to read it. Several suggestions are offered, but the one that is the most profound and exemplifies what Fratney is about comes from Oscar, the brash, dark-haired boy who came to school this year unable to read at age nine, whose family was traumatized by an alcoholic father prone to violent outbursts. Oscar proudly holds up his alphabet book, complete with pictures and sentences using each letter, the first book he's finished this year: "This is an alphabet book in Spanish and English. I wrote it to give to the first graders that I tutor. They think I'm great."

Beyond the curriculum, the staff at Fratney works to organize the entire school in ways that are consistent with its philosophy. There are the obvious things—the school newsletter is produced in both Spanish and English, side by side. By design the faculty works to avoid stereotypical roles in the school, as in not having male teachers always enforce disciplinary policies. And school resources are multicultural and often drawn directly from the Riverwest neighborhood, which is, as one parent puts it, "integrated, not desegregated." But the difference really shows in the deliberate attempt to aban-

don traditional forms of school discipline. We have heard too often
that the way to deal with children in schools, especially those from
impoverished neighborhoods, is to bear down on them with strict
disciplinary rules. Joe Clark, the baseball-bat, bullhorn-toting former
principal of a high school in Paterson, New Jersey, has become a
media star by whipping minority kids into shape or throwing them
out of school. (However, reports indicate that academic achievement and staff morale appear to have deteriorated during his tenure.)

Reasons why discipline does not work →

La Escuela Fratney has chosen a different route. First, the staff
takes seriously the challenge of eliminating the reasons many discipline problems occur in the first place: "boring curricula, low self-
esteem, and failure." Second, they believe that people are most
willing to live with rules that they set for themselves. Thus, every
classroom engages students in the process of setting their own rules,
a tactic also used by many Athens County teachers. Third, the
emphasis in the classroom is on cooperation, not competition. Tasks
are designed that reward collaboration and teamwork, in academic
and nonacademic areas. Finally, every room in some way has a
classroom meeting structure where problems that do occur are resolved within the spirit of maintaining the classroom community.
Let's listen in on part of a meeting in Becky's class where students
are trying to resolve how to work out a system so that all class
members get a turn at one of their favorite jobs, helping with the
kindergarten students:

BECKY: Remember the rules you all set for meetings. You can't
  speak unless you get the talking rock and everyone who wants
  to speak can do so at least once before anybody speaks a second time. *(She starts the rock around.)*

HANNAH: Well, I don't like it [the suggestion] when you say just
  the good kids. If you give all the kids responsibility, maybe
  they will do better.

EVA: But I don't like alphabetical either. That's just an easy way
  out. . . .

STEVE: I wouldn't like alphabet either if my name was on the
  bottom of the list, or good kids if I got in trouble, so that
  doesn't seem fair to everyone.

TAMIKA: But it would be easier if we just went by alphabet.

HOSEA: Why not go by who the little kids like best? . . .

JAMES: But if they don't know all of us, how can they choose? . . .

KAREEM: The reason I like doing this is to help them and when they grow up maybe they'll want to help kindergartners too.

DAWN: This is the best thing we can do, to help other people.

This is just a piece of the conversation, a discussion that went on for nearly two hours over two days. There are faster, easier ways to settle such issues; a teacher can, of course, just take it upon her/himself to make a decision. But think about what is happening in this dialogue: students are empathetically understanding others' positions, listening to a range of opinions, dealing with issues of fairness and justice, and committing themselves to the common good. All of these things take time, time well spent at Fratney School.

Bringing all of this together is the team of people who direct the school. Parents elected by other parents, teachers and paraprofessionals appointed by the staff, and a principal form a site-based management team that runs the school. The team has control over virtually everything, from maintenance of the building to the curriculum to the hiring of administrative staff. The team members take their task seriously, meeting once a month for hours to deal with agendas similar to this list from the March 1989 meeting: new learning disabilities class to open next year, the hiring of a new principal, parent education sessions, room parents, next year's enrollment and racial makeup, whether or not the Chapter 1 Program should be a pull-out program, how special teachers who are not based in the building (for example, music, art, physical education) are working out, an upcoming parent meeting, a parent survey to be sent out, citywide school advisory councils, report cards and a new assessment model, new computers, parent committees, discipline, and how the council functions. Through it all, four hours of hard thinking and at times difficult discussion, they maintain the ease and friendliness that characterize much of the public talk at Fratney.

They maintain this spirit because they are working on something real that they care about. Bob Peterson sees it this way: "Whenever parents and teachers genuinely have control, many more energies are unleashed and the potential for success for students is much greater." According to Rita, "Having some say over how I teach makes me feel wonderful. I feel people are trusting me to know what is best for my kids. I feel I am recognized as a professional." Hard as it may be to believe, parents win in this process as well. Dawn Luebke, who has her three children travel to Fratney from the far West Side of Milwaukee, put it this way: "I don't feel here any of the intimidation that sometimes comes from people who tell you they are professional educators. I'm a professional parent, and I feel I deserve the same respect as the staff does. At Fratney it really does go two ways."

Why Fratney? Better yet, why shouldn't every school in every city, town, or rural community reflect the commitment to children and a better world displayed so boldly by these educators? Schools like La Escuela Fratney are the type of schools we should hope for, the type of school that parents passionately support with the conviction the way Fratney parent Amy Kirkland does in this column taken from the school newsletter.

WHY FRATNEY

When time grew near for [our daughter] to begin her school year we were concerned. She was on the waiting list for several schools, but not high enough. Then we heard about Fratney. A group of parents, frustrated with even some of the best schools in the system, and some "young Turk" teachers, some of the most talented and principled educators in the city, were coming together to form a school where decisions would be made on site. Those involved consciously decided to have an anti-racist, non-sexist curriculum. The children would learn that we are all together on this planet and that what we and our teachers do every day affects every person and place. Our responsibility to each other is to care and nurture and provide a successful experience for all our students.

Winnetka, Illinois: Creating a Community of Learners

The North Shore suburbs of Chicago are about as far away economically, socially, and culturally as is possible from Athens County, Ohio, or the Fratney School neighborhood in Milwaukee. Here, high-powered accountants, lawyers, doctors, and architects live next to the CEOs of major corporations and managers of Fortune 500 companies. In the midst of these suburban villages is Winnetka, with its small-town ambience of tree-lined streets, a one-street shopping district, and schools surrounded by homes and parks (as opposed to being isolated by vast fields of asphalt). It is virtually another world in comparison to the communities we have already visited. A world of well-financed schools, ample social amenities, nice, comfortable childhoods. So why look here for schools that work? Can't these schools just do what they want, bringing to bear the wealth and support of the community? Would that it were so. In fact, the long-standing history of progressive, democratic education in the Village of Winnetka is threatened by the same legislated-excellence movement that challenges educators in Athens County and Milwaukee.

Winnetka is blessed with a long history of progressive education. Carleton Washburn, superintendent of Winnetka Schools from 1917 to 1943, was, along with John Dewey, Frances Parker, and Ella Flagg Young, one of the leaders of the Progressive Education Movement in the first half of this century. Everything about the schools was viewed through the lens of progressive education. The curriculum was to be child-centered, with daily activities growing out of the experiences of children and academics taught as children needed them to complete real tasks. The schools and playgrounds themselves were models for the rest of the country—built to accommodate child-sized bodies with plenty of room for active learning (Winnetka's Crow Island school building is still the touchstone for school architecture). The teaching staff was treated as the primary source of educational decision making, engaging in curriculum development, school scheduling, budget direction, in sum assisting in all the educational decisions in the district. The goal then, as it is now, was to build a community of learners.

* * *

"A community of learners." This is the watchword of the Winnetka school district. It graces the cover of the most recent district
curriculum report, appears frequently in newsletters home, and is
often referred to by the staff as a guiding principle. It is not mere
rhetoric. The notion of the school as a learning community directs
virtually all aspects of the school—from the length of the school
day, to teaching, to staff relations, to the very layout of the buildings. Though one could easily pick any of the districts' four schools
(three elementary, one middle) to see this philosophy in practice,
we will focus on Hubbard Woods Elementary and its principal,
Dick Streedain.

You have to arrive at Hubbard Woods early, well before the
day's official 9:00 A.M. starting time, to begin to grasp how this
community works. At 7:15 Dick walks us through the halls, pointing out the art projects, commenting on each classroom and the
strengths of the teacher in it. He often refers to the recent conference or in-service attended by the teacher, and points with pride to
the curriculum, which the staff, not textbook manufacturers, has
created. Staff development is of major importance here. "We think
that we all have a lot to learn," Dick Streedain comments on his
own development with the teaching staff. "We bring people to the
school and we send our people to a lot of workshops, conferences,
and all the rest. It's only when the staff is learning, is excited about
learning, that the place comes alive for the kids. That goes for me
too. You've got to take in if you're going to give out. The most
powerful relationship between a teacher and student comes when
they are both learners."

On the wall there are pictures of whole-school celebrations. In
1987 the sky was filled with the colors of the Hubbard Woods
Balloon Launch (an activity discontinued today because of its environmental impact). The 1988 school year began with a sunrise
breakfast and sing on the sandy shores of Lake Michigan. These
celebrations serve to nurture the sense of community at Hubbard
Woods, and to heal the occasional tears in the fabric of childhood,
an issue we'll return to later.

There is not long to linger over this feast for one's eyes; at 8:00
A.M. the first of the "Early Birds" begin to arrive. For students who

choose to come, the doors open for a variety of activities. The gym is open for free play, the music and foreign language lessons commence, and virtually every classroom is available for students to come in early and work with their teachers. Today the art teacher, Charlotte Bond, and several students are working on the mural in the entrance foyer. The scene depicts a forest, with flora and fauna changing with the seasons. By 8:45 the group has grown to include over a dozen students, male and female, from several grade levels. By 9:00 what had been a colorful fall scene has begun to take on the stark whites and blacks of winter.

In the classrooms the notion of a learning community is carried out in a multiplicity of ways, all devoted to lowering or reducing in any way possible the rigid barriers that so often fragment schools. Dick Streedain describes it as "honoring diversity. Every child, every teacher is different. So we try to create a family setting in the classroom where we all are accepted for our uniqueness." The first barrier to drop is age; virtually all the classrooms are multiaged groups, with, for example, groups of first and second, second and third, or third and fourth graders, and so on, together. Age, Dick explains, is not a very precise indicator of a child's psychological, intellectual, or social development. With multiaged classrooms students can be organized by maturity and not be forced to take on tasks for which they are not ready. The results are classrooms virtually without failure. Additionally, throughout the building you are likely to find older students working as volunteers with younger students. Helping with academic or social tasks, the older children develop a sense of responsibility for the younger ones in the building. Seldom, if ever, is there a problem on the playground with older students picking on younger ones.

The nature of the learning experiences in each room eliminates another barrier, competitiveness. Most tasks are taken on collaboratively, with students working in teams to solve problems, create large-scale displays, or write plays, for example. Much of this is possible because the curriculum is geared to the developmental needs of children. Rather than workbooks and worksheets which require only the ability to manipulate a pencil and to copy, most classroom tasks involve a hands-on experience. Math games, tools for mea-

How can we do this in HS2

Reading Raiders

suring or counting, costumes for plays, plants and animals all fill the rooms so that students can touch, feel, and experiment as they learn. Such learning does not require that students memorize "correct" answers, compiling enough of them to earn a grade; in fact, letter grades are not given. Rather, students learn through collaboration how to help one another find out, how to ask good questions, in short, how to learn. The notion of competitiveness on abstract tasks only hinders learning, and so these teachers break away from that orientation. Katy Beck, a fourth/fifth-grade teacher, explains it this way: "I found that when I was in school I couldn't wait to get out so I could start learning. I want that type of learning to go on here."

Families aren't ability grouped, and neither are the students at Hubbard Woods. While observing Mary Anne Tindall's class we talk about how the children are divided during math. Some of the students have gone off to work on the computers, others are still in the room playing a math game. Has she formed these groups by ability? "Oh no. It really doesn't help to ability group, so I avoid all the social problems with ability grouping by assigning the students to random groups. Then they get to learn from one another." Indeed, random as opposed to ability grouping is the norm at Hubbard Woods. Efforts in this area have been extended to handicapped students as well. In one room a young child suffering from cerebral palsy, a quadriplegic, is just another member of the first-grade class, just as likely to be helped with her work by another student as by the teacher. Another barrier crumbles.

As with any good family or any viable community, there is enough barrier-free space in this school to accommodate all children—physically and psychologically. It's inherent in the minimization of rules of conduct, most of which are set by students. Katy points out, "It's hard to live up to things when the rules are just to keep you in line." It flows through the learning activities that offer every child a way to demonstrate his or her skills on a variety of tasks. You can see it in the form of the *Mayflower* re-created in two classrooms, built to approximate scale, on which the students and teachers spent sixty-six hours re-creating the sixty-six days spent by the Pilgrims.

Hubbard Woods' community of learners extends to the staff as

well. At the noon staff meeting Dick Streedain asks who would like
to facilitate the gathering. A teacher volunteers and works the staff
through a brainstorming session, listing all the issues that they feel
should be discussed. Items are then prioritized and the group works
through the list until the hour-and-a-quarter session is over. What
about the items that are not taken up? "Well, maybe they just aren't
that important," muses Dick, in an approach similar to that of Mick
Cummings when he talks about parts of the science curriculum.
"But we always deal with the real stuff, the curriculum, kids' needs,
and the rest."

The staff at Hubbard Woods, because they deal with the real
stuff, works hard to stay current in the field of education. Their
requests to attend conferences, visit other schools, and take advanced course work are supported and encouraged by the school
administration. Through careful scheduling and use of parent volunteers and aides, the entire faculty has seventy-five minutes for
lunch, all at the same time, a luxury almost unheard of in other
schools. That time is used for staff meetings, grade-level meetings,
and frequent drop-in sessions when a guest joins the staff to share
research or information. The consequence of this availability of time
and support for professional development is not a homogeneous
staff. Rather, every staff member feels free to pursue his or her
special interests, which can then be shared with other staff members.
Thus, you are just as likely to see two members of the staff leading
an in-service program on science as you are to see a so-called outside
expert doing the same thing. While outside wisdom does influence
the staff's work, the majority of curriculum development and writing, school organizational changes, and new approaches to teaching
come from within. The people closest to the students thus make
the crucial decisions about teaching and learning. The community
of learners teaches itself.

Parents are a part of this community as well. In the weekly school
newsletter we find more than lists of important dates and calls for
volunteers to help with fund-raisers. To remind the community of
the school's roots, a section titled "Getting in Touch with Our
History" features selections from the writings of Carleton Washburn. One page includes entries from Washburn's book *What*

Is Progressive Education? Featured are pieces on cooperative learning; the whole-language approach to reading; democracy, and play. Additionally, articles on current topics of concern to the school are copied and sent home advising parents that "Tests Pressure Kids Too Much" or that provide insights about "How Children Learn."

Just sending home materials isn't the only way that the school includes the parents. Not long into the school day you become aware of the great number of adults in the school. Parent volunteers are busy serving as tutors, demonstrators, library assistants, classroom aides, instructors of special subjects (such as drama and movement), and helpers on the playground. They frequent the building for visits with the principal in his "Second Cup of Coffee" morning seminars where educational, safety, and community issues are casually discussed. And on any given evening you can find Dick and several teachers at a parent's home for one of Dick's "Fireside Chats," a chance for parents to meet one another informally, hear the staff discuss the school's program, and ask a wide range of questions. These are not complaint sessions, nor are they times when the staff "sells" the school. Rather, it is, as Dick put it at a meeting in November, "a chance to dream dreams about what the school, what we, might become and can accomplish."

At the end of the school day, as he sits on the front steps chatting with parents, celebrating children's work, thanking the teachers for another good day, Dick Streedain looks to be at peace with his world. "It is," he says, describing his position, "the best job in the world." Indeed. In fact, it's the best job in the world for all of those, teachers, students, staff, who inhabit Hubbard Woods daily. It is a family place in the best sense, honoring the diversity of all its members, providing a community where all can flourish. It is the type of community that makes democracy possible, a community of learners.

Holding on Amidst Waves of Reform

Each of these excellent schools is at risk from the reform movement of the 1980s and 1990s. What the educators in these schools accomplish with the young people in their care goes on unnoticed and often in spite of the reformers who occupy statehouses and sit on blue-ribbon committees. Each of these teachers and administrators has dozens of stories to tell about how state mandates, testing programs, and local bureaucracies work to thwart what they are doing.

For example, near the end of the year Marcia Burchby is expected to test her first graders to see if they are making adequate educational progress. Not content to trust the classroom expert and her inventory of an entire year's work for each student, the district administers a timed, standardized test to each child. This year the test results were not good enough.

"Actually, the scores were fine if you trust these," Marcia smiles in the retelling. "You see, half my students scored above the median score and half below.[4] In other words, we were average. But I was told that wasn't good enough, that a majority of our kids should score better than average. I'm not sure the people who evaluate these tests really know what they are doing."

But the real crime was that several of Marcia's children were being placed in remedial classes for reading on the basis of the test. Marcia contested the placements. "I knew they were reading, and reading well. They just didn't score well on the test." So she launched a campaign against the test results.

The story of her campaign to get Jacob put back in the regular classroom sums up the entire battle.

> I went to [the administrator in charge of the tests] with Jacob's work. The test said he wasn't even ready to learn to read. But I went in with books that he was reading to me in class, samples of his writing, even an entire book he had written. But none of it mattered, I was just told "look at the test scores." And when I pointed out that there wasn't even any reading on this so-called reading-readiness test, well then [the administrator] said maybe that was the problem—that I should spend more time getting them ready to read than having the kids read. It was so frustrating. They really trust these silly, one-shot tests more than they trust me!

Assessment

Amazing)

There is a happy ending, of sorts, to the story. Marcia was able to convince the district to readminister the test and most of the students formerly placed in remedial classes were shifted to regular classes. Miraculously, scores had skyrocketed in only three weeks. "Don't tell anybody," Marcia confided (she's since said that it's all right to tell this story—the kids have moved on), "but I coached them. See, what had happened is that since I don't use workbooks, dittos, and all that stuff my kids had had very little practice with the skills test makers want—filling in small dots, sitting for hours, etc. So I just taught them how to do it. I called it 'reading-test reading,' and explained that people who make these tests aren't very smart and can't always figure out what kids mean when they fill out a paper. So we had to do it exactly like the instructions to help these poor people out. And Jacob said, 'Oh, so you mean we're not supposed to fill in all the dots and color all the pictures and write down the answers?' I just laughed, but when I think about what could have happened to him, I could cry."

In Milwaukee the struggle for Fratney Elementary to come into being is hard to believe. Even after school board approval, roadblock after roadblock was thrown in the way of Bob Peterson and his colleagues. Local school officials, trying desperately to maintain control over school reform through "official channels," nearly prevented Fratney from ever opening its doors. Peterson tells it this way:

When we finally received school board approval we were informed that we would have to order *everything* for the new school in a two-week time period so materials would be in place for the beginning of school. It was difficult working at central office among people who had bitterly opposed our plan. One of the teachers involved remarked that us working on the Fratney project at central office was like three peace activists working in the Pentagon. When we returned in mid-August, we found that necessary renovation construction had only just begun and that the school building still needed to be cleaned from the previous spring. Nothing that we had ordered had yet arrived at the school.

We started calling the vendors and they told us they had no records of our orders. Upon further investigation, we discovered that although the requisition forms had been signed on July 18 (or before) by a deputy superintendent, they had sat on a shelf in the purchasing division for the following month because the department did not have an authorization card with the deputy superintendent's signature. The error was particularly annoying because many books and materials had disappeared when the school closed. Our bilingual program necessitated new materials and the few library books that remained at Fratney were in boxes because of the delayed renovation of the library. We started school with virtually no materials. At the time we figured, "Well, at least we ordered a high-quality Xerox machine so we can rely on that for the first few weeks of school." We called to check on that order. It had never been placed. Somehow it had been lost too.

Ultimately, with the help of a new superintendent, Fratney's materials arrived—about forty-eight hours before the kids. "Unfortunately, of course, the consequence of the many months of inaction and planning were acutely felt throughout the first year," Bob remembers.

It is too easy just to chalk this struggle up to bureaucratic bungling. Instead we should see it as the natural consequence of trying to change schools from the top down. Good schools struggle daily against the dictates of reformers who know nothing of the day-to-day life of the classroom—and they often engender the ire of central office bureaucrats in doing so. The problem would not be so acute if it were not for the fact that these paper pushers can foul the works as badly as they did at Fratney.

Even Winnetka is not immune to the growing desire to control schools from the outside. Here the pressures for such a move come, not surprisingly, from a few of the parents in the district. Hopeful that their children will do well in high school (Winnetka is a K-8 district) and then in college (leading to a high-status profession), they push the academic curriculum lower and lower. Not willing to trust the staff to insure that the appropriate content will be covered (that is, that it will prepare kids to score well on tests), the pressure mounts for changes that will reflect the legislated-excellence agenda.

At a school board meeting when the district's mathematics curriculum was presented, this conflict, always polite, came to the fore. The math curriculum has been developed by the teaching staff, and virtually no textbooks are used. Workbooks are nonexistent. The staff made their presentation on the "developmentally appropriate" nature of the curriculum, a sequence that involves real-life examples, creative problem solving, and hands-on math experiences. It is not a program designed with an eye toward the mere memorization of facts. Instead, it's intended to engage children's curiosity about how numbers function and their use in the world. The teachers presenting the program put it best: "We are really about discovery. We want to keep children's curiosity up, help them ask what they can use this for . . . The fun of using this [the math program] is the patterns and helping kids see them . . . Helping kids develop number concepts and problem-solving concepts without dragging them through endless equations is the agenda." Do the kids learn math? Most certainly: they do better than national averages on the math tests given at the high school.

But several board members act as if they haven't heard a word the teachers have said. Their main question: Why don't we have more algebra at the middle (and maybe even the elementary) school? The staff responds that algebra is not appropriate for the children and they are already doing quite well at math, thank you. That is not answer enough, as board members suggest that algebra would facilitate better job and college preparedness, and besides, the neighboring districts offer it. Superintendent Donald Monroe demurs, pointing out to the board members that pushing more algebra into the middle school curriculum is developmentally inappropriate. "We don't move faster than we believe the child is ready to move," he states. Further, adding algebra to the program would necessitate ability grouping of students, and "we think, as a district, that it is detrimental to put young children into ability groups."

The debate ends, at best, as a draw. The board requests a survey ("Yet another one," notes one teacher) of students and parents as to satisfaction with the math curriculum. Several hours later the meeting draws to a close and the board members file out of the building. Tonight's meeting was held in the Hubbard Woods Elementary School building—a school in which the halls are filled with displays and art, demonstrating the work of the pre-K through fifth graders. Sadly, these same board members who were so concerned about the smallest of details in the math program or special education funding (another item on the night's agenda) do not say a word about these displays. They walk by them without noticing, without knowing the quality of the work this community of learners produces.

Not only do we put our best schools at risk by trying to straitjacket them in the name of reform, we also push them to the breaking point by refusing to deal with many of the social problems children face. For example, at Fratney, a persistent problem throughout the school day is the struggle for the child's attention. The discipline here is not based on a model of control, where children are merely forced to behave through either the threats or power of adults. The many struggles this group of kids have with life often impinge on the work at hand, and thus discipline is problematic. Certainly this was to be expected, as children and staff adjust to new, more cooperative, ways of working together. (The intention was not to open an entire kindergarten-through-fifth-grade building but to begin with lower grades and add one grade each year. However, lack of classroom space in the Milwaukee public schools forced Fratney to open at all grade levels at once.)

Peterson points out that while the Milwaukee city average for free lunches is about 60 percent, and at specialty or open enrollment schools that number drops to 30 percent, at Fratney nearly 90 percent of the students qualify for free lunch. Additionally, a great many children came to Fratney from other schools, hoping to find the success they had not experienced elsewhere. "Some principals saw it as a great way to get rid of their biggest problem," muses Peterson. "We prefer to see them as possibilities." That's where the staff at Fratney differs greatly from so many other professionals; they don't blame the kids.

Tamika was struggling today, with the text, the teacher, and other students. Time after time as her own attention wandered she would cause a disturbance, distracting not only the kids around her but Becky, her teacher, as well. Later that afternoon Becky relaxed with a cup of tea, and talked about Tamika's life: "Three weeks ago her mom left Tamika and her cousin, just left them in their house. They are both only nine. It was a few days before anyone even knew they were living alone. . . . They have now moved in with a grandmother; nobody knows yet where the mother is, and Tamika's just been back at school for a few days. Reading just wasn't on her agenda today. But we'll give it another try tomorrow." And they will. Not once did I hear a Fratney teacher blame a child for not learning.

At Hubbard Woods Elementary an even more graphic example of the troubled world our children face reared its ugly head. To dwell on the details of the specific event would only be sensationalizing the tragedy. In brief, in the spring of 1988 a deranged young woman entered the school and, with concealed handguns, took the life of one young boy and wounded and psychologically scarred many other children. No one would have been surprised to see the school turn into a fortress, complete with the guards and metal detectors that grace other school buildings. But in some way the staff and administration knew that such arrangements would only serve to violate the school community.

Today if you visit the school you notice only one difference. All visitors are greeted by an unarmed and hardly uniformed guard and asked to wear a visitor's tag. You might notice, if you were really astute, an extra psychologist and social worker, but they simply blend in as part of the staff. And if you sit in on a class meeting you may hear students discussing bad dreams, expressing dismay over the continued press coverage of the event, or voicing concern over the possibility of the tragedy recurring. But most of this, the openness to the needs of children and of the staff, is an extension of what was already going on at Hubbard Woods. When any member of the community needs help or support it is freely given, and it is not begrudged as a hindrance to class work. "When people hurt, they need that dealt with first," comments Dick Streedain. "That goes for the staff as well as students. So we want people to be able to say, 'Hey, I hurt, I need help,' and to be able to get that help. Sometimes that means we drop everything else, forget the lesson plan, spend time making people well." A community is only as strong as its weakest member—they remember that at Hubbard Woods.

It would be easy to put out symbolic guards against reforms and the problems of childhood. The doors could close, backs could be turned, curricular recommendations accepted, nodded at, and put on the shelf. But this turning inward would again violate the spirit of these schools. Once the process of closing down begins, it would not stop with merely excluding the bureaucratic reformers and occasional visitor. Perhaps next it would be those parents who ask well-intentioned questions, then the administrator with a new idea, and finally the fellow teacher who wanted to collaborate on a classroom project. The process of building barriers is difficult to halt once it is begun, and at each of the schools we have visited the staff has decided not to start it.

Responding to the pressure for legislated excellence, these educators in Athens County, Milwaukee, and Winnetka continue to work at expanding their base in the community. Newsletters are designed to put forth the vision of the school and systems. Teachers actively engage in working for progressive education, defending the curriculum they developed and finding ways to expand it. Doors to these schools and classrooms are open to all, and board members, parents, and community members are issued invitations to come see the program at work. In all, it is an approach to potential criticism that typifies the healthy community—welcome the critic, listen and learn, take from him/her what we can use, reject that which is inconsistent with our aims and goals.

The response to the changing needs of childhood is just as aggressive. Rather than embracing a reactionary get-tough stance, Joette Weber, Bob Peterson, Dick Sheedain and their colleagues take the needs of their students seriously and work to maintain the space necessary to meet them. By allowing children to play a part in creating their own environment, establishing their academic agenda, asking the important questions, each of these schools, each classroom, each teacher and his or her students, maintain a sense of connection and compassion for children who often have too little of either. As we shall see, compassion and connection, while often overlooked in calls for school reform, form the backbone of schools that work.

CHAPTER 2

Secondary Schools, Primary Lessons

At Central Park East Secondary School in New York City's Harlem neighborhood, four students are crowded over a set of observation notes. They have been conducting a series of experiments and observations on the topic of nutrition. Their work has included measuring and calculating the calories in various foods, identifying parts of the tongue that respond to various tastes, and researching the differences in eating habits over generations.

Today the team is exploring how best to exhibit their findings. A slide-tape show is discarded because not enough people would see it. Posters are judged inadequate as well: too many posters are already on display. "What about flyers for preschools and things like senior centers?" Sherri, thirteen and ready to change the world, suggests. The group seizes on the idea and within minutes they've divided the tasks. Two students begin layout work, while Sherri and Loretta head out to get prices for printing and lists of possible distribution points.

Somewhere near Thayer Junior/Senior High School in Winchester, New Hampshire, a team of students with a video camera and notebooks walks slowly through an open field. The land is slated to become a hazardous waste dump, and the kids are anxious to find out what it is the town would be covering up. A spring is discovered, filmed, and noted, as are several species of wildflowers and tracks and other signs of animals. These findings, analyzed back in the school's science room, become the basis for a communitywide hearing on the proposed dump—and its ultimate rejection.

Back at Central Park East yet another team of kids is tackling a complex math problem. They've been asked to construct their own instrument for measuring the movement of stars and planets. But first they have to come up with a formula that allows for the earth's movement as well. It's quite a puzzle, and they tackle it again and again, each false start seeming to redouble their determination. Finally they hit upon an idea, take what they already know about the speed of the earth, measure the movement of the sun, and begin computing the earth's effect on another object's movement through the sky. An imperfect start, but one that over time will reveal a great deal about mathematics, astronomy, and science.

In Rabun Gap, Georgia a group of high school students publish the quarterly *Foxfire* magazine. Over the past quarter-century they and their predecessors have also published nearly a dozen books— each researched, written, edited, and sold to publishers by the kids themselves. In class today there is a debate over whether to put a picture of a husband and wife who had not been traditionally well-respected in the community on the cover. A poor family, they supported themselves through doing odd jobs and producing unusual whirligigs for lawns—over one hundred of which occupied the lawn in front of their converted-boxcar home. Several of the students had taken an interest in the family and their work and had developed a deeper appreciation of their life and craft. But putting their picture on the cover of *Foxfire* magazine would raise more than a few eyebrows in the area. After a long discussion, the issue was put to rest when Kim rose to speak:

> Growing up in Rabun County and knowin' about the ———s, it's kinda like Polish jokes, a thing you take for granted. . . . But once I got into the article, I saw how his work is artistic, it's

folk art, it's valuable. . . . He's a proud man, and he has lots of character . . . and they deserve some respect.

So do Kim and all of her colleagues, because they show us what kids can do if only given a chance. And giving every kid this chance is a measure of how well each of the schools discussed in this chapter works.

Harlem, New York City: Less Is More

On the corner of Madison Avenue and East 103rd Street stands a moderate-size, relatively unattractive brick school building. It is the Jackie Robinson School Building and it houses what many think is one of the best secondary schools in New York or perhaps the entire United States—Central Park East Secondary School (CPESS). This is not a likely location for such a school. The campus is run-down, hemmed in by busy Madison Avenue on one side, an elevated mass transit train track on the other, and the large towers of overcrowded subsidized housing projects all around. The view out any first- or second-floor window is impeded by metal screening over the windows to prevent breakins, and in case that fails, all the computers are wheeled every night to locked closets for which only teachers have keys. To get to school students often negotiate piles of garbage, homeless people asleep on the sidewalk, and the occasional offer of illicit drugs.

Once inside the school it is as if you have entered another world. The halls are spotless. Science rooms bubble with ongoing student experiments, math rooms are cluttered with models and physical shapes, and humanities rooms hold back avalanches of books and ideas. Your attention is always drawn inward, and for a while you forget the street outside.

The students here are not those who come to mind for most of us when we think about school success. The makeup of the student body is a prototype of schools that fail. The school draws the majority of its students from east and central Harlem, two of New York's poorest neighborhoods. As is to be expected, approximately

75 percent of the children come from poor families. The students also come from ethnic groups that are not traditionally successful in the New York school system. Approximately 45 percent of the students are black and 30 percent are Hispanic, groups that in the city of New York have drop-out rates of 78 percent and 72 percent respectively.

And yet these children are succeeding at CPESS. One indication of that success is that virtually no one drops out of school. Another is that CPESS students do as well or better than children in any other New York City school on citywide standardized tests. But there is yet another, more important indicator—the kids themselves. You notice first that they arrive early, some more than an hour before school, so that they can use the library or attend the optional foreign language classes. Follow them through the day and watch the excitement in their eyes as they prepare a video on executive power to show other students, or their concentration as they build instruments to measure the motion of the planets and stars, or their sorrow as Lennie brings George to his "farm" in the closing pages of Steinbeck's *Of Mice and Men*. In the halls the chatter is happy, friendly, good-natured—you are greeted with smiles and offers of help. Herb Rosenfeld, the teacher who doubles as assistant principal, tests your observational skills: "Have you found the place where the kids go off to hide and smoke during the day?" You admit that, no, maybe you're not such a good observer, you have not yet found such a spot. And Herb grins: "There isn't one."

How can this be? Amidst all the horror stories about inner-city schools, here is a school (and there are many others) that succeeds, both by conventional measures and by the clear indications kids themselves give. But this school doesn't have the back-to-the-basics, sit-in-the-desk-and-be-quiet environment that many have come to equate with teaching and learning. Instead, it is an active, busy place, with students coming and going, working in groups, seldom if ever reading a textbook, and engaged in a wide variety of tasks. Two things make this possible: a sense of community that is built here, and a narrowed yet richer curriculum. These two things lead to students who care about their learning, themselves, and each other.

The sense of community at CPESS is built through both the

internal organization of the school and links to the community outside the school walls. CPESS was started in 1985, and Deborah Meier, the school's principal (called Debbie by staff and students alike), makes it clear that the desire to see kids more connected to a school was a driving force behind its founding. She and the staff wanted to be different from the "huge and impersonal" high schools that dot the city: "Places with thousands of kids, hundreds of teachers, a vast array of complex schedules, no cohesion, and little sense of community—where many kids get lost, lose hope, are uninspired."

To combat this alienation, CPESS is kept small and made smaller still by dividing it up into "houses." Each house of around 80 students and four teachers holds two grade levels, seventh/eighth, ninth/tenth, or eleventh/twelfth (also called the Senior Institute). The relatively low student/teacher ratio is accomplished by having *everyone* teach; you won't find teams of administrators huddled over coffee or behind closed office doors in this building.

To make the school even smaller and more personal, there is its basic building block—advisory. According to Herb, to understand CPESS you have to "start with what happens in advisory." Each teacher is assigned a group of about fourteen students (that's how many fit in a school-district van), all from the same grade level, all in his or her house. Unlike the usual homeroom setup, where kids show up in the morning, hear announcements, and leave, advisory groups meet for nearly three hours a week. The time is occupied with the usual housekeeping chores—attendance, announcements, materials to be sent home. But more important, advisory is where kids connect with the school through a single adult.

"The advisory is a group arrangement in which one adult develops a relationship with a number of students that allows him to paint a complete picture of each of these students, at least in school," explains Herb. "In order to do that, you have to know what kids are feeling. So, through a variety of different devices—journal writing, small group discussion—kids are pushed to express themselves. Express themselves in detail and at length and to reach for what they may be thinking or feeling that normally they may not express." Advisory groups take trips together, and the advisor is the one who reports all academic progress to families and maintains contact with a child's home. This structure is a clear and deliberate attempt to create community, to support children and integrate them into the life of the school.

The students themselves speak most eloquently about the system. "Ricky [Harris, a teacher in the seventh/eighth grade house] cares about us. That's why he's always calling us at home when we're absent, and pushing us to get our work done to our best. He treats me like a little brother, and I love him like a brother, too." A tenth-grade student who attended another high school for two years echoes Debbie Meier's observation: "At [the other school] we were just numbers. Here everybody knows you, especially your advisor. We can go to Herb for help with school, home, whatever; he's always there." Small classes, houses, advisory: that is what community at CPESS is all about—someone is always there.

Of course, the danger with any tight-knit community is that it can turn in on itself to the exclusion of others, encouraging members not to build relationships with outsiders (say, for example, communities built on racism, religious intolerance, or age). Unfortunately, many of the "communities" to which our children belong do just that. Formally, think about single-sex organizations, religious groups of believers only, athletic teams from which many students are cut, and social groups based on academic criteria. Informally, think of the cliques children form which ostracize some students, making them untouchables who can socially contaminate any student who offers help or support. Then think of the school—when the door swings shut at the start of the day, virtually no one is let out without passes, in triplicate signed three days before, virtually no one comes in, and all life is segregated by age as teenagers find only other teens for models. Here the main form of interaction children have with other "communities" is to cheer for their defeat and humiliation on the athletic field. And we wonder why young people seem so unwilling to be "involved" in the community. How did adults get so dumb?

Students are not kept in isolation at CPESS. Every Monday through Thursday morning, if you stand outside the school, you see what seems to be a steady stream of truants, kids who stopped

really interesting!

by to be counted as present but are now slipping back out for a day. In fact, these are some of the most responsible young people around: students on the way to their community service placement. For half a day each week every student works as a volunteer in one of over forty-five different community service placements throughout the Upper East and West Sides of New York City. Working as a teacher's aide, organizing games for children in a pediatric emergency unit, getting out a mailing for a community theater, writing for a neighborhood newspaper, talking, or more important, listening, to senior citizens at a nursing home, all these tasks and more are taken on by the students.

The school day is structured so that an entire house is gone from the school at the same time, so students do not miss classes and staff have extended planning time together. While students do not receive a grade for their work, it is a vital part of their educational experience that must be completed for graduation. The students are responsible for getting to and from the placement on their own—and they do, either walking, taking a subway, or riding a bus. Seldom, if ever, do they miss a day. There is a simple lesson here: give a student a real responsibility, and he or she will act responsibly.

Naomi Danzig, coordinator of the service program, was there at the beginning when Debbie Meier suggested that it would be good if students left CPESS with a marketable skill and some real-life experience in the world of work. The program has developed in ways that go well beyond that original goal, as students have developed links to their own community that help them see the contribution they can make. Naomi puts it this way: "We want them to see how they are powerful people right now. That they can contribute and be effective now, not at some far-off date in the future. In other words, this has very little to do with credentials. We live in a highly credentialed society that can only assess people on the basis of pieces of paper. We say all of our kids can contribute now, that they are all capable of understanding the difference they can make. The students are more spontaneous [in the program]; they are generally on their own so it allows them to be who they are, caring, warm, insightful; these are not attributes that normally early or middle adolescents praise in one another. The peer pressures are as strong here as anywhere else: how you dress, how you walk, what you do in or out of school. . . . We hope, we know, this gives them an opportunity to be themselves."

But does the academic agenda of the classroom get slighted in all this? Kids out of school, advisory meetings during the day, what about all the calls we hear for more "time on task," more hours in the school day? CPESS has an answer for its doubters on this agenda: less is more.

Unlike the comprehensive high schools so many of us know or knew in our hometowns, students at CPESS do not choose their courses from a list of electives. Every student takes the same core of courses. But it is not a core curriculum like that being touted by test-and-measure statehouse reformers. You won't find endless lists of names and dates to memorize, or sheets of math problems to work. The curriculum at CPESS is, in Herb's words, "thematically developed through essential questions, and learning and growth are assessed by kids doing things." The best way to look at the thematic and narrowed nature of the curriculum is to follow one student through a day at CPESS. Remember, though, there is no such thing as a typical day; some days start with advisory and some end with it; community service is scheduled once a week; and academic classes may take the entire morning, or afternoon, or both. We'll follow Jimi, a seventh grader in the East House of Division I (seventh and eighth graders). In other schools Jimi would be in a pull-out program for children with special needs. Living with his unemployed mother in one of the area's many housing projects, he came to CPESS after not finding success in several other New York City schools. Here, he began the year by attempting to burn down the school. Today, halfway through the school year, he's our tour guide and you would never have picked him out as a "problem" student.

Jimi's school day can begin as early as 8 A.M., when the school building opens. Jimi makes a point of arriving at 8:15, when the school is already buzzing with activity. He finds a corner in the library and spends about half an hour on his schoolwork. The next fifteen minutes are spent on the rapid-fire give and take that only another teenager could understand.

The academic day begins at 9, and today that means Jimi is in

Ricky Harris's humanities/social studies class. This class meets for two hours, as do most of the classes, allowing extended time for real work. This year's theme is the emergence of contemporary political issues, with a focus on United States History. Next year, Jimi and his fellow seventh graders will study the peopling of America—the theme this year's eighth graders had last year. The two-year rotation of themes insures that every student in the multigraded houses gets every theme. The eighth graders will move on to the ninth/tenth-grade themes of comparative systems of law and government and non-European traditions.

Today Ricky and his students are dealing with the news media and its influence on political events. This particular topic is a spin-off of an earlier one in which the students followed the 1988 presidential election from the perspective of the issues in their community and the influence of people of color on electoral politics. Ricky has cast backward today, using the Boston Massacre and accounts of it to discuss propaganda. Listening in on the discussion you hear the same questions repeated several times—how do we know that, what evidence do you have, where would we find out? These and other questions have a familiar ring because versions of these same questions are posted in various places on the walls. On one wall are the "essential questions," which all of the humanities teachers utilize to organize the subject matter under consideration. They are:

- How do people achieve power?
- How do people respond to being deprived of power?
- How does power change hands?
- What gives laws their power?

Of course, these questions change each year as the humanities theme changes. Another set of questions is located near the door in every room in the school. These questions form the "Habits of Mind" that all teachers in all subject matters focus on:

- How do we know what we know?
- What's the evidence?
- What's the viewpoint?

- How else may it be considered?
- What difference does it make?

So when Ricky asks if Paul Revere's etching and poem about the Boston Massacre are accurate, it makes sense that these twelve- and thirteen-year-olds ask fairly sophisticated questions in response. For instance, what news accounts of the event are available, what did British papers report, and what would be a credible source for information about the actual events? And when students are grappling with the underlying issue here, it makes sense that they see propaganda as a tool some people use to get power. Building from one theme, they have not only developed a complex understanding of a historical event but have also begun to grasp a concept that will serve them well for their lives as citizens: propaganda and its uses.

At 11:00 Jimi and his friends move on to the two-hour math/science block. For the most part students receive an hour of each subject, changing rooms and teachers halfway through the period. However, the block does allow for the teachers to collaborate and extend the time as needed. In Bridget Bellettiere's math class students are working on a variety of tasks around the theme of patterns in numbers. All of them will make either a slide rule or an abacus as a way of presenting how number sets work. Their projects will be accompanied by reports on the principles behind their exhibits. Similar exhibitions are used in all subject areas to evaluate what students know. Several times during the class Bridget is approached by a student who has found an easier way to unlock the problems presented by the slide rule or abacus. Each time she smiles and responds that of course it's all right to use the "easier" way; after all, the students have just unlocked another pattern in math.

Science follows immediately, and the students quickly gather in groups to work on their exhibition in this area. For two years the science curriculum in Division I focuses on the human being, teaching basic biology through the questions of who and what we are, how we work, and how we fit into the environment. Utilizing scientific methods of inquiry, students explore issues in fitness, nutrition, reproduction, growth, the brain and senses, and ecology. Jimi's group is working on an exhibition that involves devising an experiment to determine the salt and sugar threshold for twenty other students. This work requires two additional skills, computer science and art, that we haven't seen earlier today and that seem to have been missing from the curriculum.

In fact, both of these subjects are woven into the core courses Jimi has had today. Studio art is taught directly through a ten-week course that introduces students to a variety of media. But the real art instruction comes as students visit Joel Handorff's art room to integrate artistic endeavors into their exhibitions. And art and music appreciation are taught in the humanities classes as those topics naturally arise through the students' studies. Computer science is approached in a similar way, taught when the students need computer skills for computation, graphing, word processing, or similar tasks. Again, less is more. By taking just two or three subjects, utilizing a limited number of questions about them, and pursuing those questions thematically, students gain a wide range of skills that help them do something real with what they are learning.

At 1:00 Jimi is off to lunch. This is when the physical education program takes place as well, including a fair number of intramural sports. Jimi returns to Ricky's room for advisory for the last hour of the day. Advisory today deals with academics, in particular how often students are writing in their journals, what books they are reading for leisure, how well they are doing their homework. They also need to discuss how to raise money for their advisory trip. Ricky checks in with each young person and offers suggestions for improvement. Next time advisory may cover health and family education (including sex education and drug abuse), career exploration, or social and ethical concerns. Each advisor builds a program around these issues as his/her group needs them.

After school Jimi heads home. Other students linger in the library (open until 5:00), some stay for instrumental music, still others for team sports. Jimi and his colleagues have had another good day at a very special school. It's a place where people care about one another, where students gain in-depth understandings of the world around them, where what they do matters. It's a school where Lindsay, a tenth grader, claims she has "learned to learn for myself. I'll think of something that wasn't there; I'll figure it out my own way. I'm learning stuff that wasn't even asked." And it's the answers to those unasked questions that make all the difference—in this school and in our lives.

Winchester, New Hampshire: Getting the Climate Right

The New England states: picture-postcard perfect, a mecca for nature lovers of all sorts, fall foliage, winter skiing, spring maple sugaring, summer backpacking. Dotted with small villages distinguished by their general stores and village greens, parts of New England seem to be stuck in time; a simpler, slower, more genteel era of town meetings, yeoman farmers, small merchants, and face-to-face democracy. Indeed, these enduring traditions of communal life do still exist here, and at their best they remind us of what democratic life can promise. But the problems of the modern world know no geographic boundary—and they show up in the lives of New England's young people just as they do in New York City.

At the end of Park Street in the village of Winchester, New Hampshire, sits Thayer Junior/Senior High School. It is a school that only a decade ago had a drop-out rate of nearly 50 percent, and fewer than 15 percent of the graduates went on to higher education of any form. Underlying all this was a feeling that many students at Thayer just were not connected to the school. Faced with fairly limited employment possibilities when they left school, students saw few reasons to attend to the curriculum or the life of the school.

Into this setting entered Dennis Littky, an educator taking time out from his career to rebuild a cabin and nurture a community newspaper. When the Thayer principalship came open in the summer of 1981, Littky applied and reentered the educational world. He came with a vision: "I knew that I wanted the kids to be good thinkers, to use their minds, to like school; I knew I wanted the relationship between teachers and kids to be good—I wanted us to not be fighting but to work together; so there was all that stuff that I knew. . . . But now the question was, how do you go about doing that?" The answer to that question presented itself as Dennis spent the summer meeting with every student, teacher, and most of the parents in the community. Simply put, says Dennis, "Everyone knew the atmosphere had to get better. And that was my first thing. I don't think you can move on to other areas until you get the climate right."

Getting the climate right meant a number of things at Thayer. First it meant turning the physical space of the building into a place that invited students rather than repulsed them. The work started in the common spaces of the school—the cafeteria, the entryways, the halls. Not only were tables and ceilings repaired, walls painted, and floors patched, but a special project began as well. One student, a returning senior, had indicated little interest in school in his summer meeting with Dennis. Dennis searched to find an activity to keep the young man in school, and he found it in art. Dennis offered him a cafeteria wall as a canvas. After a summer of work, the Pegasus, a life-size mural exploding with color, emerged. Given Thayer's history it isn't surprising that bets were placed among the local townspeople as to when the Pegasus would be defaced. It watches over the cafeteria today, however, untouched, serving as the unofficial mascot for the school. Almost every year it is joined by another mural, just as dramatic, somewhere in the school, a mural always initiated and designed by a student (or students).

The message in this seemingly simple act of environmental enhancement (apparently not so obvious when we look at the drab, sterile, or often outright ugly school interiors in so many communities) was to tell students that someone cared about them, that someone was willing to take a risk to make their space more pleasant. But beauty wasn't enough, and the next move was to challenge and change the academic structures that create the inhospitable environments in so many schools. It was these changes that protected the murals as well as raised Thayer's graduation rate to nearly 95 percent, with over 60 percent of those graduates going on to some form of higher education.

Much of the conventional wisdom today is that school days need to be longer. Littky started in the other direction: "I figured it made no sense to do more of what we already weren't doing right. So one of the first things I did was to call the state [education office] to find out what the minimum amount of time was that we could spend in school." The answer was six and a half hours, so Thayer went to a six-period day, one hour per period, and *no* study halls. Then every student met with Littky to work out a schedule, and as needs arose—say students wanting to intern in a day-care center or a local senior citizen center—they were worked into the schedule.

When you visit Thayer you immediately pick up the relaxed tempo that hour-long class periods generate. Students are not lugging around seven sets of books, racing from room to room at thirty-seven minutes after, or eight minutes until, the hour. Rather, classes move easily into extended projects and teachers and students savor the time available to settle in, focus, read, discuss, or write about the topic at hand. At the end of the period there is not the usual flurry of books slapping shut, quickly scribbled assignments, work tossed on the desk, and a mad dash for the door. In fact, there are not even any bells ringing to mark the passing of a period, and more likely than not someone will forget to ring the only bell of the day, the one at the day's close.

The Spectrum Program

Not satisfied, always seeing the school as "a living organism that has got to be changing all the time," Littky and his staff have begun moving toward using even larger blocks of time for extended study. One of the most interesting of these projects, and something of a model for other parts of the school, is the Spectrum program. The idea behind Spectrum is simple: take a team of teachers from different subject areas, give them the first four hours of the day and the same number of students they would normally see during that time, and let them design their own program. What has emerged is a group of eleventh and twelfth graders of all abilities (admitted on a first come, first serve basis), three teachers (in natural history, English, and math), and a schedule that leaves you wondering why everyone doesn't do it this way.

Dan Bisaccio, Julie Gainsburg, and Val Cole are the Spectrum teachers. Every week they work with fifty-five students, the same students they have shared as a team all year. The students are divided into three subgroups and rotate between teachers, some days seeing all three, others seeing just one or two for extended periods of time. In addition, one period a day is set aside as a "coaching period," a time when the students are not formally scheduled into a room but can work in small groups on projects or meet one-on-one with a teacher for extra help. Often they learn from a curriculum that is woven together by a theme. Like their experience with Thoreau's *Walden*—they first read the book in English class and then studied the pond's geologic origins in natural history class.

Aside from linking the curriculum together, there are two additional benefits from altering the usual schedule of the high school day. The first and most obvious is the ability to make the daily schedule respond to the curriculum, not the curriculum respond to the schedule. Dan, who teaches natural history, provides us with a simple example: "I wanted to go out collecting fossils at a place about a mile from here. It didn't make sense to bring all the kids to the site; it would be somewhat dangerous for one thing, and, two, a lot of people would get lost in the shuffle. So we were able to work out a schedule where for three days I was able to take one group of kids per day for the whole morning to the site. It didn't interfere with their academic schedule at all because the three of us just arranged it so the other two would take kids for longer periods of time." Time, such a precious commodity in a child's life; how important to be able to spend it wisely and with care. The second benefit is a by-product of the time issue, but an intended one. Spectrum makes the school smaller and gives the students another point of connection with it. While in some high schools students see seven or eight teachers a day, these kids spend virtually all of their time with three. While some high school students rotate through seven classes with upward of thirty different companions per session, these students spend most of their day with just several dozen people.

But the students' connection with the program is not left to chance. A special space—an abandoned barn behind the school—has become the group's "home" away from the school; group outings are a regular part of the program; and parents are involved in both social and planning activities. Spectrum provides a special place where kids and teachers have time not only to pursue subjects but also to get to know one another. It is a way of connecting the student with the school community, letting each student know that he or she counts.

But what of the other students at Thayer? Are they connected as well? Indeed, long before Spectrum [or the similar teaming efforts that are under way], Littky and his faculty had instituted an advisory system at Thayer. Similar in intent to the program at Central Park East, it was another part of Littky's agenda to get the climate right. Each Thayer staff member, including the principal and guidance counselor, is assigned a group of advisees. Since all faculty members are involved, each advisory group consists of only ten students. It stays together throughout the students' two junior high and four high school years at Thayer. Each advisor is responsible for all communication home about his/her students, arranging parent conferences, compiling report cards, and the general life of each advisee at school.

Don Weisberger, a special education teacher at Thayer, describes the system's effect this way: "Advisory in one word is communication. It makes the school smaller. . . . [Students] know someone's there for them, they are not getting lost among all the other students. . . . In advisory we don't talk *at* kids, we talk *with* kids."

For Greg, a senior, the system has meant that an "advisor is there if we have problems, say, like with another teacher, or school, or whatever, or if we just need someone to talk to. [My advisor] wants to know as much as he can about each person so he knows their weaknesses and their strengths and he is always willing to help. . . . He looks out for us as much as he can."

Beyond these formal structures, the folks at Thayer challenge yet one more notion that often shapes the structures of schooling. Inherent in much school organization is the assumption that individuals cannot be responsible for their own behavior, that it takes suspensions, assistant principals, student handbooks, and grades to keep students in line.

The school Littky came to was plagued with discipline problems. Teachers felt they had no control; kids felt overwhelmed by the rules. The solution was, first, to assume that student misbehavior and teacher frustration weren't necessarily the "fault" of either party. Rather, as Dennis puts it, any time a student was in trouble, "I assumed it wasn't just the kid's fault but a problem of the environment." So the staff and the students took a long look at the school rules, giving here, taking there, but really looking at what is necessary to make a school run. Finally they came up with a few rules that everyone could agree on—at which point they were hardly needed. The cycle of mistrust and tension was broken merely by everyone "getting clear that the priority was the kids. That we would do whatever we could for the kids, and were doing it, through advisory and the schedule and all the other stuff. And when you treat them with respect, with dignity, they act responsibly." The gospel according to Littky.

And it works. Dan Bisaccio points out that one of the big differences between Thayer and other schools he knows of is that you "don't find the kids rowdy to the extent you might expect; there's virtually no vandalism or theft here." That explains why there are *no locks* on the lockers in the hall. Stephanie, a junior, explains that "kids here aren't into stealing and stuff. It just won't be right to do that to your friends." When I'm walking down the hall with Dennis I point out several locks on a row of lockers. "Oh, yeah," he chuckles, "those are seventh graders, they haven't figured out where they are yet."

The responsible nature of the students flows outside the school as well. At one time, as hard as I find this to believe after my visits to Thayer, the kids at the school were apparently referred to by some as the "Thayer animals." Disaffected, angry, alienated, they were unwelcome in many places and feared in others. But now the name "Thayer" on a letter jacket or windbreaker marks a student as someone special. Thayer students are recognized as valuable members of the community, as people who make Winchester's junior and senior high schools among the best around. Dan mentioned this to me as we were traveling on the field trip to Walden. "Most of the time we are told that our students are some of the most knowledgeable and best-behaved students that the host has ever met." At the end of that day's visit as we were leaving Walden Pond, the naturalist who had been our guide caught up with Dan and me as we returned to our car. "You know," he said, "we get hundreds of groups through here every year. But I can't remember one that was this well-mannered, asked so many questions, and treated the place with such respect. Would you please thank your students for me?" Dan just looked at me and smiled.

Of course, changing a school's character and structure is never easy. In some ways it may be even harder to change in the often very conservative and close-knit communities of New England. Such was the case in Winchester, as Littky found when he was fired in 1987. It took several court challenges and the election of a new school board to reinstate him, but in the end the majority of the community rallied around him. It wasn't an easy time for Dennis, his teachers, or the students. But he never entertained the thought of just walking away. He and his staff are driven by a vision that makes their work possible, and that makes coming to school every day a challenge they want to face: "When it all works, I'd like the kid to be an inquisitive learner. To be somebody who is excited about reading a book or learning something, or seeing something. A person who is strong enough to stand up and speak for what he or she wants. A person . . . who is continuing to learn and to grow. Somebody who understands him or herself and understands learning. That's what is important."

Rabun Gap, Georgia: Making Connections

It would be fair to call Georgia schools at the end of the 1980s the most overregulated in the United States. In one of the most wrongheaded educational reform programs in the country, the Georgia state legislature has seen fit to mandate all of the following, and more:

- Standardized testing of all kindergarten children to be the sole criterion for advancement to first grade (since withdrawn under a firestorm of criticism by educators of young children from around the country; the tests, however, as developmentally inappropriate as they are, are still used as one indicator for promotion).
- A standardized teacher evaluation form that reduces good

teaching to a checklist of behaviors and the ability to fill out a formulaic lesson plan. Teachers report simply altering their teaching style to fit the guidelines, which reward lecture and passive student behavior, on the days they are to be observed.

- Standardized testing for all students on a yearly basis, with test scores to be reported in the media. These scores are then used by ill-informed news reporters to rank schools as the tests lose their diagnostic function and become evaluation tools.

- Tightly regulated standards for schools, including the number of minutes that are to be spent studying a subject. This strait-jacket approach limits such valuable activities as field trips or extended periods, as every subject matter can only be allotted its state-mandated proportion of time.

- The crowning glory of all this, a statewide curriculum, down to the objectives students are to learn, has been written by those farthest away from children and teaching in the educa-tional hierarchy—state department of education bureaucrats.

It would be hard to imagine a scenario that reflects the legislated-excellence movement more completely than the Georgia Quality Basic Education (QBE) scheme. Top-down mandates that attempt to control everything from what children learn to how teachers teach, from the number of computer-scored questions five-year-olds have to get right to go to first grade to the parts of speech a high school sophomore has to master, all the reforms resound with the more-is-better refrain we hear from the official voices of school re-form. In the end, there is little change in terms of what children learn. What does change is the life of the teacher—for the worse.

In the face of all this, one of the nation's most innovative and progressive educational endeavors continues, now well into its third decade—the Foxfire program. Many of us know of Foxfire through its successful publishing enterprises, beginning with *The Foxfire Book* and continuing through *Foxfire 9*, which have captured the public's attention with their interviews of Appalachian elders helping to pre-serve traditional ways of life. But what many people do not know is that these books, and others on selected topics such as cooking and wine making, are taken from the *Foxfire* magazine, written by students in Eliot Wigginton's high school English classes at Rabun County High School in Clayton, Georgia. That fact, not the books' contents, is what the *Foxfire* program is really about.

Wigginton literally stumbled onto the publishing idea in the way most truly valuable educational innovation occurs—by trying to find a way to motivate kids to learn. As he tells it, his students in Rabun Gap were so bored with his lectures on English that they decided to warm them up a little, by setting his lectern on fire. The collective boredom and rebellion of the students grew as he used the classic teacher control tactics of threatening to lower grades and tossing kids out of class. He began "to regard them collectively as the enemy—and I became the prisoner—not they."[1] Before the warfare had gone on too long, Wigginton, to save himself as a teacher as much as to reach his students, called for a truce and proposed that he and his students figure out some way to make "Englas," as one of the students spelled it, more interesting. What followed were long brainstorming sessions that finally yielded the *Foxfire* magazine in its original form as a school literary magazine. Later, at the suggestion of community members and students, the notion of utilizing interviews with community elders gradually took over the entire publishing venture.

Today the *Foxfire* magazine is still written, edited, and published by students. Royalties earned from the publications have purchased land upon which students have reconstructed cabins and preserved cultural artifacts. The Foxfire project has increased to include Foxfire music, radio and video, and storytelling programs. But the program's success has not affected the core practices and beliefs that originally inspired it. These ideas are that students learn best when they are engaged in real experiences yielding genuine products, that these experiences should be related to the student's daily life and locale, and that students themselves should play a major part in making decisions about their work. It is this type of education that will have a long-term effect on students, teaching them how to learn, linking them to their community, and showing them they can make a difference.

When Wigginton first began to explore with his students how to change the dynamics in his English class, he began by making a list of times he felt he really learned something in school. Key to that list was the following simple item: "Times when things we did, as students, had an audience beyond the teacher." Reflecting on this, Wigginton applied it to his own teaching: "In what ways, as a new teacher, had I created opportunities for my students to have that affirmation that could bring them to a new and serious sense that the work we were doing together could have utility and function and worth and purpose and the potential for reward far beyond an entry in my grade book? None." Unfortunately, Wigginton's answer to his own challenge would probably be repeated by many teachers if asked the same question. Students sense this when they ask, "Why do we have to know this?" and the only answer is that they will see it on the quiz. The work at school is left at school, and it doesn't seem to matter in the real world.[2]

In asking the question, Wigginton forced himself to act upon it. One of the things he and his students were looking for was a way in which English could be a tool for learning something large, not merely an end in itself: grammar and reading and interpretation could become means to doing something valuable. After numerous false starts that "something valuable" has become the Foxfire books and magazines. Now students do need to know how to write, edit, compose, rewrite, summarize, and a host of other academic skills because these skills are put to use every day in producing something for a real audience that students care about. The range of skills students use goes well beyond English: they take and develop their own pictures for publication, keep financial records on the magazine, and utilize communications skills in setting up interviews, making contacts with grant agencies, hosting visitors, giving tours of the Foxfire grounds, and giving speeches about Foxfire at numerous meetings and conventions. Students do these things well because *their* names are on it, not the teacher's.

The academic side of the publishing venture is not left to chance, however. In order to insure that students pick up on the elements of grammar, Wigginton carefully marks all classroom work, drawing attention to common mistakes and conducting quick mini-lessons on how to avoid them. Also posted clearly in the room are the state of Georgia's QBE objectives for the English class. Whenever one is covered in the course of class work Wigginton makes note of it for everyone.

It is important to point out that the grammar lessons or QBE objectives are secondary to the publishing aspects of the course, at least for the students. Rather than spend the year driving students through the chapters in the grammar book so that they might write an essay in the spring, Wigginton begins with writing for a purpose and draws the grammar lessons out of that. Thus, students don't ask, "Why are we learning this?"; they see why from the very first day of class and are reminded of the reason every time their names go on a new publication.

For example, when Johnny Eller visits the classroom to demonstrate toy making, it's not just for the sake of the interview. Shortly after he leaves, Wigginton bounds to the front of the room and begins. "OK, you guys, every interview we publish has to have an introduction. It's how you make sure people really understand who Johnny is. And since we know that part of who he is is what he looks like, we need to get that down. So, right now, while it's still fresh, let's get a description of him." He goes to the board and solicits descriptions from around the room, gradually filling up the board. "Now, I want all you guys to take this home and come back tomorrow with a paragraph describing Johnny." After several more sessions the class checks off the ability to "Write a Descriptive Paragraph" from the list of QBE objectives. Just one more task accomplished on the way to becoming a published author.

One Foxfire alumnus put it this way:

> Somehow I learned to write more creatively as a result of Foxfire . . . . It was the culmination of all I did at Foxfire, having to pick out a word or a phrase that would catch the reader's eye, listening to a tape you have to edit to make it readable, observing the environment, learning how to connect paragraphs and how to get from one paragraph to another to make an article flow. When you listened to a tape you had to learn to use commas, exclamation marks, and [quotation marks] correctly, even spelling.[3]

The other side of writing for an audience is writing about some-thing real. Again, from Wigginton's notes on his own schooling, here are two more types of experiences that make a difference: "times when there were visitors to our class from the world outside the classroom"; "times when, as students, we left the classroom on assignments or field trips."[4] School does tend to be an artificial environment for students. It is age-segregated and cut off from the community, with a few contacts for six to eight hours beyond the walls of the building. Such an environment only fuels the "why know this?" question as students see little connection between school and the rest of their lives. The point is not that everything we do in school leads to a job-related skill or is "relevant" in some sim-plistic sense. At issue, rather, is insuring that what students learn in school is not gained in an environment so artificial that they are unable to use those skills in any other setting.

For Wigginton's students, all of the southern Appalachian region is their classroom. The premise of Foxfire is that students are on a mission to collect, record, and preserve the history and heritage of their area. To do this, students seek out what are known as "community contacts," senior members of the community who are willing to share their skills, insights, and wisdom with students. Interviews with these contacts are then transcribed, edited, and, with the introductory material written by students, published in the magazine and books.

What students gain from this is more than a chance to produce something real. They are reclaiming a heritage, their own heritage, which has been historically demeaned through cartoon characters and national stereotypes. What these students are discovering is that their homes, their neighbors and relatives, are a valuable natural treasure. What they learn in school about writing helps to preserve and reclaim that heritage. The experience is real—not contrived, not simulated—but real in the sense of using what they learn to make sense of the world. Perhaps it is easiest to grasp how important this is through some comments by Wigginton's students:

- I never really ever knew what my heritage was until I got in Foxfire. Seems like I had a lot more in common with these old people than I thought.[5]

- I'm sure she [Aunt Arie, a regular Foxfire contact] knew she fed me, shared her life experience with me, and once gave me a place to sleep in a bed that was stacked one foot high with quilts. But I doubt that she knew that she renewed my faith in mankind and taught me what unselfish generosity was.[6]
- I've learned that I'm Appalachian. And that's a good thing. We've got a good tradition, a heritage, a home. Just like everybody else, we deserve the respect due all human beings.

There is one more element involved in Foxfire's work that makes the experience so valuable: the role students play in making decisions about their work. Wigginton, again drawing on his own experiences as a student, argues that students really learn when they "are given responsibility of an adult nature and are trusted to fulfill it." Students in the Foxfire program are given such responsibilities every day. At the individual level students select their own contacts, arrange their own interviews, and are responsible for their own editorial choices. At the classroom level, collaborative decisions are made about the content and organization of each issue of the magazine. On the contents page of each issue you will find a listing of "Editors" that includes every member of the class. Indeed, the entire class debates such issues as the cover photograph and the order of the interviews.

Beyond the class, students have been and continue to be involved in the major decisions that face the Foxfire project. Students often join the school's weekly staff meetings and are consulted on a range of organizational issues. They are involved in the relatively straightforward items, such as whether a visitation request from a school or teacher can be honored. The norm of involving students in decision making extends into some of the most important issues Foxfire has faced. As Wigginton himself describes:

When the JFG Coffee Company wanted to make a series of coffee and tea commercials showing our community contacts demonstrating various traditional crafts (the theme begins, "Just as these people take pride and care in their work, so too does

JFG''), I was against the idea, but the students wanted to pursue it. Writers from the ad agency flew up from New Orleans, presented their story boards, and then the students fanned out across the country to poll contacts and community advisory board members as to their thoughts. The final decision, the result of heated class debates, was to allow the company to proceed provided that

- Teams of students would actually participate in the filming process.

- Students would locate all contacts and set filming dates in advance to minimize strain on the participating community people and make sure all went smoothly and no one was inconvenienced or put in an awkward position.

- All contacts would be paid on the spot at the completion of filming their segment.

- No contacts would be asked to comment on JFG products at all, or "taste" them for reaction, etc. Thus a contact would be shown making butter or bottoming a chair, for example, and would talk briefly about that process, and then at the end of the commercial the JFG message would be added.

The company agreed, a dozen people were filmed, each was paid on the spot, and all concerned were pleased. The company admitted it was their most successful series of commercials ever; and one of the contacts told the students involved, "That's the most money I ever made at one time in my life. That will pay for my seeds and fertilizer this year and pull me out of the hole, and I want to thank you for that." And in our part of the country—which is JFG territory anyway—the commercials were watched eagerly by families and friends and were very popular. I would have vetoed the project if the decision had been left to me, but the students wanted to do it, they proved to me that people in the community wanted to try it, and they convinced me that it would be a worthwhile project. Had I voted no, they would have outvoted me, and they stood ready to take the consequences had the whole thing proved to have been a mistake. And so I backed them, and I'm glad now that I did.

As people who come to us with ideas have found, they get put through some of the toughest questioning they've ever faced, and as likely as not, if their ideas are flawed or they aren't willing to let the students participate fully and have some control, they'll be sent packing.[7]

How does Foxfire go on, swimming against the tide of the legislated-excellence movement in Georgia? Certainly partly because of the program's historic success. Since it is recognized internationally as one of the most outstanding educational programs in the country, anyone, the state of Georgia included, would be hard-pressed to challenge it. Yet you have to wonder in today's climate if such a program, which focuses on actual writing, not just getting through a writing book, and which takes students out of school so they can pursue topics in depth, would even get off the ground. How easily the entire project could have been stifled in its early years, with Wigginton off to succeed in some other area, if he had been obligated to cover an English QBE course of study before being allowed to pursue an actual writing program with his students.

On the other hand, Wigginton does not ignore the demands put on classroom teachers today. He is, after all, among their numbers. Foxfire is not a separate school; it is an English elective within the Rabun County High School curriculum. He faces all the same daily frustrations any teacher does—short periods, classes interrupted for announcements, limited supplies. He also has to meet the QBE objectives for his course just like any other teacher. But in his teaching the QBE objectives are secondary, not primary. It is after he and the students decide upon the next project or challenge that he turns to the QBE handbook and identifies the next set of objectives to be mastered. It is after the students show a need to learn how to avoid dangling prepositions through their writing that he goes to work teaching it. In this way the real work of the class, the daily projects and experiences of kids, drives the curriculum and meets the objectives.

Unfortunately, faced with a list of objectives that must be met, many school systems simply order teachers to march through the list. Compare the lifeless memorization of grammar (or math, history, science, language, or whatever) with the experience of recording and publishing one's history, learning these same concepts through usage. Clearly the latter approach develops citizens who use academic skills as tools and who will come to value their heritage and themselves.

Two from Illinois

Like Wigginton, the final two teachers in this discussion of secondary schools work largely by themselves. They are not fortunate enough to find themselves in a high school that totally shares their vision for students. In fact, they are even more isolated than Wigginton, having achieved neither national notoriety nor the funds to build a support staff. Yet they survive, flourish in fact, and continue to do good things with their students. They are islands of democracy in large high schools, and they make a difference by being there.

It's hard to imagine a public school that could better represent the various mistakes we have made in education than Proviso East High School in Maywood, Illinois. The school holds over 2,500 young people in a massive brick structure that can only be described as foreboding. To enter the school, students have to pass a series of hall guards, displaying their photo ID cards. An office just for the guards is located near the front door, while the administrative offices are out of sight on the second floor.

The school is desegregated, and the growing population of students of color has led many white parents to seek alternatives for their children. Certainly, some of this is simply due to racism. However, one wonders why anyone would choose to send their children to a large, overcrowded school, where guards patrol every door and hallway, where there are so many staff that most of them do not know each other. It's as much the school itself as race that drives people away and leads teachers to despair.

In an attempt to hold the white population, the strategy has been to resegregate children once they are in the school. Virtually the entire curriculum is "tracked," or ability-grouped. This means that students are separated by perceived ability level within classes, and instruction in, say, U.S. history will then vary greatly between "high"-ability and "low"-ability tracks. The fact that this system of instruction, so deeply ingrained in American schools, doesn't work, will be discussed later. But here, at Proviso East, we can see in one classroom the insidious effects of the system and one teacher's struggle, against mounting odds, to turn the tide.

It's first period on a Tuesday, and the kids in John Duffy's low-track U.S. history class wander in. Thirteen students are here today, out of a class list of nearly twenty-five. As will be the case with the rest of Duffy's classes, this one contains overwhelmingly students of color; twelve out of the thirteen attending are black. Many slump into seats, some catching up on a little sleep before the day begins. Their faces are expressionless, their eyes betray little, if any, interest in being in school. It's a situation that overwhelms many teachers.

But John Duffy refuses to give up. "I don't treat them as low-ability kids." For example, they are working on an interpretive art project—a poster contest that displays some school-based application of the Bill of Rights. It's an enrichment activity, Duffy points out, "you know, like all the high-ability classes get to do." And he has organized his U.S. history course around current events being used to illuminate and explore historical issues. No lectures, no drill, no mere memorization activities. Duffy refuses to fall into the trap of spoon-feeding the material to passive students, which only increases their passivity.

The cases he selects to use with his students have a particular resonance with their lives. Today they read aloud an affirmative action case about to be heard by the Supreme Court. The content for the day is the Thirteenth, Fourteenth, and Fifteenth Amendments (quick, raise your hand if you know what they are). But rather than lecture on their history and have students memorize their ratification dates, the task is to learn the ramifications of those important words in today's world. "Why do we have affirmative action?" The discussion is suddenly animated with historical accounts of Jim Crow laws, Rosa Parks, Martin Luther King, Jr. What is amazing is how few of these high school juniors, now seventeen or eighteen, soon on their way into the world, know anything about this history. Not only has the school failed them, but their families, communities, and the media do little to inform them of their history and the power that lies within it. So John Duffy, a white city kid, attempts to kindle in them a sense of who they are by exploring what is happening to them today.

"Jim Crow laws—were they positive or negative?"

"What kind of group is the NAACP?"

"Should companies be allowed to discriminate? What are the laws?"

"Would an opponent or someone for affirmative action call it reverse discrimination?"

Most of the students join in, though some are only physically present, their minds more on girlfriends, jobs, the gang. "So what about it? Put your thoughts into words. Right now write an introductory paragraph to an essay stating your opinion on affirmative action." Now virtually all of the class is writing, and within five minutes they are sharing their positions.

"Wallace, what say you?"

"I'm for it."

"Why?"

"We got to tell our reasons why?"

"Sure, I want to know that, I'm interested." And so it goes around the room . . .

"I think it's fair, it offers equal opportunity."

"It's not fair, the best qualified should be hired." Back and forth until this exchange.

DWAYNE: I'm against it, you can't tell a company not to discriminate.

JOHN: What would you say about the company being allowed to discriminate?

ANGIE: If you said that, we'd still be slaves!

JOEL: It doesn't matter what race you are, it depends on qualifications.

DWAYNE: I'm sayin' he can tell you whatever he wants because
    he's got the jobs to give out.
JOHN: Is that the way it should be?
DWAYNE: No, just the way it is.

Just the way it is for these kids has not been very good, but like
Dwayne most of them see nothing different in their future. "That's
my job," John Duffy says. "Not so much to teach U.S. history, but
to teach them their own personal history. I don't mean ignoring all
the textbook stuff. But I gotta find some way to help these kids know
who they are, feel better about that, feel like they can do something.
Heck, kids in the advanced tracks know that, so anybody can teach
them. This is where the real work goes on. And it's harder because
we segregate them. If I could just get the tracking system dumped,
then we'd do some stuff. But in the meantime I got these kids and
we're goin' for it."

By now the class is in small groups, preparing oral defenses of
their positions on affirmative action that they will present the following day. Duffy works with each group, coaching, working out
interpersonal relations, helping students find resources in his well-
stocked (from his own collection) classroom. He works for them to
be real teams. "What can you learn from other people?" And he
encourages every effort to go further: "We think too often that
unless you're the best, you're nobody. Well, you don't get to be
the best unless you work at it. So watch what other people are
doing, learn from your mistakes, and move on."

The next day in class some of the fruits of his labors show up.
The presentations are clear, dramatic, and filled with detail. The
same group of kids who sleepwalked in the door are avidly involved
in the discussion as issues fly around the room and the debate far
outstrips what passes for information on the various talk show programs the networks provide. Duffy cheerleads: "What you are doing
is excellent. You have researched your ideas, thought about them,
and are enthusiastic. What you have to do now is tighten up how
you *all* present it."

This leads to bringing in even more of the class, the quiet or
more alienated students. David is urged to the front: "Come on

David, you did a very nice job of putting that together." When David falters, a fellow student stands beside him and whispers, "Come on now, you're representing us." He finishes, with her arm around his shoulder, and you wonder why this act, a black female teenager helping a shy white male fellow student, seems so natural in this room but so out of place in much of the rest of our world.

Picture in your mind the typical suburban, high school campus. A semi-modern brick building, surrounded by asphalt that opens out into a neatly trimmed lawn embracing athletic fields and marching-band practice areas. Now throw into that scene a damp depression of sorts, complete with cattails, weeds, some standing water, and a variety of interesting wildlife. Better yet, park this wetland area near the football field and allow it on occasion to run over quite near the path parents walk to get to the Friday night game. Now, what would be the logical course of action in *most* schools? Simple: drain the swamp, cut down the cattails, and plant grass in order to extend the pristine albeit unnatural green carpet. Simple, that is, unless your school is blessed with a teacher like Richard Cargill, who teaches English at Willowbrook High School.

In 1986, the "Battle of the Cattails" ensued in the west Chicago suburb of Villa Park. Its 2,200-student school is not much different from most high schools; you'll find the same regimented day split into short periods and the same menu of courses. But there, in the middle of all this sameness, is something, someone actually, very different. Richard Cargill, who was not about to sit back and watch something so precious to him and his students as a wetland habitat be destroyed, no matter whose aesthetic senses it offended.

Cargill's English class, titled "Man in Harmony with Nature," had long used the site as a place for investigating the environmental issues about which they were writing and reading. One of the issues stressed throughout the course is not mere academic awareness or skill, but a sense of commitment and action. So when it appeared that yet another habitat was to be destroyed, Cargill led by example, enlisting the local teachers' union, public sentiment, and his own energies in a struggle to remove the drainpipe that had been installed to clear the wetland.

It wasn't an easy battle by any means, what with weekend mowings of the cattails and unclear administrative messages. But when the smoke cleared, and the school board and administration had read enough letters from Cargill's former students, not only was a wetland left, but a commitment to entertain a proposal for an entire nature sanctuary on one end of the campus was won. Today students continue to develop that nature sanctuary along the lines of a plan established by Cargill's 1987 class.

It is often said that good teachers do not teach subject matter, they teach who they are. This is certainly true in Cargill's case. Entering his room you might be surprised to realize that it houses an English class. The room is stuffed with material that seems to be more in line with a science class—posters of the environment, rocks, recycling materials, and the like. But the class is indeed an English credit, and the stuff you see is the material about which students read and write. "If you want kids to be good at something like reading, writing, and research, you teach that thing through something they can have a commitment to. Here we use the environment," Cargill points out. Indeed, students do become committed, to testing so-called biodegradable plastic bags, measuring and reporting on various strategies for cutting down the amount of water used in their toilets, or saving tracts of Canadian wilderness.

We are all surrounded by these issues, and most of us do little about them. Why do these teenagers, so often pictured as apathetic or just lazy, get so involved? Quite simply, it's thanks to the example of the man with the soft voice and big heart. "He lives what he says." "He doesn't teach out of the book." "He tells the truth." Who wouldn't follow him?

But do the students learn English? Or is this just another blow-off elective, designed to pad the students' schedules? Not according to test results, which show that Cargill's students do just fine. And not according to the kids either, who certainly know a blow-off course when they see one. Listen to their voices again: "No one misses this class. My other English teacher lives to take attendance, and she needs to." "We learn because he relates this to life; you can do it now. I feel I'll never have to use the stuff from other classes, so why learn it?" "This is a tough course; I work hours on this to get it right. Most of the rest of my homework I do on the bus." There is nothing like publishing your work in a newsletter, sending your findings to your congressperson, or presenting your concerns to the community through a newspaper article to make sure you get it right. Beyond academics, the course nurtures that all-too-rare commodity in today's world: a sense of commitment to make this a better place for us all.

The overflow of that commitment beyond the bounds of the classroom led in 1988 to the formation of Students for a Better Environment (SBE). Cargill, as the club's sponsor, is nominally "in charge" of the organization. But if you sit in on one of SBE's meetings it becomes clear the students run the show. They are the ones who choose each issue, which then goes through a three-step process. First, research: making sure they understand what is at stake, what the evidence is on competing claims, and what can be done. Second, awareness: making sure that in their own lives they are acting in environmentally sound ways in terms of the issue at hand. Third, action: petition campaigns, recycling programs, trips to field sites, clean-up efforts, letters to authorities and the press, all with the intent of making a difference *now*. Their range of success is as varied as the targets they select: local grocery stores are shifting back to paper bags from plastic, but the local Burger King still uses Icelandic fish (Iceland harvests whales, an action SBE opposes);[8] a local developer was prevented from draining a natural wetland for his golf course, but Canadian timber interests continue to harvest rain forests; not everybody in the school recycles, but due to an SBE program over twenty-nine thousand pounds of paper were re-cycled from the school during just the second half of the school year. "It's not that we win all the time," explains Chris Curtis, this year's SBE president. "It's that we make a difference and that we keep on trying." But they win often enough that the sarcophagus in the classroom is slowly filling up with symbols of each victory. Each plastic bag and drainage tile dropped in the coffin makes the world just that much more beautiful.

When students talk about Richard Cargill, which they love to do, the conversation always comes back to the person, not the teacher. "He loves it when we stump him, when he has to go look up something. I know teachers who will never admit they don't know, even when they are wrong." "He values everyone, he wants each of us to succeed." "He is in the habit of treating all his students as respected individuals with unique talents, abilities, and desires." When you watch him teach you see all of this in action, as he strives to set up experiences for each student that make success possible in a deeper way than the student even imagined.

Al was in Cargill's class during the 1988/89 school year. He is, as he points out himself, sort of the head "greaser" in the school. After a class discussion on the deforestation of Canada, Cargill arranged for Al and another student to spend a week visiting a logging camp in British Columbia to witness what was going on firsthand. Today Al is the resident school expert on the issue. Ignoring the snickers of students (who see him as a hood) as he is introduced, Al demonstrates to them the expert he has become with a slide show that leaves his audiences speechless. But he is more than just an expert; he is a changed young man. "I guess I usta just blow off school," Al says and you're almost surprised to hear the words that follow from this hulking, leather-and-jean-clad, unshaven young man. "I really didn't care about it or anything. But now, like after seeing that, it's part of me, I really care about those forests, it's gotten inside of me. . . . Mr. Cargill, he really turned me on to this stuff. Without him I wouldn't care about anything. Now I do."

Rethinking Schooling

What goes on at Thayer and CPESS, and in the classrooms of Eliot Wigginton, John Duffy, and Richard Cargill, is the stuff of genuine school reform. What is done here with and for high school students will make a difference in who they are when they leave school. This is because, unlike most of the official school reform agenda, the very assumptions about how to "do" school are challenged in these places.

Let's take another look at the outside of Thayer Junior/Senior High School. It is an old, squat, three-story (if you count the basement) building built in the classic school-as-factory architectural style.

This school, and thousands of other schools built from 1910 to 1940, was deliberately patterned after the factories that were springing up during our Industrial Revolution. There is probably one in your town, and I can describe it without seeing it: built of red brick, three stories high, with tall, large windows and one or two huge entryway doors. It is topped off with a cement scroll of some sort and you enter the school at the end of a long walkway that leads to a plaza or steps directing all traffic to the main entrance. All the building needs is to have its flag replaced with smokestacks and it would be an exact replica of the small- to mid-size factories that were, at the turn of the century, symbols of economic development throughout the midwestern and eastern states.

Unfortunately, this drab architecture was reflected in the teaching styles and organization of the schools. Public schooling did not become commonplace until the 1920s and '30s. During the same period the efficiency movement in manufacturing had grasped the business community. The assembly line, with each worker endlessly repeating the same task without control over his or her work, and its emphasis on uniform standardized products, became the new icon of American society. Citing the success of American industry, educational and civic leaders applied the lessons of the factory to the schools. Students were to be processed in batches, with the curriculum chopped into small pieces and administered at each step by a worker (teacher) with little or no control over the process.[9]

Think for a minute of the school as assembly line. Every child enters at a set age and is expected to proceed at the same pace. At each step of the way the child is tested to see if he/she has mastered the necessary content. The teacher, stuck at a certain grade level or subject matter while the children move on to the next treatment, only sees one part of the child's development. All products (children) are pushed to the norm, and those who come with less "raw material" are dropped into lower tracks and become substandard products. Textbooks that chop information up are used. This was the dominant motif for schools in the first half of the century.

Today industry knows better, and workers are more involved in making decisions about the production processes. The assembly line is giving way to quality circles, and *quality* rather than *quantity* is becoming the watchword. Unfortunately, many schools have yet to learn this, and the consequences are disastrous.

Starting with the daily schedule, we can see how deeply entrenched the factory model of schooling is in most secondary schools. All day students are shuttled from room to room for forty two- to fifty five-minute periods of unrelated subject matter. A typical student might start the day diagramming sentences, move on to linear equations, then to the Civil War, a quick session of volleyball, a break for lunch, then continue dissecting the frog started two days prior, then on to a session on irregular French verbs, and finish with computer programming. As with an assembly line, the entire school moves on a set schedule regardless of the fact that sometimes learning doesn't happen in short, fragmented blocks of time.

Almost everywhere we turn in our secondary schools we see the model of the factory reproduced. Students, like raw materials, are batch-processed as an undifferentiated mass, with only a few high achievers or troublemakers gaining any special attention. Teachers have to deal with a schedule that treats all subject matter equally, kids moving past in a dizzying blur, never able to exert control over their time with students. And in the end an external quality-control panel steps in, administering a standard measure (the standardized test) to judge the worth of the school's work.

Most of our would be school reformers never stop to consider that the very nature of the school experience is what inhibits student achievement. If they really want more student learning in schools, they have to find ways to change the context in which such learning occurs. Simply calling for more hours, subjects, and tests will not make anything good happen.

But there is a deeper issue here. Schooling is about more than just subject matter. It is about inculcating in our young a set of dispositions, attitudes, and behaviors that they take with them into their communities. As long as official reformers are primarily concerned with producing workers, making the school experience like life in a factory makes sense. Using the school to teach passivity, moving in crowds, taking orders, and following a preset agenda make great sense if your main agenda is to get kids ready to work in the growing service sectors of our economy.

But in the New Hampshire and Georgia countrysides, New York and Chicago, and in hundreds of other locales, a different agenda drives a special breed of teachers and administrators. They have set their sights on insuring that we will have among us young people with the habits of heart and mind that make democracy possible. Young people who can think carefully and clearly, who can understand the world around them in all its complexity, who can work together, and who have a desire to make a difference. To do this has meant changing the very environment of the schools, restructuring the experience of teachers as well as of students. It involves making room for communities to develop, for students to engage in real experiences, for connections to grow and develop, and for genuine engagement in the world outside the school.

PART TWO

Changing the Norms

What attributes facilitate democratic citizenship?

T his book is concerned with schools that do a good job of preparing democratic citizens. While many school reformers have directed their attention toward schools as sites of vocational preparation, I have gone in search of schools that work to nurture the attributes of democratic citizenship. What those schools have in common, how they have challenged and changed long-standing assumptions about schooling in order to make a difference in the lives of our children. Before going on, it is necessary to explore what attributes facilitate democratic citizenship. The term *democracy* is frequently used but seldom understood. In recent times it has been stripped of its participatory basis, as voting and representation come to replace the active involvement of citizens in making public policy and community decisions. The consequences of this weak, shadowy notion of democracy are all too obvious: voter turnout continues to decline; political debate over difficult issues is reduced to shouting matches; and an individualistic notion of freedom dominates political debate, leading to more and more programs to privatize life rather than to facilitate community values.

In private life, similar signs of decay are apparent. From Wall Street lawyers and brokers to school officials, the search for private advancement replaces any sense of public service. Courts are filled with white-collar cases as our public servants and professionals are caught with their hands in the public till. In neighborhoods, groups of disaffected young people vandalize property, public and private alike, and seek gratification in a myriad of transitory ways. And the most privileged of our youth on college campuses are locked in competition with one another over grades in order to see who will get the most lucrative jobs. No longer does service play a large part in their future plans.

When the legislated-excellence reforms do speak of citizenship, this most private and individualized sense of it is what they have in mind. To be a good citizen means to be able to pick out on a standardized test how many senators or representatives come from a state, the name of the governor, or perhaps the steps by which a bill becomes a law. Most of these ideas are reserved for the social studies or history courses. But when citizenship is just social studies, when politics and community are reduced to test-taking skills, schools produce spectators, not citizens. We are trained to watch and observe, to drop our franchise in a box, to support interest groups, and to seek private satisfaction while shunning the public world.

But entry into the public world is what democratic citizenship, that is, democratic life, requires. Since the beginning of the American democratic experiment, the belief was that ordinary people, engaged in everyday talk, could resolve public problems and issues. Representation was a part of that; but that meant representation of genuine community desire, informed by the ongoing active participation of citizens in the maintenance of civic life. A full discussion of democracy takes us far away from the main focus of this work. It is important to note, however, that the assumption that electing representatives is all democracy requires is a faulty one. In fact, democracy requires the continual expansion of the range of decisions that citizens make, the broadening of access to political activity, and the creation of institutions and opportunities for expanded public participation in answering the pressing social questions of our day. The expansion of citizen participation is greatly threatened today by government secrecy, industrial monopolies, and a closed media. Without this expansion democracy will wither and die, consumed by individual passions that go unchecked by any notion of the common good.

If we take democracy seriously, if it is more than a mere slogan, what would it require of citizens? This is where we must start in considering the work of the schools and teachers we have just met. Consideration of the requirements of good workers—promptness, ability to follow orders and rules, perseverance at a task, capacity for memorized information—is where the legislated-excellence reformers begin. These reformers also have some notion of what citizenship requires—memorization of the rudiments of representative government, a knowledge of American history, and patriotism. But such a store of knowledge is shallow and limited, leading not to a commitment to democracy but rather to a tolerance of the status quo. Participatory democracy requires much more.

Although not exhaustive, the following list presents some of the characteristics that democratic life requires of us all:

- Ability to make judgments about public issues, giving full consideration not only to private interests but to the public good as well.
- Commitment to having one's actions informed by the accumulated wisdom of the past while not allowing tradition to blind one to the realities of the present.
- Ability to use the written and spoken word in order to enter into public debate.
- Ability to gain access to information, and to desire information from a variety of points of view.
- Commitment to the ideals of equity, justice, and community, without discriminating on the basis of race, creed, color, gender, or any other criteria.
- Willingness to experiment, to take risks, to try new approaches to old and new problems.

What emerges from this partial listing is the notion of citizens who are courageous enough to act on behalf of the common good in confronting and resolving the dilemmas of modern social life.

Certainly the school experience cannot carry the weight of all the demands of democratic citizenship. We need a revitalization of many public spaces where the attributes of democratic citizens can be developed. Communities, town halls, city governments, and the various media all need to play a part in nurturing and reviving democracy. But common to all of our experience is schooling, and it must be, in its very essence, an experience that promotes democratic life.

We often tend to limit what schools can do to nurture a democratic disposition because of the limited way we think about what people learn at school. We look at the textbooks, the curriculum guides, and lists of goals and objectives and assume that the transmission of this material is the meat of the school experience. But this attitude hides more than it tells us. What students learn in school is not what shows up on the standardized tests. More important is what they learn from the daily treatment they receive in school; this is what tells them who they are, what they can be, how their world is ordered.

Thus, students don't really learn about democracy by being pummeled with endless lists of dates, facts, and great names. While such information is valuable, it is in how students are taught this material, how they use it, how they interact with one another and the adults in school that they will learn about their role in social life. The entire school experience, the organization of the school day, the types of evaluation used, the rhetoric of the classroom, the way students use what they know, the structure of authority, the ringing of bells, all tell children every day what the social world is like in this, their first extended interaction with a community larger than their families. It is in the daily lives children lead in schools that the characteristics of schools that work are found.

very, very true!

CHAPTER 3

🍎

School Climate

Our school—we think about it as our community.

"OK, who's next?"

It's David Smith's humanities class at Central Park East on a Tuesday morning in December. The task is an oral recitation of e. e. cummings's poem "in Just." Kareem, a tall, lanky thirteen-year-old black youth has just finished a performance that brought down the house. Having watched him regale the class with his interpretation, as he strode around the room, pantomiming the characters, one is hard-pressed to believe David's later claim that this is virtually the first time Kareem has contributed to the class. But then, knowing this, the excitement of his peers seems all the more real. Several students get through adequate, but not nearly as theatrical, renditions. Others pass, choosing to recite another day. We move around the room, coming to a quiet, reluctant face locked in concentration on his desktop in the hope that he will not be noticed.

"Hua," David asks, "would you like to try?"

The shy southeast Asian youth shakes his head no, still avoiding David's eyes.

"He's new, he's only been here a couple of weeks," I'm informed in hushed tones by the young woman sitting to my left.

"Are you sure?" David tries again, but Hua, obviously a bit ill at ease, doesn't look up. "Well, try this with me. Go get your copy of the poem . . . now, read it out loud, don't worry about it, just try; we're here to help you."

Hua hesitates, and he looks around the room. It's as if he is trying to gauge us all, to see if we are to be trusted. He clears his throat, throws one more protesting look at David and prepares to begin.

Before he starts, the young man on my right leans over to me and instructs, "Look, he doesn't speak English real well, so you need to pay attention, listen closely, and don't make fun. OK?" I nod, wondering where his savvy comes from. It's silent in here now; for some reason even the noise of the commuter trains outside can't penetrate the room.

"in Just—

spring," Hua begins, cautiously, quietly.

"when the world is," he falters, stuck on a cummings-invented word.

"mudluscious," coaches David, softly.

"mudluscious the little

lame balloonman

whistles far and wee

and . . ." he falters again.

"eddieandbill," this time from a fellow student, whispered as encouragement, not bellowed as one-upmanship.

Hua pushes on with these and other whispered aids. And as he does the room is almost thick with a sense of triumph. Every member of the class is on the edge of his/her chair, silently cheering Hua on, hanging on his every word, nodding encouragement, struggling with him on each difficult pronunciation. None of this is lost on Hua. He picks up confidence with each line, until even he is smiling as he brings the verse home.

> "its
> spring
> and
> the
>   goat-footed
> balloon Man whistles

far
and
wee"

There is silence as we all realize what a moment of personal history this is for Hua. It is, literally, the first English he has spoken to more than one person since arriving in the United States. Then, sensing it is their history, their victory as well, cheers and shouts of congratulations fill the room as Hua grins shyly at his friends and then hides his bespectacled face.

David, visibly moved (as am I, busily trying to hide tears of emotion behind my field notebook), first thanks Hua, then addresses everyone.

"I think this group can do anything it wants to if it puts its mind to it. And I want to thank you for being so supportive of your new classmate. . . . You are a real family. Thanks."

In David Smith's classroom the spirit of community that permeates Central Park East Secondary School is demonstrated by the respect, caring, and commitment with which students treat one another. This spirit underpins democratic life. Our ability to live together as neighbors, to tolerate our differences, and to arrive at mutually satisfactory solutions to common problems determines our ability to sustain and nurture democracy. The basic building block of democracy is a deep sense of commitment to community, including an obligation to think of the common good over individual good.

The strains and cracks in this commitment are all too apparent. Press reports trumpet the most obvious of these: racially motivated attacks in major cities, stock traders and bankers who cheat their clients, military suppliers who cheat the government. Many of us in smaller ways choose to ignore those communal obligations that we think were actually meant for "the other guy." Thus, we purchase radar detectors for our cars so we can break the speed limit without fear, subscribe to newsletters that help us avoid taxes in a quasi-legal manner (or just outright lie when we file), and think nothing of littering or choosing disposable over returnable containers. Seen individually each act is a mere personal choice—or failing. When taken collectively these acts signify a deeper, more threatening tendency.

Schools are one of the first places we learn about community. Children must operate for the first time in close contact with individuals to whom they are not related. What they learn about living together as a community, about accepting and working with those who are different, is learned first in school. For that reason, among others, we have attempted to racially desegregate schools, bring handicapped children into the mainstream, and eliminate barriers to women's full participation in schools.

This requires that we think carefully about the ways we organize schools and the daily experiences children have within them. It necessitates rethinking our approaches to discipline, classroom organization, school climate, and our connections with the community outside the school. Unfortunately, we are seldom encouraged to think of school as community, and thus much of what young people experience in schools is more a reflection of our general lack of community. Child-assault-prevention programs teach them to be fearful of all strangers; hall monitors and passes teach them that big brother is always watching; and their mass movement teaches them more about being members of a crowd than of a community. But it can be different, as demonstrated by schools and teachers who work daily to build schools into communities.

Classrooms as Community

COLLECTIVELY SETTING THE NORMS

Remember the list of rules in Marcia Burchby's classroom, a list that starts, surprisingly, with "No Smoking"? When asked, Marcia smiles, and allows that "the kids made the rules," explaining rule number two: "No throwing books at the lights." While making the classroom rules may seem like a simple thing, to many children it offers a genuine experience in building a community. For most of us, time spent in institutions means that all the rules are set and in place; our job is just to follow them. In classrooms like Marcia's, however, the very rules of conduct are set by students, so that they will develop an ownership of the room.

"Somebody else is always the boss, and they don't have much power over anything in their lives," Marcia says about her kids. "But what I want them to accomplish is responsibility for themselves and also a respect for others. They only get that if they have some practice at running their own lives. So, they're here for a good half of the day, let's do it here."

Making the rules is only part of it. How the rules are carried out during the day, how the classroom "feels" to students, is the other side of the coin. On a Tuesday afternoon Tabatha and Shelly run to Marcia, each with their own tale of woe about who took whose missing piece for the Lego houses they are building. As soon as she can, Marcia intercedes: "Is this a butter battle?" To the uninitiated the obvious answer to this question is, "Of course not, it's about Legos." But to the kids in Marcia's room, this secret code seems to solve many problems. This time Tabatha and Shelly smile shyly, first at Marcia, then at each other, and quickly return to their project, which now involves them in joining the two houses into one large one—connected by the disputed piece.

Earlier in the year Marcia read Dr. Seuss's *The Butter Battle Book* to the class. In it, Seuss builds a world whose very existence is threatened by an escalating conflict between the Zooks and the Yooks over which side of the bread the butter should be spread. The debate of butter-side-up versus butter-side-down becomes a metaphor for many of the conflicts in the classroom. "When they stop and think, they realize that what they are arguing over is nowhere near as important as their friendship. . . . I want to give them the tools and the space to solve their own problems, without violence, without anger. It takes some time, but so does trying to straighten out every little dispute or argument that comes up during the day . . . I'm surprised you're asking about this; it seems pretty simple to me."

Perhaps it seems simple to Marcia, but working to build community in a classroom is anything but simple in many schools. The current "get-tough" attitude that celebrates baseball-bat-carrying principals leaves little room for hearing students out and helping them solve their own disputes. Instead, strict adherence to predetermined rules, enforced silence or stillness, and multiple threats of punishment are used to keep kids in line. In these settings we teach children obedience, not community.

"We do not want to have an oppressive situation where there is peace but no justice in that peace," Rita Tenorio explains at a meeting of the Fratney School's School-Based Management Committee (SBMC). At the meeting a concern has been voiced about student discipline, an issue the school has struggled with. Explicitly committed to democratic models of classroom discipline, staff members have found that many students referred to Fratney from other schools were sent because of discipline problems. Additionally, many students have brought with them to school the chaos that surrounds their life outside school. The mix at times has been difficult, but the staff does not plan to abandon its approach. As one of the school paraprofessionals put it at the SBMC meeting, "Discipline in the long run at Fratney is to get children to be responsible for their own actions."

This sense of self-responsibility does not lead to a set formula of classroom management at Fratney. Instead, in each room, careful attention is paid to how to build a just community. As we saw earlier, each Fratney classroom has a specific time set aside for classroom meetings. Here is where problems are solved, rules set, decisions made. Each teacher conducts the meetings in his/her own style, but the intent is always the same: to build in students a sense of personal and collective responsibility.

In Becky Trayser's room the class meeting takes on a formal structure. "The talking rock" is passed from student to student, and one can only speak when holding it. Every student has an opportunity to speak, and no one can speak a second time before each is heard from once. Each speaker has to preface his or her comments with a paraphrase of what was said by the preceding speaker, and decisions are made by consensus more often than by formal majority vote. The students set the agenda; a list on which they can place items of concern for the weekly meeting is posted on the bulletin board in the front of the room. All this is designed to help students build a sense of community, to be able to resolve their own problems without the intercession of others.

It was from Becky's class that the discussion of kindergarten helpers in chapter 1 was taken. An extra class meeting had to be scheduled to solve the problem that arose when kids felt that there was no fair system in place enabling all the class members to work with the younger kids. The discussion was always intense, but never angry. Suggestions offered were put on the board, each one worked through and dealt with on its ability to solve the problem for everyone.

Finally, on the second day, a student surfaced with a new idea: "Look, the problem is that we all want to work with the little kids. So there are too many of us for too few of them. Well, look, let's get more of them!"

Suddenly the rock is forgotten as a chorus of voices chime in their agreement. "Right, more kids for us to work with." "We could all go down and take all the kids." "Then Becky and Rita [the kindergarten teacher] could go take a nap while we do their jobs." At this we all collapse in laughter. A committee of volunteers is formed to meet with Rita and see if she would like more helpers for more kids. And Becky and I both wonder why we didn't think of that sooner.

In Rita's kindergarten the class meetings are less structured and often more personal. Problems with toys, with games or books, with possessions dominate most classroom conflicts. At other times the class meets just to share what they are working on, sometimes with the entire class, other times in pairs. At every transition in the classroom there is a time to share and to talk about how the day is going. Today the class is sharing news in general at the beginning of the day. Students are gathered in a circle in front of Rita, who is sitting comfortably in her rocking chair, listening intently to every child as he or she speaks. For the first few minutes the conversation drifts from favorite television shows to pets and on to new toys at home.

Then, a big-eyed little guy offers this:

"Some kids are making fun of people on the playground."

"What do you mean by that, Antonio?" Rita now joins in the discussion.

"I mean they do things like call kids names and stuff. Like fatty or stupid or stuff like that."

"Or they make fun of how you walk or something," Gina joins in. "They say you walk like a monkey or an elephant and walk like that and say it's you."

Rita asks the class, "Do you have to join in with that?"

A chorus of nos and shaking heads answers her. "Why not?"

A torrent of stories about how someone made fun of each of them at sometime is offered. Personal tales of pain and offense.

"So what can you do about it?"

"You can tell the kids saying it not to say it," one sweatsuit-clad boy offers, while drawing himself up to his full kneeling height to demonstrate that he is serious.

"You need to tell those kids that they should ignore the other kids and that you like them and that they are not like that, that they are your friends." All that before Ramona even stops for breath.

"That's right," says Rita. "I hope you'll all grow up to be strong people and do what you know is right."

In both Rita's and Becky's classes at Fratney, the teachers are working to build a sense of community. Becky sees that she and her students are "going through a system to solve issues that (the students) bring up. . . . We deal with what the problem is, and then brainstorm possible solutions and evaluate those solutions and choose one to try and then go back and see if it works . . . That's very simple and it's something that I encourage them to do on a personal level as well, with a problem they have with a brother or sister or a problem they have of their own." Rita's students are taking "more responsibility for the group. It's interesting because they'll tell each other to please be quiet or they'll tell each other, you know, it's time to sit down now, which they did not used to do and that's good . . . They are developing a sense of a group." Solving their own problems, developing a sense of the group, these children are learning what it means to be members of a community.

* * *

Similar lessons are learned in the Primary Forum at Chauncey Elementary. Here, once a week, children gather from the first- and second-grade classrooms to share, learn, and work together. Eighty or so chattery five- to eight-year-olds sit on the floor or curl up next to a teacher in the building's multipurpose room first thing Monday morning. The agenda is largely, if not entirely, theirs. After an introductory presentation, Charlotte Newman opens the floor for discussion:

"Any old business for our wing?"

"Some kids are still pushing on the slide," C.J. sings out.

"When do you mean, C.J.?"

"During recess and lunch. Kids just push to get you out of the way."

"Well, we talked about this before, I think; what should we do this time?"

"Have the teachers make 'em stand against the wall," Melissa offers.

"You could take away their recess," Charles adds. After a series of suggestions, all of which involve a teacher in enforcing a rule, one little girl reminds the group: "But the teacher isn't always there."

"That's right," Charlotte joins in, "most of the time no adults are around when you are playing."

"So we have to do something ourselves," Patti begins, "and I think kids have to tell each other not to push."

"But what if they still do?" Michelle, new this year, asks.

"Then we all ask them not to push and we stop playing until we get it worked out."

When today's forum goes on to new business, a personal issue comes to the floor. Benji has asked to speak. "My best friend don't play with me anymore." What seems like a small problem to you and me quickly grasps the attention of all the young people in the room. More than likely this is an experience to which they can all relate.

"Can you tell us any more?" Charlotte asks.

"Well, we used to play together a lot; we played every day. But now he doesn't come to my house and when I go to his house he says that he wants me to go away," Benji tells her; he is now near tears.

"Why won't he play with you anymore?" Brittany asks. Joey has moved over to put his hand on Benji's shoulder.

"I don't know. I think he plays with the new boy that moved in. And when he's with my friend he's really mean to me and he acts like he doesn't really know me or like me . . . He makes fun of me and he calls me names."

"Is your friend older than you?" Charlotte again joins the discussion.

"He's in fifth grade," Benji, who is in second grade, replies.

"Well, friends," Charlotte addresses the entire room. "Benji has asked us for help. What do you think he ought to do?"

"You could tell his mom."

"Or you could tell your mom."

"But then he would just get mad," Benji replies.

"Ignore him."

"Play by yourself."

"Why don't you just come and play at my house tonight?" Tony asks.

Arrangements are made, other kids plan on joining them, and excitedly they organize a group bike ride for that evening.

Pushing on the slide, best friends leaving us, these are the often seemingly mundane problems of childhood. But what seems insignificant in our eyes is often of vital importance in the eyes of a child. What Primary Forum does is honor those important issues and teach children how to deal with them as a group. Any of the teachers could have decided to go and play "police officer" at the slide, and they could have counseled Benji on their own. Instead, they chose to let students work on these issues themselves, as a group, in order to find solutions they can all live with. As Joette Weber puts it, "We want the little guys to relate well with each other, relate well with all people . . . Sometimes they are able to and sometimes they are not able to, but they really move it in that direction. We can't do it for them, but we can set up, get them in a situation, where they have to solve their own problems . . . And sometimes you just watch it happen and it feels so good."

All of this group problem solving pays off in these classrooms in Athens County and Milwaukee. While many teachers struggle with classroom management, and books fill the market offering quick tricks to keep kids in their seats, these teachers see discipline as a much larger issue. It's not just keeping kids at their desks, mouths closed, eyes forward, and, often as not, brains turned off. Discipline comes from enticing and exciting classroom activity and a genuine commitment to the classroom as a community. For these teachers classroom management is not an "add-on"; rather, everything they do works to foster the sort of self-discipline necessary to make communal life possible.

This focus on community occurs informally as well. When Damien complained to Becky that "someone stole my stuff," she reminds him that maybe he didn't put it away, and if it's really a problem he should put it on the list for class meeting. When two students approach Charlotte on the playground about a third child bothering them, she reminds them of how the class decided to deal with playground problems (call the person by name, tell him/her what he/she did and how you feel about it; if that doesn't work, then get an adult). Reminded, they head back to their game, resuming it without any problem.

The communities that exist in these elementary classrooms are self-sustaining because these teachers pay so much attention to community building at the outset. They come to their classrooms with a vision of who they want their students to become, and that vision is reflected in nearly all they do. Charlotte echoes the words of Marcia, Rita, and Joette: "My biggest goal is that they are thinking and caring people. You can be very intelligent but yet not really able to live in a social environment . . . So the bottom line is I want them to be good people, good neighbors."

TAKING THE TIME TO LISTEN

For a variety of reasons the emphasis on classrooms as communities receives less attention in secondary schools than in elementary settings. Frequent class changes, with a teacher seeing as many as 150 students a day, a young person having as many as 8 different teachers a day: these circumstances and more work against building group spirit. They all suggest the value of restructuring the school day (discussed later in this chapter and developed more extensively in chapters 6 and 8). But short of changing an entire school, what can one teacher or a group of teachers do to build community?

Inside Georgia's Rabun County High School there is no doubt that real communities exist within the Foxfire program's classrooms. Expanded beyond the magazine classes (Foxfire I and II), students may additionally choose classes in music (with George Reynolds) and video/radio production (with Mike Cook). In all of these classrooms a genuine sense of community is apparent from the moment you enter the door. On reflection it's clear that the physical setup of their rooms makes it feel more like home than school. Desks, tables, chairs, work stations, are arranged so that people face one another or a small group rather than the teacher's lectern. The rooms are filled with the tools of the trade. George's music room is filled with instruments and records; Mike's room with tape machines, cameras, and tape recorders that students are encouraged to touch and use. The walls and shelves are filled not with the work of experts, but with the work of students. These are spaces that students own; they are homes away from home that invite participation and community.

The adults in these rooms invite the students they work with to be part of a community as well. There is the informality of students using teacher's first names and of teachers being in close physical contact with kids. In this day of the lawsuit, touching a student is often actively discouraged by school administrators. At Foxfire people just care about each other so much that not touching one another seems absurd.

These rudiments of space and close personal relationships grow out of the tasks set forth in the classroom. Virtually all instruction is in small groups or one on one. Class may begin as the teacher checks in with everyone to find out what is going on. But almost immediately every student is at work on editing his/her most recent interview for publication, mastering a new string instrument, or mapping out the next video production. As the students pull out their work and settle in, Wig (or George or Mike) pulls up a chair and starts coaching. They provide direct instruction, new leads, editorial comments, advice, questions, and always a supportive pat on the back.

If we compare this to the traditional approach to high school teaching, the teacher lecturing while students take notes, it's easy to see the new space made available for community. These teachers know every student well, as who they are and what they care about comes through clearly in their classroom work. The way they organize instruction provides the time to talk with, not to, students, to push each student to reach new insights in his/her work, to just listen to every young person in the room. The feeling in the classroom is one of the teacher as partner, as collaborator, not as manager or competitor. Together teachers and students strive to make *their* work as good as possible. This communitarian environment also makes it that much easier to trust students to make decisions. Earlier in chapter 2 we saw the major decisions that the students in the Foxfire program are expected to make. Just as important are the hundreds of daily decisions students make about the program. A student from each class attends and participates in decision making at weekly staff meetings: from dates for events, to whose request to visit the school will be accepted, to what the next year's program will look like. (More recently, due to after-school scheduling problems, this discussion takes place in each class during the day.) Students share in charting the course of the program and their educational experiences, and because of that they belong.

What goes on in this program is more than learning academics: it is also about making genuine human connections. Because of the organization of the class, Wig and his colleagues find the time to work with each student, honing skills, building self-confidence. The outcome of this is that every student learns that he/she counts, that each is a part of a dynamic group of young people working together with a common mission. This sense of community makes the informal room decor and demeanor, the student-based decision making possible. And it helps students see themselves as participants in, not observers of, the life of the classroom.

SOLVING THEIR OWN PROBLEMS

Making space available for building a sense of community is also on the agenda at Thayer's Spectrum program. Just as in the Foxfire program, this space is both temporal and physical. The physical space, as mentioned before, includes a barn at the back of the school's land that has been turned into a meeting center for students and faculty in the program. Dan Bisaccio describes what the space has come to mean to the program:

> We asked Dennis [Littky, the principal] if we could have the barn as a home for the project. Then we scheduled a day in July when the students and their parents came in and joined us and fixed the place up. At the end of the day we had a cookout and spent some time admiring our work and talking, just informally, about the program and what we hoped we could do.
>
> After about the second time we worked on it, I think the kids realized that it really was their space. They took ownership of it, so they started to go get things for the place on their own. Like the new benches that were made, or the new brick chimney for the stove.

The cohesion that comes out of this space is extended by taking frequent trips with the group. Some of the trips, like the trip to Walden Pond described earlier, are directly linked to academics. But others are just taken in order to build a closer sense of community among the group. Dan describes one such trip taken the first day of school:

> We took all the kids to Mount Monadnock [a local landmark, the highest peak in the area] and we hiked to the top of it. It's not a hard hike, but for some people it's not that easy either. It was really a way to say this is something we can do together, you are a team, we want to spend time with you. It is part of the history we are building for this program and this group of kids.

Indeed, this history is proudly displayed on a bulletin board filled with photos of the event—including those of teachers and students alike rubbing tired feet at the end of the day.

The result of such close attention being paid to community is a growing sense of responsibility on the part of the students. But this is not left to chance, as the Spectrum program is designed to make space in the form of time for students to exercise programmatic responsibility. Every Wednesday during "D" period, the Spectrum Council meets. The council's founding and its evolution show how students can take responsibility when given a chance.

The council was initially just an open meeting, held every Wednesday from 11 A.M. to noon, the time when students were also working independently or with a teacher in any of the Spectrum content areas. The goal was to get the students more involved in the actual planning of the program. Dan put it this way: "We want them to have a stake in the program, to know it's *our* program, not *your* program or *their* program. To do that means giving them space to exercise control." Of course, such space is not always effectively used.

"You know, it started with chaos," Julie Gainsburg describes the council's early days. "Mostly there were a lot of . . . bitch sessions." But even at the beginning, everyone agrees, the students were starting to catch on. "They were getting the idea that we really wanted them involved. And they were continuing to evolve, heading for a deeper sense of responsibility. What we often had a hard time doing was working out what important things they would be deciding," reports Dan, who works with the council. "At first they just focused on the fun part, the social events. We had to help them move on to the curricular and teaching issues."

A meeting in October demonstrated both the students' growing awareness of a sense of group responsibility and their frustration. The council was asked to deal with a problem that had occurred on their field trip to Walden Pond. To make such trips affordable, students drive their own cars, following the teachers. Imagine my surprise when we were leaving on the field trip to find no buses waiting for us. When I asked how we were going to travel, Dan replied, "By car, of course." Many school districts won't let teachers, let alone other students, transport students. But Dan explains: "We knew that to give kids the experiences we wanted them to have, and to build a spirit of the group, we would have to take trips together. But the school budget is too tight to afford a lot of bus trips. So we went to the parents and the kids, explained the situation, and told them we would be giving them the responsibility to see that it works. And it does; like this trip today, the kids organized it all, made reservations with the naturalist, planned the route and [meal] stops, and arranged cars. All we [the teachers] have to worry about are the educational details, not the mechanics." This time there had been some confusion in driving. The caravan of cars had been broken up and there was some concern about the quality of the driving. Dan, speaking for the teachers, started the meeting:

> The other teachers have asked me to have you discuss the driving issue. . . . It looked like to us that some people were driving recklessly and not staying in line. . . . The problem with driving jeopardizes the future of field trips. We're taking a risk when we take trips like this.

With that it was left for the council to come up with a way to preserve the trips. The discussion was heated, split along gender lines, and disorganized:

JEAN: Toby was driving like an idiot. He cut us off twice.

SHERRI: Doug was playing chicken with Al; they just missed hitting each other several times.

DOUG: You just don't know how to drive. I was just trying to change lanes to pass.

JEAN: Why pass? You were supposed to stay in line.

DOUG: Well, did *you* ever try to stay in line on the highway? You don't even stay under the speed limit in town.

CAROL: The problem is the guys all want to drive . . .

PATRICK: No, the girls don't want to drive, they just want to ride with their boyfriends.

CAROL: . . . and they show off. They drive like jerks. We need to have a rule that if they don't drive right, they won't be allowed to drive next time.

RITCHIE: And who is going to decide that, you?

DOUG: By the way, have any of you ever tried to stay in a

caravan of fifteen cars? It wasn't easy you know, especially on the interstate.

CAROL: All you have to do is slow down a little bit . . .

At this point chaos ruled. Kids wandered in and out. Small groups broke off from the main discussion, insults were freely traded. All the while, Dan, at his desk on the other side of the room, while seeming to pay no attention, was keeping an eye on how things developed. Finally, one girl called the discussion to a halt:

SHERRI: Look, let's have a committee to come up with some guidelines. Then we can give them to everybody on Friday . . . How about Carol, Jean, and Melanie. Now . . .

DOUG: Who put you in charge?

SHERRI: Nobody, but who else would do it?

At that the discussion again broke down, but somehow they stumbled on to plans for a dance and a party.

With ten minutes left in the period, Dan asked to be recognized again:

DAN: You guys rate the meeting.

CHORUS: Terrible. Waste of time. Stupid.

DAN: So let's take some time out here and look at what was causing problems.

MATT: Kids talking.

SHERRI: Nobody will listen.

DOUG: Arguing.

DAN: Well, how does one even address the group? It almost seems like a mob. What's the point of having a council?

MATT: To solve problems.

DAN: But why not have the whole group do that?

PATRICK: It would be chaos.

DAN: But so is this. What could you do differently?

MATT: Say nobody else could come in.

JODY: But we said they could.

MATT: OK, but only to visit or present new ideas, not just to talk.

DAN: Do you have an agenda? What might be some mechanics to make the meetings go smoother?

JEAN: Sit so we can see each other.

DAN: How about a chair, someone to direct verbal traffic?

DOUG: But now it sounds too formal.

DAN: So what's the solution to it?

In a few minutes the council has decided to have a chair (they elect Sherri), to make a request for a separate room to meet in (during this period they were frequently interrupted by students returning from their field work in the land lab—often in waders and always with samples), and to request time at the Monday Spectrum meeting to discuss both driving rules and ways of running the council. At lunch later that day, Dan discusses the meeting. "I guess I could have just taken over the meeting . . . [but] they are getting to it, we just have to keep working with them. You know, they've never had this chance before . . . And besides, their idea about smaller [car] caravans for field trips is brilliant; we [the teachers] would never have thought of that."

Returning to Thayer in January, I sat in on another Spectrum Council meeting. It was hard to believe the change in organization, purpose, and content that had taken place in just two months.

A nine-member group, elected by the other students, is called together by its chairperson, Sherri. Dan suggests two topics for discussion: (1) The librarian has lunch during "D" period; since so many Spectrum kids come to the library during that time, would someone want to cover the library? (2) What about next year? What do students want the Spectrum program to be and how will other students be informed? Dan leaves after presenting both issues.

The group goes immediately to work, with Sherri consulting notes from previous meetings and an agenda prepared for this one. They consider the following topics:

1. An attendance policy for council meetings.
   The issue of fairness in terms of excused absences is dis-

cussed. Is it fair to use homework as an excuse? Several times Sherri reminds the group: "We need to decide this as a group."

Final decision: All council business will be conducted in the final fifteen minutes of the meeting. Council members are allowed only three excused absences (not counting sickness) from this part of the meeting.

2. The Spectrum class trip.
   They decide to take this to the entire group. The debate is between New York City and Boston, but the other students may have better ideas.

3. Spectrum Dance and Parents Night.
   Committees are set to deal with each of these.

4. Complaints about the program.
   Agreed that they need to continue to work on communication between students and teachers. But "we need to help distinguish between legitimate concerns and just bitching." Decide to post in each classroom a list of council members and encourage students to discuss complaints with them.

5. Next year's program.
   Three students volunteer to develop a survey to see what students want. Request an all-school assembly to dispel myths about the program.

"They started with chaos, but now they are really doing something," Julie notes, thinking out loud about council during her planning period. "It's slow, but they are going through the right processes, and the fact that they are moving forward is a good thing, you know." Yes, they are moving forward, and yes, it is a good thing, and yes, more important, it is indeed a slow process.

Schools as Communities

Building institutions is easy, building communities is not. Up to this point we have considered the process of building communities within classrooms. As any teacher can tell you, this is made much easier when the entire school works together to build this ethos. In fact, many teachers who work in America's mega-schools, often housing over 2,500 students, may find it next to impossible to develop the space or time for such activity. But it is possible for the entire school to develop a group spirit, one that makes every child feel deeply a part of the program. Schools that do this, that connect with virtually every child, think carefully about elements that build community: the overall climate of the school, the size of the school, and the accessibility of the school.

CELEBRATING WHO WE ARE

The much used and abused term *school spirit* tells us something about what a good school can be. Unfortunately, this concept is usually only involved when we talk about beating another school's athletic team or following the school rules. That is, it's a manufactured spirit that cannot sustain the community through turmoil or motivate it to excellence. There are schools that work on developing a deeper and more inclusive sense of school spirit. School spirit for them means a commitment on the part of all of those involved in the school—students, teachers, administrators, and parents—to an all-inclusive community, one that honors diversity, finds strength in collaborative action, and shares the triumphs and sorrows of each of its members. This sentiment operates daily, not just at an occasional pep rally or assembly.

It's the first day of the 1988/89 school year for the teachers, parents, and students of Hubbard Woods School. At sunrise the entire school community gathers on the Lake Michigan shoreline. A bonfire burns, songs are sung, and breakfast is served.

Every year at Hubbard Woods several all-school celebrations occur. They have nothing to do with athletics or the next fund-raiser. Rather, they are simply a time to get the entire school population together and rejoice in who they are. Just like a strong family, Hubbard Woods carries out celebrations that connect its community with the tradition from which it has come and of which it is a part.

There is no "program" for these events; they are overseen by a parent/teacher committee in charge of finding ways to bring the school together. "You have to decide you want to do these things, that they are important, that you are willing to devote time to them," explains Dick Streedain. "If you don't, if you just assume they will happen, they never do . . . We can easily get caught up in just working our own time and space and forget about the rest of the school. You can't allow that to happen if you want the entire school to be a nurturing, supportive environment."

The sunrise breakfast was more than just a school celebration; it was, also, according to Dick, "a healing experience" that year. Only four months earlier the shooting had occurred at Hubbard Woods, and wounds that will never heal were still raw and sensitive. It's important to note, though, that this gathering was not a "crisis-management" event, not merely a response to an isolated event in the school's history. It was, instead, a regular feature of community life at Hubbard Woods, and continuing it not only advanced the healing process, but further fostered the spirit of community at this school.

It's a Saturday in Milwaukee, and Bob Peterson and his colleagues are busily finishing up preparations for the first Fratney School Family Day. A Saturday? Who wants to spend a Saturday at school? "We were warned about that," muses Bob. "We were told by another principal, in a very successful middle-class school, that he would never try to organize something on a Saturday. They were afraid nobody would show up. That never crossed our minds."

The Family Day idea came from the parents at Fratney. They wanted a time to meet one another informally, to build a school spirit. A sense of community in the school doesn't just happen; it is worked at, nurtured, and promoted. The Family Day, an extension of what we saw earlier in Rita and Becky's classrooms, was a success beyond anyone's wildest dreams. Bob Peterson tells the story:

We worked to have an activity where people could bring their entire family, not just the children who were in school, but all of the kids. . . . It started at 9 A.M. and it went until

1:30 P.M. . . . The parents organized a phone bank a week
before the event and every family in the school who had a tele-
phone was called. You know we have both English- and Spanish-
speaking parents to do the phone calling. So on that Saturday,
by 9:30, there were about 150 people here in our gym, the only
room in our school where groups of people can gather. We
began with a story by Maggie, our librarian, on the theme of
the Family Day: "Peace and Global Awareness." We had a poetry reading by a group of students that was organized by one
of our first-grade teachers. And then we broke into workshops.

There were ten workshops organized in each of the classrooms
and they went for forty-five minutes, then a break, and another
series of workshops. Some of the parents were involved in conducting those workshops, some of the community artists were
involved. [They covered] everything from tie-dying to button
making to juggling to storytelling to arts and crafts and singing
of songs. They were very successful.

By the time the two workshop sessions were over at about
12:00, the people reassembled up in the gymnasium on the third
floor. There were about 275 people here at that time and we
had a presentation by a local African-American dance troupe [on]
West African dancing. By 12:30 that was completed and we had
a pot luck lunch for 275 people up in the gym without any
tables and chairs and so on [laughs]. And that was a smashing
success.

Parents had organized it and people thought it was really fine,
but I went home depressed, however, because we had forgotten
to invite the superintendent and school board members. And that
would have been a nice showing. But our strength lies in our
own internal will and organization so I guess I felt very positive
about the whole thing . . . [it] really built the sense of family.

Institutions have regulations, codified systems of behavior, organizational flow charts, and job descriptions. Communities have histories, a memory of who they are, and a vision of what they can be.
Through celebrations such as the ones at Hubbard Woods and Fratney Street, a storehouse of memory and a sense of family is built
that will sustain community.

GIVING KIDS THE KEY

Occasional community celebrations are only the tip of the ice-berg. Such events will ring hollow if they are not markers for some-thing larger and deeper that is going on in the school. Perhaps the reason some schools do not venture to have meetings on Saturdays is precisely because the rest of the school week does not invite connection. The school is not always a full-time extension of the community. Often, it operates instead with tightly regulated hours of access, not allowing children in until the appointed hour and quickly shooing them out (except for athletes) at the end of the day. But if a school is to be a community, it must adapt its hours and access.

At Central Park East this means that the school doors are open to students from 8 in the morning until 5 in the evening, even though classes are only scheduled from 9 to 3. What can kids do the rest of the time? The main focus of attention is the library. During a recent visit, the library was full of students by 8:30, work-ing in teams on projects, reading by themselves, searching the card catalog for sources. The same happens after school: At 4:40, while a faculty meeting goes on in half of the library, the other half still has nearly a dozen students working in it. Who operates this won-derful resource? Don't teacher contracts limit the number of hours on the job? "Our teachers are wonderful, they come early and stay late," Debbie Meier explains. "But the work before and after hours is all done by students. They are in charge of the facility; they circulate books, supervise, and organize. It's a great place to be, isn't it?" She smiles, shrugs her shoulders with motherly pride and warmth, and then heads off to catch another student or teacher in the act of being good.

This sort of open access to school resources goes on throughout the day. As in any genuine community, special permission is not required to utilize all the school has to offer. At CPESS students frequently visit the library, using it to supplement classroom re-sources. Teachers do not have to obtain special permission for stu-dents to go to the library and no hall passes are required. "The library here isn't an escape from class, it's an extension of class," explains Mike Goldman, a humanities teacher. "It is open all day to all the kids so that they can get to information when they need it, not when we decide it is to be available."

This user-friendliness of school resources echoes through the halls of Thayer as well. On a visit to the library I found students paging through recent periodicals, setting up a videotape camera to record this week's edition of the Thayer news broadcast (which is played during lunch), a group working on a project for math class, two students working with a teacher on a concept they were having difficulty with in English, and several students searching the card catalog and the shelves for resources. Unlike many libraries, it is not silent here, but it is not noisy either. The hum of voices is purposeful; all are actively engaged. I mention this to Ann Ladam, the librarian, commenting on the hands-on nature of the setting. She replies, "Yes, I think the students are really coming to own this place."

A sense of ownership does run through these school settings. At Thayer it means that at 7:15 A.M., nearly an hour before school is to start, I find Vince Tom in his room with a group of students working on some difficult math material. "Well, they asked if we could get together and this is the time we came up with," Vince explains, with a look that seems to say "Doesn't every teacher do this?" Obviously they do at Thayer, as a quick check around the building identifies ten other teachers here early, working with students or setting up their rooms. Twelve hours later the lights are still on at the school. The library and computer lab are open and about twenty-five students are working in both settings on a wide variety of subjects and projects. Several teachers are there; they have volunteered on a rotating basis to keep the place open. The atmosphere is loose, open, relaxed, and inviting. Students of every ilk, the ones who find school easy and the ones who find it difficult, are here. "It's a good place to be," says one. "You know, we like it around here and so it's *almost* fun to come back."

Similarly, at Hubbard Woods the doors open at 8:15 (often earlier, unofficially), and the school invites students to use it as a base for their interests. On a walk around the building you are likely to find up to a couple of dozen kids playing basketball in the gym, a group in the computer room working on their writing, others working on group or individual art projects, and still others in classrooms fixing up a display or taking care of their class pets. It is important to note that there is very little supervision during this time. The students are on their own and expected to choose their own activities.

The best way to describe what happens at Hubbard Woods from 8:15 to 9:00 is that the school is slowly waking up, taking stock of itself, getting ready for another day. It is all done in the name of making the school more like a community and less like an institution. Dick Streedain reflects on what he hopes happens at his school: "In a lot of ways, when I was a kid, I would think, 'Wouldn't it be nice if I had a key to the school and I could go there and shoot baskets between eight and nine' and not because I would be destructive but because this was how I wanted to use my time . . . In a sense we are giving the kids the key, and I love that."

Making It Smaller

The lack of connection with the school, the lack of a sense of community, is often due to the sheer size of the school. When we herd together 2,000 to 3,000 young people in a building, we should be surprised by the existence of community rather than the lack of it. While this is more a problem in secondary schools, many elementary schools also struggle with populations of over 1,000. Yet the answer to the issue of size is easier for the self-contained classrooms found in grades K–6. In the previous section on classrooms, the ways in which individual elementary-grade teachers try to connect with students through classroom meetings, rule setting, and decision making were pointed out. When coupled with the other schoolwide strategies seen in this section, the school does become smaller and more personal for each student. However, in secondary schools, with their departmentalized offerings and staff, with students frequently changing class and spending only part of the day with each teacher, community is all the more difficult to build and sustain.

Of all of the ways in which community is nurtured in schools, reducing the school's size can often be the hardest to envision. We are, unfortunately, stuck with the huge, unpleasant, and often downright ugly school buildings that we have. With barely enough money to keep many districts afloat, it is not reasonable to talk about building new, smaller schools. Further, smallness at times leads to exclusion, as with drives for neighborhood schools that were often thinly veiled attempts to thwart desegregation. Returning to our sample schools, we can find examples of how to make schools smaller within existing structures. Two approaches to reducing the size of the school are shared by Thayer and CPESS: advisory and instructional divisions.

We all remember homeroom from our high school days: the five or so minutes before school when a teacher took attendance and we listened to announcements. Usually we were grouped alphabetically and had a different homeroom teacher every year. This was where report cards and letters home were distributed, and it was not much more than a holding pen before the start of the day. In an effort to make schools more personal, to make them smaller, Thayer and CPESS have abandoned the traditional homeroom concept for advisory.

At Thayer, advisory was one of the few things that Dennis Littky insisted on when he took over as principal. "I believe in the concept of advisory . . . it's a simple way of breaking down the school into a smaller school and making sure that you are on top of each kid. The details of it depends on the school and the kids and the teachers. So I basically said, 'We are going to have this advisory system which means that every teacher is going to have a group of kids and get to know them. . . . [The advisor] will be the communication with the home, will be the one doing the parent conferences.' From there we worked the rest out as a faculty."

What they worked out is that every staff member is assigned about ten advisees (the number is low because everyone, principal, guidance counselor, as well as classroom teacher, librarian, takes an advisory) with whom he/she meets every morning for ten minutes. This time is taken up with the conventional homeroom topics: announcements and the like. Additionally, each advisee has an hour-long conference with his/her advisor once a month to check on academic, personal, and social issues. Further, the advisor compiles the grade cards and reports on each advisee to be sent home as well as acting as the main person parents schedule conferences with. The entire system, according to the Thayer Advisory Handbook, is about communication. This concept is developed well beyond the usual understanding teachers have of their students, given that a Thayer student will stay with an advisor through both junior and senior high school. "The concept," according to Littky, "is just trying to help kids so they don't get lost."

Of course, some teachers go well beyond making sure that kids don't get lost. Don Weisberger takes his advisory group on yearly outings to Boston Red Sox games, Christmas dinners, and skiing trips. Littky and many other advisors have advisees in their homes for meals or holiday get-togethers. The point is not how much is done with the students, it is, as Don Weisberger explains, that "[we] are supporting kids and are advocates for them in school. For the one principal and one guidance counselor to have constant contact with all our kids would be an impossibility. What advisory does is make the school very small, it makes the school about a one-to-ten ratio where you as an advisor are responsible for ten kids. You are their advocate in the school. You are the person that they go to for support, for anything that they need . . . It is important for kids to know that they have someone to go to when they need help; they are not just numbers, but they matter to us."

If student reports are anything to go on, the system does appear to work at Thayer. Stephanie, a junior in Don's advisory, sees it this way: "There's someone there who is not a parent who will talk to you. Sometimes it's just like a parent and sometimes it's hard because just like a parent you don't want them there, you know? But other times it's good because it's not a parent . . . and so you can go tell them something that you wouldn't tell your mother." Greg, from another advisory, adds, "It is a great idea. There is another person you can count on because you are going to have meetings with him . . . He is also there if we have problems with another teacher. Like we can count on meetings where the advisor will be there and like be the moderator."

These comments echo those we heard earlier from Herb Rosenfeld of CPESS, which has its own version of advisory. In chapter 2 we saw the range of issues that were covered in advisory at CPESS. The numbers in each group are small, about fourteen, as *all* the staff members take an advisory group, as at Thayer. Unlike Thayer, however, advisory at CPESS takes up several hours a week of class time and is a place for one-on-one academic tutoring, journal writing, and instruction in some school subjects, such as family life education. Following are notes from one of Ricky Harris's advisory meetings:

> The session starts with a discussion of their upcoming skating trip and moves on to a possible New Year's Eve Party at the school (are the kids interested?), announcements, and distribution of the school newsletter.
>
> Ricky then comments on the family conferences that were just completed. "I met with the families of all of you. For some of them it was the first time I had met with them. And I want you to know that I was quite impressed by all of them."
>
> Then he brings up a concern that he has had and that several students have raised with him. It seems that they are still working on how to use their time and some students are falling behind in their work. The students suggest that they need more time in advisory to work on academics. They all agree that on Thursdays advisory will be a one-hour concentrated study session, Fridays will be for "stuff," and on alternating Mondays Ricky will choose a topic for discussion while students will choose the topic on the other Mondays.
>
> The session finishes with a videotape entitled "The Dating Game," which leads into a discussion of boy/girl relationships, specifically concerning what boys do to try and impress girls. The final admonition from Ricky is: "What I want you to realize is that standing on the corner yelling at girls does not impress them and is degrading to other human beings."

The range of topics in Ricky's advisory is typical. This free give-and-take, the personalization of the school, gives it what Herb calls "a private school quality." It is a quality that comes not only from advisory, but from the organization of instruction as well.

At both Thayer and CPESS an attempt is also made to reduce the school's perceived size through instructional organization. Previously we saw how at Thayer that attempt means team-teaching programs such as Spectrum and at CPESS it means extended time in each class, fewer subjects, and organizing the school into houses.

The consequence of these strategies is that students get to know a few teachers very well rather than a lot of teachers superficially. Time and time again the teachers at both Thayer and CPESS talk about the extended time they have with students and how much better they are able to know them because of that.

> I think the whole idea behind teaming was to let students know that several teachers know them well . . . well, I don't know if it was to let the students know but it is a lot easier for us to keep track of the students. To know how they are doing. (Vince Tom, Thayer)

> I'd like [the students] to feel like a group and I think they do; feel like a little family and feel like there are three teachers that are really concerned about them. I hope they feel that way. (Julie Gainsburg, Thayer)

> Because of the time we have I have a sense that I have found a way to build enough support in the class to have them take something which can be very risky and try it—something I wouldn't want to do unless I knew them very well. The idea is that things go well in here because there is time to know a student deeply and the student knows me also. (David Smith, CPESS)

Through advisory and the organization of the school day, Thayer and CPESS have become smaller. Each student is connected and feels that someone knows him/her, is watching out for him/her, cares about him/her. Every child in every school deserves such attention, but too often the size of the institutions we have built get in the way. When we find ways around the size of the school, the ultimate reward is a climate that fosters community.

Rethinking Schools as Communities

The climate of a school is not likely to show up on the legislated-excellence agenda. But the climate of the schools and classrooms described here makes all the rest of the outstanding things, the excellent things that these educators do, possible. As Dennis Littky put it, "Everyone knows the atmosphere has to be right first before you can move on to other things."

It is hard to pin down something as elusive as a good school climate. It is similar to that classic definition of pornography: one knows it when one sees it. A climate of community flows through everything these teachers do, and it is so deeply ingrained that many of them almost take it for granted. This sense of family, of belonging, is just the way school is supposed to be. Even at that, there are some particular ways in which this spirit manifests itself through the schools' atmosphere that are important to point out.

There is the very feel one gets from the physical appearance of the school. The schools proudly display the students' work in virtually every available space. Any space can have art; doctors' waiting rooms and corporate offices have art and beauty, but they do not have community. That is because the public display of children's work in these schools represents something much deeper: the genuine compassion and respect the adults in these schools display for their charges and one another. You see it daily in all of these schools.

At Thayer every student is greeted by Dennis and a group of teachers the moment he/she walks in the school. Dennis's voice, distinctive in any crowd, rings out above the others: "Hey Timmy, how are you, my man? Heard you did real well on that presentation in Mr. B's class. What are ya' tryin' to do, show up your brother?" "Come here, Shelly, you're movin' too slow; it's a beautiful day, smile for me . . . that's it." "Steve, where did you learn to shoot foul shots? That one was a brick last night. How 'bout a little one-on-one after school?" No one gets past him without an encouraging word, a pat on the back, a smile. It is the same with the other teachers. Only one or two of them are actually on hall duty; the rest are just there to welcome their students to the school.

Melanie Zwolinski, guidance counselor at Thayer, describes the morning scene as one full of "playfulness. There is lots of touching, and I think touching, in our society, is a real no-no. But there is lots of it going on in the hall. That's what I love, the way the school says 'Welcome,' or 'It's OK, we're glad you're here.' We need to do a lot more of that in schools, a lot more."

At Chauncey, Joette Weber sees the half an hour or so before school, when kids in the primary wing at Chauncey mix freely from room to room, as part of a family time. "All the kids see all of us as their teachers, and we see all of them as our students. But more importantly, they see every child in the wing as a potential friend, playmate, as someone to be with. We have opened up the wing so that we are all a family here." Obviously, Joette, Joyce, and Charlotte's former students have a hard time leaving this home away from home: you are likely to find them visiting during this part of the morning with former students from throughout the building who wander back just to talk.

All this talk about family and community has a purpose. It is, as Dick Streedain puts it, "basically about trying to create a family setting within the classroom." Or as Herb Rosenfeld relates, "It's not me against them and I'm not the surrogate father. If I am, I am the good part of the surrogate father, the reasonable, decent, helping part." The point is to get the atmosphere of the school comfortable, so that kids (and teachers, too) naturally feel responsible for it, feel that it is worth contributing to, that it is a good place to be.

Of course, this concept goes beyond the openness and warmness of space; it flows into the personal relationships between teachers and students as well. In all of these schools there is a good-natured informality; teachers are often referred to with nicknames that are terms of endearment ("Doc," Mr. B, Ms. G, and so on) or are addressed by their first names by students. There is a lot of physical contact between the people in the building: teachers with their arms over students as they work together, students and teachers on the floor working together on a project, the casual touch on the arm as a teacher concentrates on a student's words. People laugh easily. In the lunchroom, teachers can be found sitting with students sharing stories; and on the playground or during breaks in the day, teachers and students carry on animated conversations about life, about the sports pages, about who they are and where they are going.

This ease with which teachers and students treat one another arises directly from the willingness of these schools to deal with children as people, not just empty vessels into which to pour knowledge. Formal structures, such as advisory, tell students that they are valued for who they are, not for what they score on an achievement test. This comes out in a discussion in Herb's advisory when students are asked to compare CPESS to other schools that they know of or have attended in the past.

ROBERT: Here I have learned how to respect adults better; the system has helped me work with people who are trying to help me. I want people by my side, I don't want people working against me.

HERB: What made you arrive at that conclusion?

ROBERT: Being rude and loud was a way of getting attention, that was the worst way of getting it. Here, I've found out that you can get attention other ways.

STACIA: You have a close relationship with the teachers, through advisory and all the other things.

JULIUS: Here a teacher pays attention to you as an individual. Why you get so mad at teachers is because you don't relate to them, you don't understand them. We're all so close here, compared to other schools.

STEVEN: They don't have a close relationship with teachers the way we do. I don't think the teachers want to be there. . . . People they can't handle they just send to another school.

JULIUS: Those kids are the same as us, if we'd been in their situation we might be different. Our school, we think about it as our community. We know we need to work together. Even

if we don't like one another, we get over that because we want
to work together.

HERB: How does that happen?

ROBERT: It's because we really know each other. You can be
together for a long time, but that doesn't mean you get to
know each other better.

After the session, Herb talks about why CPESS rejects much of
the legislated-excellence reform movement in order to create the
type of community his students have just described:

I have been interested for years, and I have taught for twenty-
nine years and have three children of my own, in being a part
of a project in which an environment would be created to take
into account the different ways in which people process information. And this is just one way to do that. What I would call
good-natured personalization I think sort of clears the decks, because so much energy that goes into the war you have otherwise
between the adults and the kids. Setting aside any principled
notions that I have, which I do have, you know, it is purely
pragmatic business. Kids aren't angry at me all of the time. I can
talk to them, I can point out their mistakes, we can learn new
things together. That's what Julius meant about our community
here; we work with each other, not against each other.

This sentiment is echoed by Melanie Zwolinski when she talks
about the spirit built at Thayer:

It's my hope that when they leave here they know that even
though the world is so big and often empty and lonely, that
there are people who will be there for them. . . . In addition to
the push to get kids to think well, we've got to really concentrate
on the social, emotional aspects of these kids as well. To prepare
them to go into a world that does seem pretty lonely and unkind
and cold. That there are certain things that we need to communicate to other human beings like, "Hey, I'm hurt. I'm really
lost." That people do care. And if they can make that one connection here, that will carry with them.

Obviously it does carry them. Greg, the senior we met earlier, talks about the effect Thayer has had on him: "I have learned to be independent and I have learned that there is always going to be someone that I can fall back on if I ever get into trouble or need real help . . . It seems like the school is here for anyone who has been here and wants to work or anyone outside of the school who wants to come in and learn about it."

Less-formal activities, such as taking time out of the school day to deal with children's problems, relays the same message. Dick Streedain relates that the time he spent in a classroom just talking with students, hearing what is on their minds, is now a regular feature of his work that has taken on new importance in light of the shooting accident:

> Today when I was in a classroom I asked the kids if they observed any changes in themselves that weren't there before the shooting. And I would say that twelve out of the twenty students shared and the other kids might have been sharing and participating nonverbally. And they were all saying some very intimate things. One kid was saying "I shoot baskets and I see a car coming down. Lots of times I will quit shooting and I'll kind of watch the car." Another kid is saying, "Gee, me too. I do that." Another girl said every time she sees a stranger she feels a little on edge. So I asked, "Do you feel any differently toward adults or your teachers after the incident?" They all said, "Gee, they came through for us so much that we don't want to goof them up; we don't want to harass them. You know, you did stuff for us. We want to protect you." And I felt we were both saying [here he pauses, as if to savor the intensity of the moment, and to compose himself] it's a good feeling, and we could talk about that. The kids say, "You always let us have time to talk about this. It is so important to us." Here it is ten months later and they are able to say thanks, we are healing . . .

Excellent schools and classrooms are clearly distinguishable by the spirit of community that pervades all they do. As we have seen, theirs is a sense of community for community's sake. These schools are where young people *and* adults come to value the strength that exists within community and learn to be contributing, concerned, and active community members. We must also see these settings as special communities of learners.

The recurring theme here is that community makes learning possible. Indeed, the strength of democratic community is that collaboration makes individual growth possible. By collectively taking care of a variety of needs and necessities, the community frees individuals to learn, grow, and develop in ways that isolated individuals find impossible. So it is with schools. As long as kids are isolated and alienated, their struggle with the structures and limits of the institution dissipates energy that could have been used for learning and involvement. When a student feels welcomed, when he or she feels that the school is his or her community, the things that get in the way of learning are put aside.

Learning is a chancy thing in an environment that is primarily about test scores, homework, time-on-task, and workbook pages. The burning issue we face today, as Richard Louv found in his investigation of childhood, "is not the academic life of the student, but the emotional life of the child."[1] Yet the legislated-excellence reformers would have us concentrate solely on academics. However, in communities of learners, where the emphasis is on support and inclusiveness, the opportunities for real learning are limitless.

Such communities do not happen by accident. Americans often settle for less in their schools. Through deliberate and concerned effort, the teachers and schools we have visited work on turning an institution into a community. Where did they start, why did these particular structures arise, how did they decide what to work on first? There is clearly no recipe here, no quick-fix solution to what ails the schools. Even when two schools utilized a similar device, advisory, the implementation of that program came out in very different ways. However, for teachers, students, and community members, there are several lessons to be learned. In each of these settings the goal was not to create a new structure. Instead, the goal was to create a new school ethic, a moral climate if you will, and the community came out of that intent. While not explicitly stated by the educators in all of these settings, three basic norms guided what they did.

First, the school itself, in terms of both physical setting and interpersonal relationships, must become more open and comfortable for students. This is what Littky meant by getting the atmosphere right first, and then working on the academic aspects of the school. To this end we have seen schools become more user-friendly through extending the hours the physical plant is available to students, filling the halls with students' work, giving teachers the time to build personal relationships with students, and setting aside time during the school day to deal with children as people, not just students.

Second, students should experience broader and deeper control over their lives in school. Rather than being passively obedient, the students we have seen are actively involved in the life of the school and, in turn, in their own learning. Thus, we see classrooms where students set the codes of acceptable behavior, meeting times made available where students solve their own problems either as groups or one on one, and classroom projects designed and carried out by students with the support, rather than the direction, of the teacher.

Third, the school needs to become a community of memory and hope.[2] Students leave the school with the experience of having been a part of something greater than themselves, realizing the strength that lies in working together for a common goal. All-school celebrations and times when students remember who they are and what they are becoming play a key role here, as do the smaller things—sharing individual victories and defeats, going on extended school trips, finding ways for young people to make a meaningful contribution to the life of the school.

Openness, self-governance, memory, and hope. These are not the buzzwords of the legislated-excellence school reform movement. But they are crucial if we are to take seriously the charge that schools become places where informed, involved, compassionate, and democratic citizens are nurtured. These schools are where young people will first make connections—to one another, to their teachers, to the school community. These connections make community in the larger sense possible.

CHAPTER 4

Life in the Classroom

We learn by doing real things.

It's a cold, gray, Saturday in early spring, and the wind whips through the wooded Appalachian valley carrying the voices of Bill Elasky and his sixth graders down through the hollow. They are in search of a very special water sample for their class project on water quality.

"We were told that there was some strange-looking water, real clear with a milky-white bottom, near the beginning of this creek," Bill explains, catching his breath while picking his way along the path blazed by several of the more adventuresome students. It's not easy to find the creek, let alone the spot they have been referred to. The woods are a tangle of briars, fallen trees, and brush. There is no path along the creek; one either wades in it or tries to fight along through the thorns and thistles on the bank.

Along the way Bill stops the group, pointing out various indicators of forest life. New growth, old animal tacks, insect homes in logs, one mini-lesson follows another. The kids and Bill exhale billows of steam as they stand around; resting up for the next charge through the brush.

It takes nearly two hours, but they finally find the spot. The six kids who have organized this trip spring into action. Two get out bottles and begin to take a variety of water samples, while a third

120

records where and how each one is made. A fourth student takes pictures of the stream and its environs, and the last two are busy making notes on the surrounding area, indicating the conditions (time, date, temperature of water and air) and setting (objects in and around the water, natural or otherwise). They confer briefly before leaving, accounting for every task.

"Did you get four samples?" asks Robert of the two girls who are still trying to get their hands warm.

"Of course," Alisha responds impatiently, with a look that says, "Don't you think I know what I'm doing?"

"Did we get pictures of the water, the way the bottom is so milky?" Kyle asks Summer, who is the photographer today.

"Yes. I even took them from both directions and walked upstream a ways to see if it looked like this anywhere else. But I think this is it."

"Well, that's it," announces Robert, the seeming team leader. "Let's get back."

In less than half the time it took to get there, Bill and his students are in his van heading back to school. Upon arrival they take the samples into the empty building and spend the next hour mapping out the collection site, performing tests that must be done immediately, and labeling and storing the samples.

Not much is said, as each young person, and Bill, is hard at work at the task at hand. After about twenty minutes the busy silence is broken by Darryl, looking up from his test-tubes, charts, and chemicals, who pronounces:

"This is great. It's like being a *real* scientist."

Active learning, doing real things, being real scientists, these things typify classroom and school communities that work. Unfortunately, according to recent reports on schools, these terms do not apply to the experiences of most students. Instead, as one researcher has put it, the tone of much of what goes on in classrooms is emotionally "flat."[1]

Study after study of American classrooms reveals a disappointing sameness in the way children are taught. Nearly 60 percent of a student's time is spent listening to a teacher, doing a written exercise, or preparing for an assignment. Virtually all the talk in the classroom is dominated by teachers, as they out-talk students by a three-to-one ratio. Less than 1 percent of classroom time is given over to questions that require complex student thought or responses. And the vast majority of classes are organized along the lines of large-group instruction, with students spending less than one-third of their time engaged in individual work and less than one-tenth of their time in cooperative work.

These figures are nothing new.[2] Pause for a moment and imagine the standard American classroom. Let me describe what you probably see in your mind's eye. Individual desks for students are aligned in straight rows, all facing in the same direction, usually toward the front of the room. The walls are, for the most part, bare, except for a bulletin board or two with a teacher-made display featuring the best student papers. A chalkboard in front has the day's lesson on it, and school rules are posted complete with punishments for violating them. Presiding over the entire arrangement and serving as the focal point for all interaction is the teacher's desk. Usually located in the front of the room, and even when it is in the back (a clever ploy so the teacher can watch students at work without being observed), the desk is the center of all activity and attention.[3] Around the room, depending on the subject matter and student age, there may be a few resource books, a map or globe, maybe even a fish or bird. But for the most part classrooms are sterile, reflecting neither the personality of the teacher nor the culture or interests of the students within.

We start our examination of life in the classroom with the physical environment because it sets the stage for all else that goes on. It should come as little surprise that in rooms with all desks facing the front (some bolted to floor) the predominant mode of instruction will be lecture, drill, and recitation. Hands-on experiences require classroom arrangements that facilitate movement, group work, and varied activities. Why then are classrooms so oppressively alike in arrangement and decor?

Part of the answer is in the way schools equip classrooms. Individual desks are the norm, as opposed to tables, lounge chairs, or work stations. The rooms themselves, especially in schools built during the 1950s, are a testament to the lack of imagination of most school architects. Carbon copies of one another, designed to meet square footage requirements, each room is adaptable to any program—as long as the program works well in an open square or rectangle with windows on one side, chalkboard on another, and little or no storage or private space for teachers or students.

Teacher frustration with classroom equipment is not new, and modern difficulties are best illustrated by a story told about John Dewey. In the late 1800s, Dewey opened his Laboratory School in Chicago. The first problem he encountered was finding suitable desks for the school. His fruitless search for classroom furniture to fit an active learning environment is summed up in the brief letter a school supplies dealer sent to Dewey: "I am afraid we have not [the desks] you want. You want something at which the children may work; these are all for listening."[4] Fortunately for desk manufacturers, sitting and listening is what most students do during the school day.

It's fairly easy to come up with the form and content of a child's day if we put some flesh on the studies cited earlier in this chapter. Before we do, however, keep in mind that often the passive, repetitive atmosphere in classrooms is not solely of the teacher's making. The real world of public school teaching is low-status (check the pay scales), hectic (with frequent interruptions), controlled (witness the legislated-excellence movement), and lonely (most teachers teach in isolation). It would be unfair to see these relatively uninspiring classrooms as merely products of uninspired teachers. Faced with the school-as-factory metaphor, classrooms packed with students, massive amounts of material, and the lecture/recitation approach appear to many to be the most efficient way possible to cover content and keep control. The demands for higher test scores seem to emphasize speed and coverage, not depth of understanding or commitment. As a defense against all these forces, many teachers logically retreat behind the lectern, the textbook, the standardized test to order their work. This is not an excuse, just one key to understanding why many teachers teach the way they do.[5]

Most elementary schools (kindergarten through grade six) operate with self-contained classrooms. Children spend the entire day with one teacher, who is responsible for all subject areas (with the possible exceptions of art, music, and physical education). However, this doesn't mean there is a great deal of flexibility in the content or form of the day. Taking their cue from state-mandated time allotments, many elementary teachers break up their day into time blocks for instruction. The day then resembles a high school time schedule, with the morning blocked out for (most likely) reading and language arts, the afternoon for math, science, and social studies. But what goes on during those times? As an example we'll follow Julia, an average fifth-grade student, through her day.

When the bell rings and the front doors are unlocked, Julia and her friends stream into the school and head for their classrooms. Julia finds her seat, hands in the previous day's homework, and listens to the morning announcements and lunch counts while she doodles on her notebook cover. Once the preliminaries are over it's time for reading. Julia is in the middle reading group, the Tigers, and so she starts in on the language arts worksheet the teacher hands to the class before she meets with the most advanced readers, the Lions. After twenty minutes Julia's group is called for reading and they assemble around the teacher's desk. They read a story out loud, taking turns, receive more worksheets, and head back to their seats while the lowest reading group, the Clowns, gets their group session. After reading everyone is bundled up for a fifteen-minute recess.

Back in the classroom, the entire class goes over the language arts worksheet. Julia hasn't finished hers (she was more interested in drawing on the back of it), but it goes in to be graded anyway. For the next twenty or so minutes the teacher goes over commas, or capital letters, or paragraphs, and hands out yet another worksheet to be finished after music class. For music the class goes down the hall to a music room where they spend thirty-five minutes with a music teacher (on other days it's art or physical education). Returning from music, the twenty minutes left before lunch are given over to review for a spelling test.

After lunch the remainder of Julia's day is similar to what went on all morning. She drags her science, social studies, or math book from her desk and follows along as the teacher stands at the chalkboard covering the next chapter. After the lecture the teacher asks a few questions to check and make sure everyone understands. Julia, sitting in the back of the room, starts on the next assignment, all the while finding plenty of reasons to leave her seat to sharpen a pencil, get a drink at the water fountain, or help a friend. The room is amazingly quiet. Students sit in their desks, wandering around if they're not noticed, while the teacher circulates and works with those having trouble. The peace is broken by the bell that signals the end of the day. Julia stuffs four out of the day's six worksheets into her backpack along with a book or two and joins the happy throng headed for the doors.

This picture is perhaps too bleak. In many elementary classrooms there is a good deal of affection for children and various opportunities for active, hands-on learning. There is a growing emphasis on reading real children's literature as opposed to using watered-down basal readers, and writing original stories as opposed to filling in worksheets or grammar exercises. Yet for the most part students sit in desks, work alone silently, and continue to fill in the dittos that are so much a part of school life. The really bad news is that it is even worse at the secondary or high school level.

To understand life inside an American junior or senior high school (and many middle schools as well), you have to know about the mysterious "Carnegie unit." Born around seventy years ago, the Carnegie unit was a device used to standardize the secondary school transcript. Proposed by the Carnegie Foundation, and used today virtually without adjustment, this bookkeeping formula specifies one unit of credit for every 120 hours (per year) a student spends studying a subject. That translates into time blocks of forty to sixty minutes, four to five times a week, for thirty-six to forty weeks a year. These units are amassed toward graduation, and, in most cases, become the only ticket to a high school diploma. The high school day, made up of seven to eight fifty-minute periods, is the consequence of such thinking about subject matter. This fragmentation of the school day gives rise to teaching that is mainly talking, learning that is mainly seat time.

On any normal school day in most high schools in America you can witness the Carnegie unit in action. Tag along behind a young man, call him Michael, age seventeen, in his junior year in high school. First period is algebra. He turns in the homework from the night before, and then listens, half-awake, while the teacher tells how to solve an equation for two variables. After working a few sample problems, she assigns the odd-numbered problems from a page in the math book, leaving twenty minutes for Michael and his companions to get started while she drifts among them offering assistance. Most students make some sort of effort, if only putting their name on the paper. For the most part, this is time to catch up on last night's activities with friends and plan for the rest of the day. The ubiquitous notes are passed between friends and lovers, often more interesting than anything the students will write in English later in the day.

A bell rings (or a beeper, buzzer, gong, or some other obnoxious sound—imagine having one in your home), and students scamper to lockers or to meet friends during the four-and-a-half-minute passing period. At the sound of the second bell Michael sits in his American history class with many of the same students from algebra. They are all in the college prep (as opposed to general or business) track and spend most of the day together. Michael's history teacher is entertaining, telling stories and jokes during today's lecture on the Missouri Compromise. But the method of teaching, and the amount of attention paid by students, is the same as in the algebra class. The teacher lectures, students listen and take a few notes, and they get a break at the end of the period for reading the next chapter and answering the study questions (a task most students accomplish by reading the questions first and then skimming the text for answers).

Third period, after the usual hallway crush, is physical education. Although most students enjoy this class, the time available for it is cut short in order to provide students with time to "dress-out" and shower afterward. Michael's teacher has "solved" this problem by having alternating lecture and practice classes. Today is a lecture class, and Michael's group watches the P.E. teacher demonstrate the proper way to serve a volleyball. Tomorrow they'll get a chance to practice the serves. Today the rest of the period (the demonstration took only twenty minutes) is given over to a study time, a euphemism for socializing.

The rest of Michael's day is strikingly similar in form. Fourth-period botany involves looking at an overhead projection of a cell structure and then labeling a matching worksheet picture with the correct terms. After a break for lunch, English class finds Michael identifying past participles in complex sentences. Sixth-period Spanish III provides a session on conjugating some new irregular verbs and beginning work on translating a new passage from a novel. Seventh period Michael has computer science, primarily seen as a way to develop word-processing skills for college. The last period of the day, eighth period, is his American literature class, where he has just finished an oral book report on *Tom Sawyer* and is now listening to an introductory lecture on *The Grapes of Wrath*. In every class the pattern has been the same: teachers lecture, students listen and practice. Perhaps Ernest Boyer put it best when he said that in secondary schools "there is a kind of unwritten, unspoken contract between the teachers and the students: keep off my back and I'll keep off yours."[6]

The legislated-excellence movement is, as is to be expected, silent about changing the *context* of classroom instruction. In fact, preoccupied with *content*, the advocates of excellence will only further flatten classroom life with their demands for more coverage. Teachers will be pushed into a corner by mandates that specify precisely the amount of time to be spent in each subject area, increased objectives to cover, and more standardized tests.

Take, for example, mandates on time spent on subject matter. What would you count Bill Elasky's students' work toward? Science, given the sampling, testing, and recording? Language arts, based on the report they write? Social studies, as they explore what governmental body is responsible for the quality of their water? According to state guidelines you can't call it all three and you must specify exactly what you are covering every minute of the day (to make sure you get the required time in). How does this project relate to the standardized testing mandate? If the test, as manufactured by experts in Chicago or New York, does not cover the types of scientific endeavors utilized in testing water quality and instead covers human anatomy, should Bill abandon his project?[7]

More than likely, faced with these problems, Bill will somehow shoehorn his program into the mandated forms and reports he spends hours filling out. Another teacher, lacking Bill's experience and the support he gets from his colleagues, students, and students' parents, could easily forsake any attempt at active learning. Instead, he/she could stay with what is safe, covering the text in lecture, assigning worksheet after worksheet to be completed, and lulling students into a passive and complacent approach to learning.

The real tragedy in this is that students learn as much, if not more, from *how* they are taught as opposed to *what* they are taught. Often referred to as the "hidden curriculum," the *context* of the school day teaches students what it means to learn, to read, to inquire, to think, and to interact with others. Thus, when children are reminded day after day, year after year, that the most important thing they can do in school is to sit quietly, obey the teacher, and repeat back verbatim what they have been told, they are learning patterns of thinking and behavior that will stay with them for life. We need look no further than classrooms of passivity to find one of the many sources of civic and intellectual passivity in daily life. The legislated-excellence movement will do little to change this phenomenon, and may only make it worse. Its proponents seem more than willing to accept the school-as-factory metaphor, which only makes sense if the products of schooling are to be passive employees rather than active citizens. But there are alternative ways to teach and learn, as witnessed by the following examples of classrooms of commitment and conviction.

Laboratories, Not Museums[8]

Let's start over. Beginning with the very decor of the room and moving on to the type of teaching that goes on in it, is there another choice for American schools? There is, and there needs to be, if we are to take seriously the civic mission of schools: helping to prepare active, self-governing members of a community.

Even with space and equipment limitations there are alternative ways to organize a room. Desks shoved together make tables; an easy chair or two saved from the junk yard makes a reading center;

the teacher's desk can be moved. Teachers who have a different agenda for their classrooms, who refuse to be limited by the space they are given or the norms of many schools, do make such changes. Instead of setting their classrooms up as museums, where children are to sit and observe, they work in laboratories, where they explore the world together with the students.

Once inside the room you will have difficulty locating the teacher. Most likely you'll look first for his or her desk, and already you are in trouble. In some of these rooms there isn't even a teacher's desk to be found! Bill Elasky, who only recently succumbed to a desk, mainly so his students could use it as a computer table, explains why he has avoided one: "It's just another place for me to clutter up. Besides, who has time to sit down?" Even when you do find a teacher's desk it lies shoved off into a corner, out of the way, never in front with all the children's desks facing it. Gone is the omnipotent teacher, the object of the museum-goer's focus. By the simple act of hiding the desk something is clearly said about teaching and learning.

Of course, if you move the teacher's desk, that frees the entire room to fit the nature of the students' activities. Mike Goldman, humanities teacher at Central Park East, explains that room arrangement has to be a logical consequence of what teachers and students are doing together: "I think definitely that the environment is us. It reflects what we are about. We want the student engaged, active, working together. So we try and create the environment that is conducive to having that." What this environment looks like varies from room to room. Following are just a few examples:

In the primary wing at Chauncey, desks are shoved together to make three large tables. Every day students choose a desk to serve as their home base and fill it with their supplies. A major part of the room is given over to an open space with a rug—the place where the class gathers to sit on the floor and share news, discuss their work, or listen to a book. The remaining space is occupied by tables covered with science projects, a writing corner, the classroom library, and a dress-up area complete with props.

In Marcia Burchby's and Bill Elasky's rooms in Amesville you won't find any student desks at all. The same goes for Dan Bisaccio's room at Thayer. Tables are the order of the day, and students sit where they want, usually with a group sharing a project. Bill has an open area in the center of the room to which students bring a table or two and chairs whenever it's time for a class meeting or an interview with a guest. Marcia has used bookshelves to cordon off a reading area complete with a sofa salvaged from the local university and a rocking chair brought from home. A similar reading area is found in Mick Cummings's room and in many of the rooms at Hubbard Woods and Fratney.

Creative use of furniture at CPESS and in the Foxfire room in Georgia allow the teachers to use different sections of the room for different purposes. For example, in Ricky Harris's room a bookshelf and sofa separate four tables used for group work from a common area used for class meetings, whole group instruction, and student presentations. David Smith's room has all the desks pushed together to form a square around which class discussions and instruction occur. On the outside of the square are tables and easy chairs for group work and independent reading. In Wigginton's Foxfire room the center area is given over to desks arranged in a semicircle for whole class work. On one side of this are three tables for students to work on magazine layout and research, in the back are carrels for working on tape transcription, and on the other side is a darkroom Wig and his students built so they could develop their own pictures.

You will usually find textbooks in these rooms somewhere. But always close at hand are supplies for active learning. Books of all types and levels, covering a range of topics and interests, best-sellers, award-winners, and those produced by students are easily accessible to every student for research, to take home, or just for pleasure reading. Manipulatives (things that provide hands-on experiences with abstract concepts like counting, sorting, and classifying), microscopes, blocks, rocks, chemicals, balances, and all the rest lie scattered about. Animals, one with fur, another feathered, and maybe one with scales, may reside in the room. Tools, including computers, tape recorders, photographic equipment, newspapers, magazines, and maps, in short, devices to get information and turn it into something to share exist everywhere. Cultural objects, such as folk art, regional or local literature, historical photographs of the area, family pictures, things giving us a sense of place, abound. You look around the room and it literally begs you to use it. Clearly there is no one best way to organize a classroom laboratory. But a pattern emerges in all of these rooms that says "we are here to work together, we are here to be involved, and we are here to enjoy what we are doing."

No room typifies the sense of laboratory better than Wigginton's room at Rabun County High School. Upon entering the door you are confronted by nearly a dozen statues, quilts, pots, and carvings donated to the Foxfire project by the artisans who have been profiled in *Foxfire* magazine. Additionally, all the walls are covered with even more quilts and wall hangings, and shelves around the room are filled with hundreds of pieces of folk art. Charts on the walls set out the class goals, and a map of the world points out all the places the *Foxfire* magazine is sent. A large bookcase in the front of the room holds copies of the students' work—the Foxfire books and magazines—and serves as a work space for handling subscriptions and reader services. Two computers in the back of the room are set up for student use, mainly as word processors. A large cabinet/bookshelf filled with layout tools, tape recorders, cameras, tapes, film, regional literature, interviews waiting to be transcribed or proofed, photos waiting to be developed or printed stands along one wall. And oh yes, back in the corner, a set of grammar books lies in wait just in case some direct instruction in verb tenses is needed.

In this room, as with all the classrooms we are visiting, you are struck by how much the setting is oriented toward action. While not all of these rooms exemplify each of the following characteristics, there are some ways to distinguish in an instant a classroom laboratory from a museum. Just look around and ask a few questions:

- Is the focus of attention the teacher's desk or places where students work?
- Is the room set up for just whole-group activity or for a variety of tasks?

- Whose space is it—the teacher's, dominated by his/her work, or the students', with their work proudly on display?
- What can you do with the "stuff" in the room—just look at it, or touch it, move it, use it to find out something new?

One last thing you'll notice about these rooms with their focus on active learning: if you arrive before school, or stop in when the room is empty, you'll immediately be caught up in a sense of anticipation. The place looks inviting, so complex, so child-centered, you can't wait to see what happens once young people are turned loose in it. So let's take a look at what keeps Bill Elasky and the teachers like him from having a chance to sit down. Let's see how the physical arrangement of these rooms both reflects and facilitates active learning. Come spend a day with Joette Weber, Bill Elasky, and Dan Bisaccio, and remember—there's no such thing as a typical day in any of these classrooms.

READING IT BETTER THAN IT WAS WRITTEN

Even though the school day does not officially begin until 8:30, by 8:15 Joette Weber's room is buzzing with activity. As the children come in they quickly hang up their coats, put their name tags and materials on desks of their choice, and head for breakfast or their current classroom project. Today most of the students are working on the large birds (up to six feet long, cut from construction paper, stuffed, and sewn together with yarn) that are soon to be hanging from the ceiling. The kids, whose fascination with birds led to the project, are following their own patterns, ultimately rejecting a book full of step-by-step instructions brought in by one student. When Jeremy turns to Joette for help on deciding whether the patterns in the book are the "right" ones to use, she replies: "There are lots of books like that one around, but they show only one way to draw things. There are lots of ways to draw, different styles. And you should choose one you are happy with." Satisfied, Jeremy rejoins the half-dozen other figures sprawled out on the floor, commenting, "You guys were right, she thinks we can do it ourselves."

Joette is always ready to talk with anyone in the room who wants to listen about how a decision she makes fits in with her overall philosophy of teaching. This time she points out that she thinks "one of the biggest mistakes primary teachers make is giving kids patterns. They are perfectly content without them, and they do better." Just then a student rings a small bell and the entire group of seven-year-olds gathers in a circle on the rug.

"OK, whose turn is it to count the lunch money?" The first task of the day is turned over to Brian, and he counts out the dollars, pennies, dimes, nickels, and quarters with the help of his fellow second graders. It is not something he is good at, but everyone gets a chance, and Brian's classmates coach him along carefully. Then he picks a buddy and off they go to drop off this vital information in the office.

"OK, how about some news?" For the next twenty minutes they go around the circle, each sharing what seems most important in their young lives this morning. The bits of information range from play dates with friends to the sometimes frightening bits and pieces of domestic violence. Today, two items draw the most attention. First, JJ pulls back a wisp of his blond hair to reveal a scar and announce, "I got shot by a BB gun."

"Oh, JJ, are you all right now?"

"Yeah, but it really hurt then! You should have seen all the blood!"

"Right, OK, but maybe we need to talk about how to use BB guns. Who knows the rules for using a gun?"

Quickly, hands go up and a list is put on the board:

1. Have something safe to shoot at.
2. Have the safety on.
3. Only shoot at a safe target.
4. Make a really big target so you can't miss it and hit a person or something. If you do it could cost you millions and millions of dollars.
5. Only use a gun with an adult.
6. Make sure there is nothing ahead of you.

7. After you are done shooting, put on the safety before you
    reload.

Gun safety isn't in the second-grade curriculum for these kids,
but it is in their lives. So is having fun around train tracks, and we
hear about it three students later.

"I put a penny on the railroad track near our house and a train
ran over it and flattened it," Jessica reports breathlessly.

"Do you have it for us to see?" Joette inquires.

"No, my brother took it."

"Well, maybe you can bring it in sometime. But who knows if
it's safe to put money on the train tracks?"

No one is positive, but plenty of opinions are voiced. After a
minute or two, Joette stops the discussion and asks, "Well, how
could we find out?"

"Call up the railroad engineers," Tony replies.

"So, you want to do that?"

And while the rest of the class continues to share news, Tony
and Jessica get out a phone book and find the number. They practice
their call several times with the class before bravely heading down
to the main office to put in a call to Amtrak.

With news time over, Joette runs through the jobs to be done
while she is working with reading groups. Several jobs are posted
on the board, which they can tackle in any order, including making
more birds for the room (they need some penguins), creating sentence strips for a sentence about a bird of their choice, or participating in pumpkin groups (see chapter 1).

Having sent them all off by 9:00 or so she is ready for her first
reading group. She sits down at the kidney-shaped table and rings
a bell while asking, "Can I have four or five readers?" As we saw
earlier, reading is not ability-grouped, and so any combination of
five children may be at the reading table at one time. Today the
first five are Angie, Michael, Willy, Toby, and Amy.

Arriving at the reading table they find a new book, *Stone Soup,*
waiting for them. This oft-told tale concerns a poor boy who offers
to help make soup from a stone in return for part of the meal. After

convincing his hostess to add a variety of vegetables to the cauldron, he feasts with his amazed friends on a meal fit for a king.

"Who wants to start reading? Willy?"

Willy starts. He's not a good reader, but he's anxious to try a new story. He stumbles, gets stuck, and stops.

"Skip it and see if you can make sense of the rest of the sentence." He does, and, going on, he picks up the missing word with a quick glance at the illustration.

"Nice work. Did you guys see what Willy did? He looked at the words and the picture. That's how you do it, use all the sources of information you can find. Who wants to read the next page?" And on they go; Joette encourages them and never corrects them when they read beyond the book. So when Toby adds "very" to the line "he was tired and hungry," Joette notes, "I think it would be fine to add 'very' there because he does look very hungry." When Amy reads "good evening" for "good lady" she is told that even though it is "good lady" her use of "good evening" makes sense because the pictures are of night time. And when Angie, who hardly reads at all, turns "ah" into "Oh, yes I can," Joette congratulates her: "You know, you read that better than the author wrote it."

Meanwhile, in the rest of the room, the hum of productive work goes on. Back in the corner one of the pumpkin groups is busy at work. It's now December, so the pumpkin specimen is just getting juicy.

Joette describes the genesis of the project, which will be displayed as a whole class' entry in the school science fair, this way. "We really used to hate science fairs—all the judging, with some kids working real hard on projects with no parental help and not doing well while other kids' moms and dads basically made the project and the kids got blue ribbons. . . . Now we just choose a project everyone is interested in and enter it as a class. Everybody works on it, and it's always a really wonderful experience." This year's project is designed in a way to help kids work together, also something Joette is very emphatic about. "I like them to work together. I couldn't stop them from working together anyway. . . . What I do is set it up so it [the project] really does lend itself to helping each other. . . . I really like them going at their own pace, and I like them asking each other 'how do I do this' rather than coming to me."

By ten, Joette has finished with reading groups and they all gather back at the rug. It's time to share the morning's work, and today the major topic are the pumpkin books. Each group shows off their work, talks about how their observations differ and why, and shares plans for putting together the class display. After about ten minutes Joette casts a look out the window and gives the kids a choice: "Time to stop and make a decision, because it looks like the kind of day that if we're going to go out, we better go now" (the forecast and the clouds call for rain). A quick discussion ensues and they decide to stay in so they can finish their penguins and the pumpkin observations.

Before returning to work, Tony and Jessica report on their phone call about trains. Tony begins the report: "Well, we went into Mr. Jarvis's room [the principal] and I got to sit in his chair while Jessica called the number. When the guy came on, I didn't know what to say [he had been thrown by the standard opening lines given by ticket agents], so I gave it to Jessica."

"And I asked him about snakes and pennies," Jessica quickly picks up the story, "and he said snakes were OK but pennies were not."

"Snakes?" Joette asks.

"Yeah, I once put a dead snake on the tracks so I thought we should know about that too. And you see, pennies can fly up and hit you in the eye but dead snakes don't fly."

"Well, I'm glad we got that straight." With that they finish up their morning's work while Joette circulates, offering help, guidance, and encouragement. As the group's interest begins to wane, and most of the work is finished, she asks them to choose an activity to get them to lunchtime. The overwhelming choice is for her to read them another chapter out of *Pippi Longstocking*. After a twenty-minute reading, with kids sprawled out on the floor or sitting at their desks, Joette announces that it's time for buddy reading. Each student takes a partner; the partners share books with each other until lunchtime. Before we know it, it's 11:10 and time for the kids to put journals on their desks, fill in the date, and head for lunch and recess.

Returning from lunch, Joette does not seem surprised to find most of the class busily writing away, a favorite tape already playing in the tape recorder. She takes her journal and sits down at one of the empty student desks and goes to work. Everyone writes about whatever they want, and it's fine to draw pictures as long as they are accompanied by a few words of explanation. The purpose of the task is to get kids to see writing as a tool, not a chore. It isn't graded or marked, and Joette only reads the entries students choose. After twenty minutes a bell goes off signaling time to stop, but when Joette looks up and notices most of the kids still busily at it, she goes right on for a minute or two (a pattern that has been repeated all year, stretching what started as a five-minute session into over twenty minutes a day). As they finish, students gather again on the rug in order to share what they have written. Only those who want to read do so; the rest form an appreciative audience.

Around noon the journals are abandoned and the class turns to a math session. Joette hands out a page of problems dealing with money, a topic they have been studying. "You can use anything you want to help you figure these things out; use the book, the play money, work with your friends. Let's see how well we can all do."

"Isn't using the book like cheating?" asks Dana, a small boy with a permanently puzzled look on his face.

"No, it's like using any reference book, like a dictionary, or calling your doctor when you are sick. The thing is to figure these things out with whatever tools you have available. You wouldn't build a house with your bare hands, would ya'?"

Dana ponders this for a moment, decides no, he wouldn't, picks up his math book, and goes to work. Again, Joette moves from student to student, asking questions, offering encouragement, never stopping even to catch her breath. Thirty minutes later, at 12:35, she gets her first real break of the day when the kids leave for either art or gym or music and she has the room to herself until 1:05.

After picking the kids up at the art room, she asks them again on the way down the hall whether they would like to take a break for recess. This time the decision is a unanimous yes, and they're out the door as soon as coats are zipped and mittens found.

One-thirty finds the group in their familiar gathering place, on the rug in a circle. It's the beginning of choice time, and kids are making their intentions known. Three are off to read, five to play with blocks, four are going to hang up the birds, and one group wants to work on their pumpkin observations. The rest are going to keep working on the play about *Stone Soup* they started that morning. That accounts for everyone except Julie. Julie needs some help with some very important writing.

Several times in the past two weeks the class has wanted to use a map. They've received postcards from friends and have had a cross-country bicyclist in to talk with them. But there is only one U.S. wall map shared among the four primary classrooms and it hasn't been in their room recently. The problem has been discussed several times during morning news, and the kids wanted to know who was in charge of such things as maps. They decided that it must be the superintendent, so Julie is now writing to her to request a map for their room. She has thought through the process carefully, surveying all the kids in the room on how they might use a map if one were available. Now, with Joette's help, she spends the next thirty minutes on the third and final draft of a letter that they will sign and send today.

"What book shall I read?" Joette asks. This question signals the end of choice time and starts kids cleaning up while they sing out suggestions. "How about this one?" calls out Alisha, holding up *Jamanji*, a new one Joette slipped into the class library today. Voices ring out in support and soon they are gathered yet again in their little group on the rug. The story is a riveting one about two children who find an adventure game which becomes real as they are playing it. Their house is ransacked by monkeys, flooded, and occupied by a variety of wild and dangerous animals. The story ends with a great deal of uncertainty, and as Joette turns the final page, she asks, "So what would happen in this story if there were another page?" The spirited debate that follows is cut off by the bell for the first bus. Forty-four little hands gather up coats and lunch boxes and forty-four little feet head down the hall to go home. They'll be back tomorrow to a classroom that is just as exciting and unpredictable as a book with no ending.

SOMEDAY THEY'LL JUST TELL ME TO GO AWAY

On the door leading into Bill Elasky's classroom is the following announcement:

Knock on this door and you may be—boiled in oil, tarred and feathered, drawn and quartered, put on the rack, taken for a ride, fitted with a cement swimsuit, used in diabolical experiments, fed to the wolves, fed to a snake, run out of town on a rail, or used to test thumbscrews.

Simply
ENTER and Wait to be seen.

"The sign was the kids' idea," explains Bill. "We're just so busy in here all the time no one wants to take the time to go answer the door."

Keeping in mind the penalties for knocking thought up by these sixth graders, I pull open the door and slip inside. The room, though full, is strangely quiet, especially for Bill, who gladly tolerates noise if it's in the name of the work at hand. Then you notice that every kid, as well as Bill, is sprawled out somewhere in the room with a book in his or her hands. It's time for morning reading, something the kids thought would be a fun way to start their day. And who could disagree? Imagine getting to spend the first part of your day, every day, curled up with a good book. The "Books We Are Reading" chart in the back of the room lists titles ranging from *The Pushcart War* and *Are You There, God, It's Me Margaret* to *Old Yeller* and *My Side of the Mountain*. On the "Books We Have Read" chart next to it we find that by mid-November every student had finished at least one book (that includes students in special education) and some are approaching their first dozen. The class average is nearly four, as this class of twenty-eight has read well over one hundred full-length novels.

"The kids read a lot because they choose what is of interest to

them from the library we have in class," comments Bill, attributing
the idea to his colleague, Mick Cummings. Bill puts together this
library once he figures out the varied interests of his students. He
buys books from his own and school funds and visits libraries as far
away as Columbus (a seventy-mile drive) to get multiple copies of
books so groups of students can read together. Then each group
gathers to discuss the work and explore ways to present it to the
rest of the class.

How do the students feel about this approach to reading? "This
is great, I didn't know there were so many good books around,"
reports Adam, who is already into novel number five. But is it
different from their other classes? "Well," Andrea begins, "we only
had to *have* a book in the other class. We didn't have to *read* any
others." "Yeah, and we don't have to bother with that other book,"
Adam indicates the reading texts on the shelf. "These boring old
things have been sitting there all year."

"OK, can we get together over here with your math books?" Bill
queries, his soft but full voice setting the group into action. The
kids emerge from corners, under tables, and behind file cabinets,
carefully marking their places in their books and heading to the
"back" of the room where Bill has posted seven sheets of newsprint.
(It's actually impossible to find a "front" or "back" of this room;
it's more of a collection of tables with three open spaces for group
gatherings. In no time at all, the kids can make the room change
into a variety of arrangements.)

Bill has just finished posting a newsprint sheet with the title "Ways
a Bank Teller Uses Math" when the cheerful group of eleven- and
twelve-year-olds have gathered around him. Those up close to Bill
are sitting on the floor. Behind them a ring of tables has been pulled
over for the session.

"Right. Let's go back to the interview with Teresa Beha on page
19." Math books, unlike any you have ever seen before, flip open.
Blue, plastic-spiral-bound, the books are entitled *Math Mania: Math
in Your Future*, and their authors are the Math Maniacs of Amesville Elementary School. It comes as no surprise that the Math
Maniacs were last year's sixth-grade class and that the text is the
product of their work with Bill.

"Now, what were the ways Teresa said she used math?"

"She first talks about making change." Bill writes "making change" on the list.

"Later she says that she has to do percentages when she does those certificate things." "Which certificate things?" Bill prompts. "You know, Mr. E, it says . . . certificates of deposit." As Bill writes "figuring percentages" he asks, "Who remembers what a certificate of deposit is?" And on they go until they have listed the seven ways Teresa uses math that came out of the interview and survey in the text.

"Everybody, which of these tasks make use of multiplying and dividing fractions?"

The young people ponder, several of them work out a few of the functions that are listed on the board. Finally, a tentative hand comes up and Jessie offers: "Figuring out quarterly payments?" "Good, come up here and show us what you mean." On another sheet of paper Jessie goes to work, creating a fictitious depositor and working out quarterly interest payments on an installment loan.

"Now, who can tell me what type of problem Jessie just made and worked for us?" After congratulating Jessie, Bill is again addressing the whole class.

"A hard one," Sam allows, to laughter by all and a bright red blush from Jessie.

"All good problems are hard," a smiling Bill replies. "But what *type* of problem is it?"

"A banking problem."

"A math problem."

"But what type of math problem?" Bill persists.

"Oh, you mean a word problem, Mr. E?"

"That's it. You remember we've done them before. But Jess did this one backward. She had the math problem and then turned around and wrote it out." Bill goes on to quiz Jessica on how she chose the particular numbers she used. He then returns their attention to the list of how Ms. Beha uses math and together they figure out what other tasks would require multiplying with fractions. Then he gives them the day's assignment.

"Get in your math groups [there are five of them, all with students of mixed abilities] and write story problems for the rest of us to work. One problem for each of the ways a bank teller multiplies by fractions in her job. Got it? Get to it." Kids scramble around the room, move the tables, and soon the five groups materialize, all in their own spaces, all at work.

"It didn't always work this well," Bill says, referring to the ease with which the groups start their work. It is working well, one person leading the group, another checking the time, another taking notes. These and other jobs rotate through the group and are clearly spelled out on a chart on the wall. The development of this chart and others throughout the room on how to cooperate has led to the success the groups now experience.

Early in the year Bill and his students engaged in several simulations that demonstrated the power of group as opposed to individual effort.[9] The lessons learned are put on charts labeled "Us, Not Me." They also brainstormed potential tasks that members of the group might have to fulfill, such as checking in with other groups or the teacher. These, too, go on a newsprint sheet and are posted on the wall. These exercises and the charts are what make the groups run as well as they do. "We develop a group ethic in here, and we work on it all the time." Indeed they do; it's only natural given the type of real work that they are about, especially when it comes to the class project, the yearly mission that sets the stage for most everything the class does.

After math and a break for gym they turn to this year's project: development of a nature study area for use by the school. Past years' projects have included production of radio spots on government services, a water-quality survey (from which the opening scenario of this chapter came), and last year's Math Mania project in which the class tried to find out how the math they study is used in real life through surveys and interviews. "What other options are there for a site and the type of nature study setting we want to develop?" The kids are all gathered in the other end of the room, one of them at the chalkboard to take notes, Bill sitting on the floor with the rest. As with most else that goes on in his class, he has started this session with a question. "I still try and start everything I do with a question. We want a spirit of finding out in the room, not one of memorizing."

Today's question is vital. The nature study project has run into a snag. The class had originally chosen a site directly across the highway from the school. This marshy wetland would have easily been converted for their use. However, the county health department vetoed that plan for a variety of reasons and the class is now back to the drawing board. "It took us a while to recover from that. We had our hearts set on that spot, it was so perfect, and you can see it right outside my window. . . . I am still attached to it, but I try not to look out the window. . . . But we've let it sit for a week now and I think we are ready to go back to it."

Clearly they are, as five new options are slowly hammered out on the board. Each will require more follow-up and investigation, so Bill helps them organize some new groups. "It would be good if we could get a representative from each of our working groups on each of the new sites. That means, that, say with the idea of doing something over at the high school, we need a group to go over there, check the site, talk to the principal, and so on. But that group should have someone from the design, finances, animal survey, all the other groups on it." Soon they are setting up new groups and making plans to visit the new sites. The rest of the morning and on into the afternoon is spent in the core groups (design, etc.) developing a list of questions to be answered by the site groups. These questions are then taken by each of the site groups and used to investigate new possibilities.

The ease with which the work comes together is due to several factors, but primarily, according to Bill, it comes from "kids getting excited about doing something real." The process is deceptively simple. At the beginning of the year, Bill and the class explored some options for whole-class projects. Sources for these options came from what Bill knows about his students and their interests. The nature study area came from a workshop Bill attended, the water-quality survey from a chemical spill in the area, and the Math Maniacs were an extension of an underground newspaper that a group of students had published as fourth graders.

Each of the projects is chosen at the beginning of the year by class consensus and by the end of the year it is clear what they have accomplished.

For example, the Math Maniacs not only learned math, they also discovered where it is used, found out how to interview and transcribe tapes, learned about photographing, printing, and graphics, and honed their writing skills. Most important, they've published a book, written something that others will read; they are in print. Two years ago the Amesville Water Chemists, the class that surveyed area water sources, developed similar skills in researching the quality of their water and providing public reports on their findings. This year's nature study project will be just as important to the kids. Again they will leave behind a mark, something that says that they made a difference. (In fact, they've now chosen a site at the high school. The high school has wanted to develop it into a nature area, but has never been able to. "Now we're doing it to show them that sixth graders can do what high school kids can't," boasts Scott with understandable pride.)

All of this goes on without Bill actually deciding what they will do or how they will do it. He is always working from behind, helping to guide their decision making, picking up the occasional loose end, keeping track of the curriculum. For example, he communicates with each group daily via letters in their group files. During one of the brief moments when Bill isn't surrounded by kids he reflects on this pattern. "As the year goes on, I do less and less, maybe by the end of the year, they'll tell me to go away." He laughs, shakes his head, and wanders to the middle of the room.

"OK, take out your writing folders." Folders filled with a story (this time fiction) that each student is writing are pulled out. "Who needs to meet with me today?" Five hands go up. Bill notes each one on his "notepad" (usually a folded-up piece of scratch paper), and then begins on the transition to writing time. Before long he's down on one knee, listening intently to a young boy describe the action he's trying to portray in his story and helping him work on dialogue. It will be a long time before these kids tell Mr. E to go away.

YOU'LL HAVE MORE QUESTIONS THAN YOU CAN ANSWER

Dan Bisaccio teaches in the Spectrum program at Thayer. His room, down in the basement of the aging school building, also serves as the meeting place for the entire Spectrum group. So it's not surprising to get there first thing Monday morning and find over sixty eleventh and twelfth graders and three teachers filling up all the available tables, chairs, lab counters, and then some. Kids and teachers chat amiably, catching up on weekend events.

"All right," Dan's voice lifts up over the others. "Regular schedule this week, council meets here on Wednesday, group meeting during D period on Friday. Any special announcements? . . . No? So let's go."

Julie Gainsburg and Val Cole take their changes upstairs to their respective math and English rooms. Dan stays with his group and they settle into their working groups around the five tables in the room. As the dust settles a chart in the back of the room catches my eye. It reads like this in October:

Natural History Perspectives: Goals

- To appreciate the universality of change and the dynamic processes of the physical and biological sciences.
- To obtain a personal standard of scientific literacy which allows for reasonable assessment of the local and global condition in terms of economic, social, legal, and applied science concepts.
- To achieve the ability to distinguish between science, personal opinion, and pseudoscience through inquiry, investigation, research, and interpretation of data.

Coming back in January, I find that Dan's students have amended the list, expanding it to include the following:

To develop independent skills
Learn more about science
To get more involved in class
Improve my science abilities and research abilities

To get as much as possible out of this class
To have fun
To be successful
How does science affect me?
To do the things we are studying
To do more professional and better disciplined science
Understand whys and hows
Understand scientific terminology

"We put those things on there," explains Lisa, who has walked over to the list. "We wanted Mr. B to see how he was helping us think. He's proud of that, you know."

On Monday each of the Spectrum classes lasts only sixty minutes. While this is longer than an average American high school class, it is shorter than the ninety minutes Dan will have with them on Tuesday through Thursday. Friday is open, usually sixty minutes again. Thus, the Monday session is often devoted to planning the midweek trips to the land lab.

"What things would you look for if you wanted to really know what was in or on a piece of land?" Sipping from his coffee cup, Dan opens the day with, as usual, a question.

"You mean like what is growing there?" questions Craig, taking the bait.

"Well, what about what is growing there?" responds Dan, with yet another question.

"Do you mean make a list?" Craig isn't answering so much as trying to find out where Dan is going.

"Try this. What would you expect to find growing on a piece of land in the land lab?" asks Dan, with his favorite type of question: "What would you expect?"

"Trees and grasses," Stephanie jumps in.

"Good. Now what if you told someone that the land you were exploring had trees and grasses on it? How might they respond?"

"Big deal," sings out Bruce, in the back. "I mean, they'd say so what, anybody can tell you that."

"Good. So, what else could we tell them given what you already know?"

There follows a forty-minute brainstorming period in which the class generates questions about the environment for Dan to put on the board:

Trees: How many, types, size (width and height), distance apart, health of

Other plants: Types, number of, concentrations and location

Animals: Tracks, damage to trees, sightings, homes

Soil: Type, wet or dry, runoff

They discuss each of these topics, making sure they understand what each one calls for, when to estimate and when to measure, how to develop a sample count into an overall estimate. The list of things to look for would daunt the ablest college undergraduate.

"Mr. B, do we have to get all these things for all of the land lab?" asks a bewildered Stephanie as the size of the task slowly dawns on her.

"That's a good question. Who wants to help Steph out on this? Obviously we can't all check for everything out there."

"Could we divide it up, like in sections or something, and each take a piece?" replies Jenny, who hasn't said much this morning, and who seems ready to go get this right now.

"We could. But what might we miss if we did that?"

"We might miss some of the best stuff," this time Nicole.

"Well, what's the best stuff?"

"You know, the stuff you always say to watch out for. The places where things change and where you find the things you don't expect to find."

"So what do you think, Steph, how can we do this?" He sends it back to the initial questioner.

"I don't know, Mr. B, that's why I asked."

Dan chuckles, then suggests they take Nicole's suggestion and choose, in teams of two, particularly interesting areas in the land lab to study. "And we'll start with trees. Come tomorrow dressed well, it's supposed to be cold and rainy, but we're going regardless." Several good-natured groans go up as the class pairs off and makes plans for tomorrow's visit.

Indeed, Tuesday is cold and rainy. But Dan is a man of his word. They head out the door equipped with notepads, tape measures, field books, coats, gloves, and boots as soon as the class begins.

The land lab, something virtually any school could have, is directly behind Thayer. Most of it is school property, but the owners of property that borders the school allow students free access. (It wasn't always this way, as Thayer students were not always welcome outside the school. But the newfound respect children have for themselves and the land due to the changes at Thayer has opened a lot of doors.)

Dan's students have indeed chosen the most interesting spots. Several teams are down near the swamp, where it emerges into hillside and changes character. Others are up on top of the hillside where trees give over to open, grassy fields. Each team stakes out a ten-foot by ten-foot plot and goes to work making notes, recording measurements, and collecting fallen leaves from the trees they cannot immediately identify.

Voices ring out back and forth through the woods. "Mr. B, come look at this." "Mr. B, what if a tree is half in and half out of your area?" "Mr. B, should we try and draw a map of the plot?" Dan goes from group to group, checking new finds, pointing out some of the subtleties the kids may have missed.

Working with one group near the field, he directs them to a stand of very small beech trees in the middle of the woods. "What would you have expected to find here?" Large trees, like the ones around them, is the obvious answer. "So how do we explain this growth, what clues do you look for?" He leaves them to puzzle over this problem while he moves on to another group. While he's away one of the students literally trips over the answer—an old stump left by beaver activity in the area.

As each group finishes, they head back to the classroom. Dan stays in the field with the last groups and then joins them in the walk back. In the classroom the groups are at work writing a summary report on the area. Using field guides, their notes, and samples, they work on producing a catalog of the plot.

Dan moves from group to group, asking questions, pointing out things they may have missed. He suggests to one group a way of graphing tree sizes and species in order to conduct comparisons. He challenges the assumptions of another group that the trees cut by the beavers on their plot were for building a dam but were too large to move. At a third table he helps students find more clues in the leaves they have collected in order to determine which types of trees they saw.

After one trip around the room he pulls the students' attention to the front. "I noticed that a lot of you were having trouble working out how to determine dominant species, especially when you have nearly equal numbers of trees. What is another way to figure out dominance aside from just counting?"

"How about looking for the oldest trees?" Steve suggests.

"But if they are older it doesn't mean they are dominant. I mean, they could be dying out with no replacements," counters Sara.

"Good, that's what you two found in your area, isn't it?" replies Dan, inviting Sara to continue.

"Yeah, we found some large beeches, but all the saplings are oak," she explains.

For the remaining ten minutes of class they continue to work on the issue of dominance. Together, continually prompted by Dan's questions, they establish that dominance is best revealed not only by numbers but by trees of a wide age range as well.

"And who remembers one of the best indicators of tree age?"

"Within a species and given the same conditions, size is usually the best predictor," sings out Karen.

"Right, bigger usually, but not always, means older," Dan responds.

"Mr. B," Stephanie calls out, "does that mean that the older you get the fatter you are?" As the room dissolves in laughter, Dan just grins and, realizing that their ninety minutes are up, reluctantly announces, "OK, I'm going to have to let you leave."

Throughout the year Dan and his charges continue to use those pieces of ground to explore and ask questions about the physical world. They make numerous other trips as well, visiting Walden Pond and going on a fossil dig, for example. But the land lab continues to function as a base for their operations.

By January the class has moved from flora to fauna. With the third quarter of the year the class is moving on to its next project: the life cycle of mammals in the area, with a focus on winter adaptations. The task begins with the class generating potential research questions. Dan starts them off by listing many of the animals that stay in the area through the difficult New England winter, carrying their offspring at the same time.

He pauses from his list and asks, "Wouldn't you think that this would be a dangerous time to carry a litter?" The class is caught up short. Again Dan has asked the type of question that causes his students to challenge their own assumptions, to rethink what they take for granted. Pressed for an answer, he refuses, suggesting instead that this is the type of question he wants them to use in putting together their project.

"So why don't you work on some other questions that you have about animals and their adaptations? For example, we know that rabbits in the area change their fur color to match the snow—but what causes that change to occur? Is it the temperature, light, or what? I want each table to generate a list of questions like these."

Within five minutes each group is filled with questions. Dan leads them through a brainstorming session during which they list these on the board for further consideration. The list, which will help direct their studies, includes, among others, questions like these:

* How do fish survive in iced-over lakes?
* How do animals "know" when to make their shelters?
* Where do animals get water if usual sources are frozen?
* If the ground is covered with snow, how does this affect the herbivores?
* If rabbits are born in winter are they brown or white?
* Are animals able to store energy?
* How do frogs and turtles maintain respiration under water?
* Do all animals respirate oxygen aerobically?
* What do water snakes do during the winter?

It's a diverse list, representing the range of interests and abilities in the class (the class is *not* ability-grouped). And the list has the entire class guessing answers and searching reference books to see who is right.

"Excellent. These are the types of questions that we'll use. Now, take a minute and read this." Capitalizing on the moment, Dan hands out an essay on the muskrat in winter that appeared in the paper just two days ago. It describes one researcher's attempt to understand an animal in concert with its environment, and it challenges many previously held assumptions about the muskrat. After the students finish reading and answering questions about the methods used, Dan gives them the assignment.

"You will each produce an essay about an animal of your choice. You'll take one animal and make field observations and do research, guided by your questions. What the author did here is very similar to what you are going to do. . . . And one of the things he found was that his study generated even more questions. And that's what will happen in your study."

With that he turns them loose to use the field manuals around the room to pick an animal to study. Each student makes a selection and begins to fill in a project sheet outlining his or her approach, the resources available, and the help he or she needs. It's hard to believe that all this is accomplished in only thirty minutes, when Dan pulls them back together for one more group exercise.

"So, let's talk about the animal you chose, your questions and your approach." For some of the students this is easy. They're well on their way and have an excellent list of questions. Others are slower, and the discussion gives them ideas and new directions.

"Good. Now you've heard a range of questions. Let's see if we can list some general questions that seem to run through all of your approaches." As students mull over what they have heard, yet another list appears on the board, this one framing much of what the students will do:

1. Nocturnal, diurnal, and crepuscular feeders: how are they affected: Which of these are active?
2. Sacrifice or trade-offs due to seasonal change?
3. Do they mate during this period?
4. How does it keep warm?

5. What adaptive changes are made?

6. How much food is consumed? Where do they get it? Ditto shelter.

7. How do aquatic animals survive the winter in relation to ice?

8. Is the size of the animal important? Is bigger better? (Surface area, volume?)

9. Why, how, and when does the fur change?

10. Do animals grow "bloomers" in the winter?

11. Gestation period—how does it operate to facilitate survival of winter?

12. Do nonhibernators eat more or less in the winter?

The following day, armed with this list, the classes head to the land lab carrying sample jars, binoculars, field guides, and measuring instruments. On the way there Jeff scoffs that they'll never see an animal this time of day. "Ah, just remember," replies Dan, "just because you *don't* see the animal doesn't mean you *can't* see the animal." His prophecy holds true as the excited group records tracks, examines a beaver lodge, collects samples of "scat," and measures the teeth marks on the trees. The world of winter wildlife, which has existed all around them for years, suddenly becomes observable, fascinating, and real in light of their new questions.

After an hour of tramping around in the cold, the class gathers back in the room to summarize their observations in the field logs. Jeff, earlier the cynic, is hard at work with a field book, trying to decipher some tracks he has sketched. As Dan approaches him to offer help, Jeff finds the pattern he was looking for, but since it isn't what he expected he shakes his head and sighs.

"Every time I think I find something out, it just makes me want to ask more questions."

At that Dan's eyes light up: "Don't feel you have to have all the answers; we will probably raise more questions than we can answer. But that's all right, that's excellent."

Classrooms of Conviction and Commitment

These three classrooms, and the others on which we have focused, take us well beyond the simplistic "more-is-better" philosophy of the legislated-excellence movement. They model for us what we can legitimately expect our schools to be. They show us the type of daily classroom work that takes students beyond mere coverage and passivity. It's not easy to distill these practices into a core list, because so much of what happens each day depends upon the interaction of the teachers and students in the room. There are some core practices that guide this flexibility, this teaching for democracy.

DOING SOMETHING MEANINGFUL

Much of what students produce in school is artificial. That is, it has no purpose, no audience, no reason for existence beyond satisfying a teacher, or, just as likely, satisfying whoever developed the dittos that go along with the prepackaged curriculum. Most kids get good at these exercises, figuring out that filling in the blanks with words or phrases copied from the text is all they need to do. As soon as these worksheets are handed back, they are wadded up and deposited in the trash, usually on the way out of the door in the afternoon.

Not so in the classrooms we've visited. In these rooms the work is purposeful, designed with a real audience in mind (often one outside the school), and intended to make a difference. Eliot Wigginton has put this principle most eloquently into words and most dramatically into practice. "There must be an audience beyond the teacher for student work," Wig argues. "It may be another individual, or a small group, or the community, but it must be an audience the students want to serve or please."[10] The Foxfire magazine and book series shows what can happen when students and their teacher hit upon an idea that captures the national imagination. Hundreds of thousands of copies of these publications can be found in homes and libraries around the country. This result in turn insures that students take their efforts seriously and work to get every detail correct. "We have to be good. Do you realize how many people depend on us?'' admonishes Jill, a junior, as she works with a team of students to finish up yet another edition of the magazine.

While Foxfire is certainly a dramatic example of how real classroom work can be, other lesser-known efforts provide examples that are just as clear. Following is a very short listing of a few such efforts from the schools we're exploring:

- Barb Ibell's Spanish students at Thayer spend one morning a week teaching Spanish in the elementary school.
- Ann Hardee's second graders write, illustrate, and bind books for their own growing classroom library at Hubbard Woods.
- Mike Goldman's humanities students at CPESS wrote a children's textbook about the American Revolution.
- Marcia Burchby's first graders at Amesville prepare books explaining the classroom and program to give to the next year's students at a welcome party in the spring.
- Richard Cargill's high school students developed, constructed, and maintain a nature area around the Willowbrook School grounds.
- Katy Beck's fifth graders develop math games that become a key part of her Hubbard Woods classroom.
- Becky Trayser's class writes alphabet books for the kindergarten classes at Fratney.

Add these to Joette Weber's pumpkin project, Bill Elasky's math book and nature study area, and Dan Bisaccio's flora and fauna surveys, and we quickly see how many different ways classroom work can be purposeful.

Why is this work so central to the life of these classrooms? Bill Elasky puts it best:

What I am interested in is a process where kids can get involved in doing something that is meaningful to them, seeing that all these things that they are supposed to be learning in language and reading and science and social studies . . . have some meaning. They empower you to do things, to affect the world around you. They allow you to do things that force people to take you seriously. They allow you to have the badge of a competent, capable, can-do person who sees the world and understands the world and does something about the world. I think even a sixth grader has the ability to do that in a lot of different ways.

MAKING CHOICES WHENEVER POSSIBLE

Of course, the real products of kids' work that Bill has in mind do not just magically spring from a classroom. Moreover, they certainly do not come from the brightly colored but shallow and dull textbook fare we feed our students. So where do the ideas come from? What so motivates these kids to turn out the high-quality, well-received work they do?

Joyce Hanenberg, from Chauncey, speaks for virtually all these teachers when she finds the genesis of this motivation in the amount of choice and control she shares with students:

> In my classroom I try to have the children make choices when-ever it is possible. We make academic choices: they're always choosing what book they want to read, and choosing what they want to write, and a lot of times they choose the project they want to work on. . . . They also make a lot of decisions about how the classroom is run. . . . I feel like the children in my classroom, they do feel powerful, because they make choices about what they want to learn or choices about something that's going on in the room. . . . I say "yes" to children in my class-room whenever possible.

The goal of having students make as many choices as possible is played out in different ways in each room. The teacher knows the concepts, facts, and skills to be covered in each area. So he/she turns the kids loose to come up with the projects they want to do that will help them gain this knowledge or skill. For example, in dealing with the Constitution, John Duffy has his students explore their own lives in high school with respect to the Bill of Rights. Mick Cummings, as we saw earlier, has his students choose and order the topics for the science curriculum. Wig's kids select the contacts and sources for their articles just as Dan's students choose the animal they are interested in as the focus of their study. At Fratney, students' production of their own books is a central part of the program, and they are always writing about topics of concern to them. The projects Bill Elasky's students take on are always derived from student interest; whether it was the chemical spill that aroused the curiosity of one class and led to the water-quality project or the frustration with the math books that led to the Math Maniacs, Bill always starts with what his kids *want* to know.

Enabling the children to make choices pays off in many ways. First, such an orientation expands what can be covered in a classroom. Traditionally, coverage has meant the number of pages the kids get through in the text. But in classrooms and schools that start with student interest, the whole notion of coverage changes. Joette Weber talks about it in her classroom:

> I think if I don't pay attention to what they are interested in, I lose out a lot on what I can teach. Now there are certain things I have to teach; say, reading. But if I don't pay attention to what they want to read about, then they are much more resistant to reading. With the science fair, our best projects are [in] the years they have told me what they want to do and I have helped get the materials and the stuff so that they could go do [it]. Now if it's, say, insects and I don't want to do insects, there is almost a mini-revolution sometimes. But if I go with insects and also weasel in what I think we ought to be learning about science, that is usually fine. They will accept a lot of that but they want to pick the topic. And I think that's real good.

In addition to covering material in more depth, using student interests to guide the curriculum induces many students to be more successful. Becky Trayser at Fratney helps her students create a web of possibilities for each topic they are covering. After showing the kids several ways of exploring a topic, she spends time with them evaluating the projects from the standpoints of interest and learning. "I ask them . . . how they thought it went, what were their favorite projects to do, and to please suggest some new and different things we could do for the next theme. . . . So in that way they help determine the direction that the theme goes and then they make the choices about which projects they do and which they won't do."

In response to this strategy a number of Becky's students, labeled troublemakers at other schools, are experiencing success at Fratney. "Even though our test scores don't show it yet, we're having some real success with our students. . . . I think of Levon David. Teachers from other schools where Levon was would say 'Oh, my God, you have Levon David' and just shudder. And he started out as a very hostile child. But now I wouldn't put him on my list of kids that have big problems. . . . I think it's because we have tapped into his interests, let him read and write about what he cares about. That was something he hadn't experienced before and it's like a whole new world to him."

When teachers take students' interest seriously, they do draw students into the class. Student interest and involvement grow as they see more ways in which they connect with the work at hand. Students also feel more powerful and responsible. Mary Ann Jiganti at Hubbard Woods reflects on her own experiences with children and their sense of power. "We need to let kids be responsible, make some choices, let them feel powerful. If they own their own education, they can become empowered to take responsibility—both for themselves and others." It simply makes sense that we'll only feel powerful if we're given power, act responsibly if we're given responsibility. It works with kids just like it does with adults.

Two students in Thayer's Spectrum program reflect on what they have learned. "Spectrum has been a chance to work harder; maybe not just work harder, but to be able, to really be able to do some things myself." "I guess their theory is that the student is the player and the teacher is the coach . . . They coach you but they can't play the game for you, you know. So we're in charge, we make a difference, we're really learning and we're responsible for ourselves and the class."

HANDS ON

Say you're a classroom teacher. You've tapped into your students' interests and settled on an approach to a topic that will yield an outstanding final product. Your first impulse? For most of us it would be to lecture until we're blue in the face in order to make sure the kids have the proper information, and then to take the project over ourselves to make sure it looks perfect. This is a sure-fire recipe for boredom on the kids' part. The alternative is to stay with what got you this far: the kids themselves. That is precisely what these teachers do by creating an active, hands-on environment for learning and teaching.

At Central Park East this means that the classes are all organized seminar-style. "The classes are all run either seminar- or peer-group style," points out Herb Rosenfeld. "Rather than emphasizing a quiet atmosphere in which a single person can hold forth, our emphasis is on an atmosphere in which there is give and take." So when you visit CPESS you are likely to find students at one of dozens of tasks, but seldom sitting and listening to a lecture. The same is true at all of these schools, where the norm is to get up and do, not sit and listen. As librarian Ann Ladam at Thayer puts it, "I think [the school] has become a more active learning environment. It is no longer just a holding station."

So what are we likely to find kids doing? If they're in the classroom we may find them building replicas, writing books, transcribing interviews, constructing mathematical models, creating dramas, developing photos, writing lab reports, or debating a class decision. If we have to catch up with them in the field they may be collecting samples, interviewing contacts, sketching and drawing, looking for tracks, measuring, recording, searching, or just asking why. The point is that they are learning through doing, through genuine experience.

Does it get out of hand? So much is written today about "controlling" kids, making them behave. The challenge is not to make kids sit still, it's to reconnect them with the classroom, to wake them up, to engage them. Visit any of these rooms and there is no doubt that kids are connected. They are not

quiet, either, a fact that bothers some teachers, but not Bill
Elasky:

> I don't worry too much about noise. You can't do these things
> without making some noise. . . . It's like the class usually, note
> that I said usually, controls itself. . . . It is often obvious that
> things going on in the class are important to [the students]. To
> have them shouting back and forth at each other about some
> decision the class has to make, some parents have been worried
> about this. These kids are shouting at each other. But it means
> something to them. The important thing is [that] after a while
> they stop shouting and then come up with some sort of compro-
> mise that everybody can key in to. They are not shouting at each
> other because they are disrespectful to each other; they are shout-
> ing because they are so excited about getting their ideas across.
> It is not something you can sit there and talk quietly about.

The reason there is so much activity in these classrooms is often
personal as well as pedagogical. Mary Anne Tindall at Hubbard
Woods is showing off the math materials used in her class, relating
that "the children need a real hands-on experience with these abstract concepts . . . I found when I was in school I couldn't wait to
get out so I could start learning . . . really doing things." Bill Elasky
had similar frustrations as a teacher: "Schools have the potential of
being a very boring place where people have no control over what
they are doing. Where you just take what is given to you and
endure it as well as you can and when it's over, you walk away
from it and that is the end of it. I have taught where students
basically had that attitude and I can't blame them. It's a place where
I couldn't take it anymore so I started asking some basic questions
about what I was doing, how it could be changed, started looking
for ideas."

What Mary Anne and others latched on to was the strength of
teaching through genuine experiences. What students learn through
these experiences is the topic of the next chapter. Here let's be clear
that teaching in an active, experiential, hands-on classroom does
generate student interest, excitement, engagement, and conviction.

Listen to these students from Richard Cargill's classes at Willow-brook:

JOHN: What Mr. Cargill teaches me, I'm going to remember forever. It will carry over through my life.

KRISTIN: [After this] experience I know I'm not ever going to sit there and watch things I don't approve of. . . . I've learned not to be afraid to speak up, not to be afraid to say, "Well, I won't do that" or to throw litter all over the place because I'm too lazy to pick it up. . . . I feel responsible, like if there's not a recycling program where I go, I want to start one.

MARK: I think the subject matter is more than just getting through a book. I would say we are learning about participating in our democracy and what we can do in the process to make a difference.

THE POWER OF WORKING TOGETHER

Part of the process of learning in all of these rooms involves working cooperatively as opposed to competitively. Much modern classroom organization fosters solitary work. Some teachers go so far as to post student grades as a way of inspiring motivation through humiliation. But what students gain from this method is how to be individualists, not individuals. Never asked to work together, seeing their gain come at the expense of others, students learn to see themselves as responsible only for their own success or failure.

It can be argued that some competition is healthy in a classroom. Yet if it comes at the expense of the ability to work collaboratively toward a common goal it is not only unhealthy, it is misleading. Most of what we accomplish in life is due to the multiple efforts of many individuals, a fact every school recognizes when children are encouraged to play together or help one another on the playground. But when students bring that same ethic inside the classroom and attempt to help one another on the real work of school, then they are accused of cheating.

In the schools we are visiting this equation is turned on its head. A norm of cooperation exists, and competitive, independent work takes the back seat. Thus, when having to administer a district-mandated achievement test, Charlotte Newman joined with her second graders in being critical of the activity: "It's no fun to think on your own, is it?" Besides, working totally by themselves in isolation is something they seldom, if ever, do.

There is a growing recognition in the educational community that cooperative, as opposed to competitive, teaching strategies best enable children to learn.[11] For Bill Elasky and the other teachers described here, that is certainly part of learning, but they structure their teaching cooperatively for yet another reason: "I am trying to teach the power of people working together. That even though one person may not have all the answers and may not be doing anything perfectly (including the teachers), all of us together can come up with something we can be proud of and that can be taken seriously by the class, the school, the community, whatever or whoever looks at it. . . . They have gained something by going through the cooperative process; the ability to work with people, to see things from a new perspective, to understand the power of working with a group."

Of course, what Bill has in mind is more than just shoving kids together for a report or activity. "I firmly believe in the cooperative ethic, I talk about it a lot. I stress it when I introduce group work at the beginning of the year. I center discussions around these themes when I feel that group problems are a result of ignoring them." That feeling explains the charts around the room with strategies for cooperative work. What is clear is that the ability to work together is not left to chance. The *need* to work together is not left to chance either. All of these rooms are physically arranged to facilitate group work. As we saw earlier, the furniture is movable and group-oriented, and materials are meant to be shared. But these are just ways of facilitating the classroom tasks and routines.

All classrooms have routines, which in turn reflect the classroom ethic. In the rooms we have examined the routines reflect the ethic of cooperation. For example, in the Chauncey primary wing, students always know to ask a buddy first for help on any task, academic or not. "Ask a friend" is number one on the list of strategies for finding out things in Ann Hardee's room at Hubbard Woods.

After Jacob tells Marcia Burchby that he had helped Jennifer write "up," she announces to the class that "if anybody needs help writing 'up' they should see Jacob." Similarly, Bill Elasky tells his class that "Tim did this for us [holding up a computer-generated graphic] with the Multiscribe program he taught himself and then taught me. If anyone wants to use the program they need to see Tim and Amy. They have more experience with it than I do."

Kids pick up on these routines quickly. When given virtually any task, they pair up, figure out how to go about it, and share the work. So it's not unusual to see a Hispanic girl teaching an African-American girl new Spanish words to use during journal writing time in Robbie McLoud's first-grade class at Fratney. Or to see Jeremy first searching Marcia Burchby's room for the spelling of a word he wants to use and then asking three of his classmates before he gets it right. Or Janelle teaching three other members of her group how to conduct a science experiment at CPESS. Or Joyce Hanenberg's students rewriting the story "Why Mosquitoes Buzz in People's Ears" in order to add enough characters so every group member has a part.

The academic tasks at hand merely build on these routines of cooperation. Work is designed so that it can best be completed by a group, with a group project being the ultimate outcome. So teams of students investigate a particular creek or animal, research voting rights laws, solve equations, construct murals, turn books into plays, and write articles. They are graded as often on how they did as a group as on how they did individually. The goals are to make sure everyone understands, everyone plays a part, and everyone shares in the credit.

JOYCE HANENBERG: My class usually works together on everything except [the standardized tests].

JOETTE WEBER: It only makes sense. In some ways they know a whole lot, in other ways they know so little. Why not share with each other to come up with the best project possible? There's only one of me, you know; there are twenty-some other ones they can go to to get the information they need.

JOYCE: It's just like adults, too. I mean, a lot of times people like to work by themselves. But other times, when you have this idea, and you do talk it over with someone, your idea is much better. As far as teaching, when Joette and I are planning or we're talking about something, it just seems the idea becomes much richer when you're able to share and talk about it. I think that's true of children, too.

JOETTE: An example of how that happened was CJ wanted to read *Little Red Riding Hood* to me. He whipped through it real well and I said, "CJ, that's amazing; you've been taking that book home haven't you, and you're learning it." And he was sitting there just saying, "Well, yeah, yeah." And he wanted to take it down to the cooks and read to them, and when he was gone to read it to the cooks, Greg came up to me and said, "CJ has been taking it home, but I taught him to read it."

Classrooms in which student work is driven by a purpose, where children's interests help shape the curriculum, where the work is active and cooperative: these classrooms of commitment and conviction hold America's future. You will not read about them in the legislated-excellence reports or hear about them from our lawmakers. These sources make it clear we will be fed yet more standardized testing and curricular standards. Tests and standards best befit museums, where children are force-fed endless lists of trivial information in order to fill in blanks on meaningless tests. Such reforms will do nothing to change the *way* our children are taught, which is just as important as *what* they are taught.

What *will* make a difference in what our children learn is rethinking classrooms along the lines taken by these teachers. That difference means substituting projects with a real audience for worksheets and quizzes, children's interests for textbook writers' agendas, student-centered/active classrooms for passive/lecture-dominated teaching, and cooperative learning tasks for competitive, individualistic arrangements.

The classrooms we have visited are not hopelessly utopian. Joette Weber, Bill Elasky, and Dan Bisaccio all teach in the schools we have today, not in some far-off classroom of the future. They have reorganized their classrooms to be places of conviction and commitment. Their students possess the conviction that they can make a difference and the commitment to learning how.

CHAPTER 5

Building a Meaningful Curriculum

*In real life no one sits around
putting commas into sentences.*

"Everybody, can you get out your project sheets so we can review where you are before we go on?" queries Becky Trayser of her fifth graders after lunchtime recess. Each student has a sheet listing the many choices that Becky has worked out for the current schoolwide theme at Fratney Street Elementary—"The Hispanic American Experience/Latinos en los Estados Unidos." The list includes interviewing a person of Hispanic heritage and writing that person's story, writing a biography of a famous Hispanic-American, memorizing a piece of poetry in Spanish and reciting it, producing a poster using Aztec, Mayan, or other Native American artwork, producing a map of a Spanish-speaking country, rewriting an historic event from a Hispanic perspective, researching and writing about a current event in the Hispanic world (i.e., Central America or the United Farmworkers' grape boycott), writing a play about a historic or current event in the Hispanic-American experience and performing it, or another idea of the student's own creation.

As Becky goes over project choices, several students share their work. Amanda and Alisha are writing the story of a woman who recently immigrated to the neighborhood. The story, in both Spanish and English, will be submitted to the school newspaper for publication. A wide range of maps are being produced, covering most of Central America. They will later be posted and studied in the classroom. Several histories are going on, including Roberto's reexamination of the Christopher Columbus story. Three students are writing news reports about the recent visit of Cesar Chavez to Milwaukee and the work of the United Farmworkers.

"Wonderful, now, if you come across dates that need to be on our class time line [it runs all the way around the room], please put them up. Also, has anyone found any important Hispanic-American scientists to write about?" When she gets no response, Becky goes on to suggest that students explore that area and maybe ask about it on their next field trip to the city arboretum.

The class goes back to their tasks. As each is finished a way of displaying the student work is found. Some of the posters and maps go on the walls of the room, the rest are proudly placed in the hall. Reports go into the computer, to be printed, bound, and, in effect, published for classroom use. Students edit and polish interviews as potential pieces for the school newspaper or community outlets.

While the class is hard at work, Becky explains why she works so hard at integrating so much of the curriculum. "With this theme, I had a hard time working in math and science. I did a better job with the neighborhood theme; we used the river for science and local jobs for math. But even without those two in this theme, think how powerful their work is. They are seeing that all the subject matters work together. Some of them are learning Spanish painlessly, and for many of them this is the first time someone has taken their heritage seriously. And we do cover the curriculum. You tell me that they are not getting language arts, history, communication skills, reading, and all the rest doing this."

In Becky Trayser's class and throughout Fratney the curriculum is connected. It is connected with the students, arising, as we saw in the last chapter, from their experiences and interests. It is also connected with itself. Subjects do not exist in isolation, but rather come together to form a coherent whole for the children. Such a vision for curriculum, for what children should learn in school, is not held by those who subscribe to the legislated-excellence agenda. Rather, their attention is directed to lists of fragmented objectives, standardized tests that examine bits of information out of context, and more so-called rigor through more seat time in academic "core" courses.[1]

The folks at Fratney and the other schools we have visited see it differently. They have opted for a curriculum that challenges the conventional wisdom, that in fact rejects the conventional wisdom on the grounds that just doing more of the same will not improve schools. They argue that the legislated-excellence movement is wrong not only about *how* children learn, but also about *what* they should learn.

Less, Not More

Perhaps the main tenet of the legislated-excellence movement is that children should learn "more." Recommendations for more time in class, more homework, more core academic subjects, and more standardized testing are all based on the assumption that exposing children to more direct instruction in more subject-matter areas will mean that children will learn more "stuff." The problem is that there is no evidence that this is true. Exposure does not equal learning. And exposure certainly does not equal retention. For example, we all took American history several times in school. Yet poll after poll points out Americans' striking lack of recall on basic facts about the Constitution or our history. Thus, the legislated-excellence movement holds within it the possibility that its reforms will make schools worse, not better. By having students cover even more material it virtually assures that nothing will be covered in depth. Students may become good Trivial Pursuit players, but they will be lousy citizens and neighbors.

"We need to remember that kids may not, probably will not, remember everything we teach," asserts Katy Beck at Hubbard Woods, as she reflects on what she hopes children learn in her room. "But they do get an attitude and sense of responsibility that they will take with them." At Central Park East David Smith talks in a similar vein when considering the current demands for students to cover more in schools.

> If you look at high schools across the country that are trying to do those things, having kids read thirty or forty required texts or something like that, the kids aren't getting a quality education. I would say that educational experiences are very, very delicate things. At a moment when a student learns something, it is not something that you can always put on a flow chart and say, "Well, he is going to have an insight on Monday. Another student will have one on Friday." I think true educational insights happen when we take the time to slow down, to look at a text deeply and give a student and everyone a chance for a moment of introspection. But that doesn't happen in a traditional high school, and it won't happen with the reforms either. That is the reason why traditional high schools in this country so often fail.

> Genuine curricular reform needs to begin by acknowledging that not all of the facts we teach children will stick with them. But a habit of mind, something much more important, will stay with young people. It takes time, not coverage, to develop these habits. It means covering less material, in more detail, and with more care. To that end, the teachers and schools I have visited have claimed that less *is* more.

HABITS OF MIND

The effort of the faculty at Central Park East to streamline the curriculum is perhaps the best example of the less-is-more philosophy. For the first four years at CPESS (grades seven through ten), students take a common core of courses in three basic areas: humanities/social sciences, math, and science. As we saw earlier, all other courses, such as foreign language and computers, are offered either before or after the regular school day. Each core has a particular set of topics for consideration each year, and students find ways to explore these in depth. Herb Rosenfeld summarizes this approach as being a "curriculum that is thematically developed through essential questions where learning and growth are assessed by kids doing real things." For example, here are the outlines of the humanities/ social science and science curricula, taken from the school's curriculum document:

Four-Year Humanities and Social Sciences Curriculum

1. The peopling of America: The discovery, exploration, and settling of the North American continent. An in-depth focus on particular periods will permit attention to special issues of American history as well as broader issues of cultural confrontation and assimilation, melting pot or patchwork quilt. Essential questions: What is an American? Whose country is this?

Such an approach also permits careful examination of basic issues of historiography—how do we know what we know.

2. The emergence of contemporary political issues with a focus on United States history. In-depth study will focus on particular periods of conflict and change as well as ongoing social movements as they relate to issues of justice, democracy, community, and individualism. Issues of governance and power will be central to this year's curriculum. Essential questions: What is power? Who has it? How does power change hands?

3. Comparative systems of law and government. Comparative political systems in the contemporary world. The meaning and implementation of different concepts of justice, fairness, conflict resolution, with a focus on the United States government compared to one or more very different systems. Essential questions: How is authority justified? Who has it? How are conflicts resolved?

4. Non-European traditions. Stability and change in selected Asian, Central American, and African states. Attention to internal continuities, traditions, and structures, and to clashes between non-Western and Western societies and ideas.

Four-Year Science Curriculum

The four-year course of science study will focus on those "critical barriers" that stand between ordinary common sense and contemporary scientific thinking. Thus while all subjects within the major scientific disciplines will not be covered, some of the critical issues essential to an understanding of advanced science will receive major attention. These will include:

1. A two-year study of human biology—how our bodies work, with comparisons to other species. How are we like and different from other living things?

2. A two-year study of physics that will include some of the following: its implications for chemistry; biology and physics; how we see; light and photography; nature and major energy sources—the theory of energy—solar, water, electromagnetic, nuclear; astronomy; geology.

After completion of the first four years, students move on to the Senior Institute, the equivalent of the junior and senior years of high school. Here, each student develops an individual portfolio for graduation. Such a plan can include courses on campus or at universities, or alternative learning arrangements. The portfolio must show that students have attained competency in fourteen areas (postgraduate plan, autobiographical essay, school/community service, ethics and philosophy, fine arts and aesthetics, practical skills, media, geography, second or third language, science and technology, math, history, literature, physical challenge) and include a final project, showing special expertise and depth of understanding, in one of the areas. The following examples from two of these areas demonstrates the focus and depth of this work:

School/Community Service

CPESS students will have had many opportunities for examining a variety of work situations through their Grade 7–10 school/community service placements, apprenticeships and internships as well as full- and part-time employment experiences.

There are two parts of this requirement, intended to tie these experiences together in a useful way:

A. An essay. The following are the kinds of presentations that would fulfill the first portion of this portfolio requirement. The student can either (1) write an in-depth assessment of what he/she gained in terms of skill or knowledge from one of his/her job experiences; (2) discuss a particular issue or problem that relates to several job experiences; or (3) using a personal work experience, discuss or outline an alternative way the work could be organized.

B. Present a formal written resume of your work and employment experience, appropriate for future job searches.

Mathematics

There is a two-part requirement to this section:

A. Overview and demonstration of Minimum Formal Competence. Students will be asked to prepare a brief overview of their past work in mathematics, as well as results of all state and city competency exams in basic arithmetic and mathematics. If there is any doubt, the faculty will devise an instrument to demonstrate that the student can do work on a level sufficient to pass the remedial non-credit courses required at any of the NYC colleges.

B. Broader Mathematical Demonstration of Competence. Students will be asked to demonstrate a higher level of competence in one of the following two areas, as well as a minimal level of familiarity in both. In each area, students can select from among a number of "in basket" items prepared by the faculty, or they can invent an alternative problem with their advisor's approval (in consultation with the math faculty).

a. Political/Civic Mathematics. Mathematics serves a variety of daily political and civic functions requiring considerable mathematical sophistication to properly interpret—in the form of statistics, assessment and evaluation data, polling and sampling, etc. All are dependent on a grasp of mathematical formulations. Students will be asked to demonstrate competence with a problem posed in this area.

b. Abstract/Scientific Mathematics. Mathematics is also the "language" of modern science. Not all citizens need to have mastered this on a high level of competence, but all students should be able to have at least a minimum/basic understanding of mathematics at this more abstract level. Problems of different degrees of difficulty will be proposed for students to select amongst.

From these examples we can see how CPESS has avoided the traditional "add-on" strategy, where every new interest or fad is added to the curriculum in the form of a new course. The staff has also refused to accept calls for going "back to the basics" that suggest students read more required books or take more required core courses. Instead, the planners have redefined the basics to mean the habits of mind that will enable students to continue learning throughout life. They are able to take the time necessary to cover these basics by refusing to fill up students' schedules with seven or eight classes a day.

No one is left to wonder what the habits of mind are that the faculty at CPESS so values. In every classroom and in every curriculum document these five habits are clearly displayed:

1. *Evidence.* How do we know what we know? What kind of evidence do we consider "good" enough?
2. *Viewpoint.* What viewpoint are we hearing, seeing, reading? Who is the author, where is he/she standing, what are her/his intentions?
3. *Connections.* How are things connected to each other? How does "it" fit in? Where have we heard or seen this before?
4. *Conjecture.* What if . . . ? Supposing that . . . ? Can we imagine alternatives?
5. *Relevance.* What difference does it make? Who cares?

At Thayer a similar effort to limit and delineate what ideas the curriculum will emphasize is reflected in the statement of philosophy and goals. A document that is frequently referred to and that guides staff discussions and work, it sets forth a specific core of "Exit Level Competencies" each student should attain by twelfth grade. In each area—problem-solving skills, skills involving general knowledge and cultural awareness, and quest (integrated skills) experience—a clear outline of what students should be able to do and not merely know is presented. The goal is not to amass facts or lists of data, but to develop the skills required to find out, to explore, to communicate, and to understand.

The usual critique of such approaches is that they are without content. It is assumed that students must first be filled up with information before they are allowed to work with it. At CPESS and Thayer the agenda focuses on learning the information while putting it to use. When you sit in on classes at these schools there is no doubt that the streamlining of the curriculum opens up the time and space for both learning "about" and learning "how to."

For example, at CPESS, after David Smith and his students have spent nearly two hours exploring Steinbeck's characters in a passage from *Of Mice and Men*, they have not only learned "about" a great American novel, they have also learned "how to" use literature to explore the human dimensions of power in a society. The list of observations and insights the students have generated during the discussion on power, powerlessness, loneliness, and even homelessness would put most university undergraduate classes to shame. The same could be said about the skill with which Dan Bisaccio's students at Thayer investigate the local habitat, carefully studying "about" biology while at the same time learning "how to" investigate the world around them.

In both these settings the point is not developing habits of the mind at the expense of learning content. The goal is to do *both*, and to reclaim the process of *learning how* to as a curricular "basic." As Herb Rosenfeld puts it, "The notion is that learning is illustrated by deeper questions. That you know you have grown when you are asking questions that are more probing."

JUST A LIST

What about schools that have not totally reorganized? What about secondary or elementary schools in which a teacher is given a district curriculum to cover and where standardized tests evaluate learning? Indeed, a number of the teachers we have met do work in such settings and yet appear relatively unconstrained by these limits.

We can start with Eliot Wigginton, who works in Georgia, a state that remains as locked into the legislated-excellence agenda as any. A state-mandated list of objectives for high school English, the course Wig teaches, does exist, and Wig's students are evaluated on this list via a standardized test. Yet he does not change his approach to teaching.

"I don't let the state-mandated curricular objectives drive my course," Wig points out. "I don't ignore them either. They are there, they are my responsibility to cover, I accepted that responsibility when I took the job. However, I don't let them dictate what we do, or how we do it. Instead, I fit them in around the tasks that arise naturally in our classroom."

The process is deceptively simple. First, Wig has posted lists of the objectives that the state of Georgia has stipulated for English classes on the classroom walls. (For the most part these objectives are ignored until much later.) Then, the real work begins. For example, in the Foxfire I course (where students learn the basics of writing for the magazine), the students need to list the steps in making wine for an article being prepared for publication. The entire class works together on listing each step in the process that they have gleaned from numerous interviews. The students then use the list to write an article for inclusion in *The Foxfire Book of Wine Making*. When the articles are finished a few days later, Wig proudly goes to the list of class objectives and checks off "Will learn to sequence events in an essay." The objective was accomplished with much more student strength and interest than had they written yet another essay describing their rooms at home.

Wig covers the entire list of state objectives this way. Kids do the real work of putting together a magazine, or book, or pamphlet, or whatever, and Wig notes when this work covers each objective.

"I have the damn things almost memorized," he jokes. "And we hit every last one of them. But they are always secondary; I only teach directly to one when the entire class or a group of students is having a problem with one that shows up in their writing. Then we might get together for a mini-lesson on, say, comma splices. But it comes as a result of the work we are doing together. Not because we are on that chapter in the grammar book."

Joyce Hanenberg at Chauncey Elementary sees it the same way. "When the district curriculum committee started working on the state-mandated PPOs [Pupil Performance Objectives] I was worried. I thought 'Oh, no, here comes even more stuff to cover.' In fact, it's been just the opposite; the district course of study covers much less than the textbooks do. Besides, it sets me free from the text—I have to cover the district list, not the textbook list. I'm really getting to love it." As an example, she pulls out the social studies list, which is only half a dozen or so items long for second grade. "Now look at this book." Holding out the social studies textbook, she continues, "I mean, I don't need to push kids through every page of that thing just to cover this list. We can really go in depth into things that I know will cover the list and that the kids are interested in. So we learn, for example, about neighborhoods by going out and exploring one, not by reading chapters in the text."

Joyce and her colleagues in the Primary Wing at Chauncey have used this freedom to organize their curriculum around themes drawn from student interests. So when the kids were interested in penguins at the onset of winter, their reading, writing, science, art, and even some of the math work centered around penguins and their environment. Books about penguins flooded the room, and penguin displays soon filled the rooms and the hall. "We knew we were covering all sorts of objectives in all of the mandated areas. We keep track of them, and discuss them among ourselves. But the most important part of this is that we were doing it through a theme that the kids enjoyed and really wanted to do. We didn't have to force them to do science, it just came naturally from their interests."

Bill Elasky discusses his similar approach at Amesville. "When I start with what the kids and I want to do, not the objectives, then the curriculum has real power. I mean I do cover the course of study, I know what is in all seven of those books of objectives, literally hundreds of them. And if I tried to teach each one of them, one at a time, we would all go crazy in here. But when we take on a real activity it is amazing how many of these areas we hit without even trying."

The richest demonstration of this approach to date was the Water Chemists' work. What had started for Bill as a way of getting students involved in their writing turned out to cover the areas of science, social studies, math, and reading. Students wrote business letters, gave speeches, produced reports and descriptions, read books, conducted experiments, formed hypotheses and tested them, constructed tables and charts to display data, found out what governmental agencies were responsible for water quality, and more—and every one of these items is included in some section of the mandated sixth-grade course of study.

"The course of study is just a list, it is not a handbook for teaching. What teachers need to do is put the stuff of the curriculum in its proper perspective. We can and should do what is on the list," Bill continues, "but only in the context of much larger, broader goals for teaching and learning. When we get the perspective straightened out, then we are really teaching."

Bill's students have just finished with a flourish a presentation to a group of teachers about their water quality project. One student had actually been conducting a water test while other students were presenting. To close the presentation, the student reports on the various chemicals found in the sample and says, "And if I were you, I wouldn't drink from that fountain in the hall." When the laughter dies down, the first question that comes from the floor is directed to the students: "How did you feel about doing your social studies curriculum this way?" Steven replies, "It wasn't social studies, it was science." Bill then adds, "That's funny, I thought it was the language arts curriculum." The point is that it was all of these, all at the same time. Less is indeed more, especially when it is connected with who the children are and all the other things they are learning.

Connections, Not Fragments

The lists of required courses, books, and objectives spewed forth by the legislated-excellence movement are, as Bill Elasky reminds us, just lists. The problem with lists is that they tend to isolate things one from another. Thus, when a state legislature mandates so many minutes to be spent on math, the belief is that math is all that can occur during that time. For many schools and teachers that means pulling out the math textbook and covering the day's lesson. The students themselves must connect the material across content areas or to their own lives. For most of them no connection is ever made. Subject areas remain separate, and school knowledge has little to do with "real life."

In the schools we have visited the curriculum does connect, both to kids and to itself. As we have seen, much of what is taught in these classrooms comes directly from, and relates to, the interests of kids. Further, the material is usually covered in such a way that the subject matter areas, the math, science, English, social studies, blend into one another, which is, after all, the way the world works.

WE DON'T NEED THOSE BOOKS, WE HAVE REAL ONES

The lack of textbooks or textbook-driven instruction in these classrooms is perhaps the single most important factor in understanding what happens with curriculum there. One of the few reliable research findings in education is that the textbooks used in a school determine the curriculum. Since textbooks are designed with only one content area in mind, and with a one-size-fits-all philosophy, we shouldn't be surprised that the school curriculum is often fragmented internally and disconnected from the real lives of students. Regardless of all the textbooks' claims, support materials, manuals, and test packages, we should remember one thing: their primary intent is coverage and uniformity (and making a profit for publishing companies).

Moving away from the textbooks, viewing them as only one among many resources, we can explore a whole world of possibilities for covering content in an experiential way. Repeatedly we have noted that an area of study begins not with what a book says is the starting point, but with what the students want to find out. This connection to the students' interests is a much richer and more meaningful way to approach learning than can be provided by any text. Just compare the standard textbook fare in math, science, English, or social studies with Bill Elasky's Water Chemists or Math Maniacs projects, the Chauncey Primary Wing's study of penguins, Fratney's Riverwest Neighborhood theme, CPESS's math curriculum, Thayer's Spectrum program, or Wigginton's Foxfire ventures. In each of these a textbook may be present as a resource, but it does not dictate the curricular program.

One particular example of teaching beyond the texts that sums up the current struggle over what schools will be is the use of the whole language approach to reading and writing instruction.[2] For years the methods of reading instruction have been dictated to teachers by the publishers of basal reading series. These books, which many people remember as the Dick and Jane series, consist of contrived stories built around word lists rather than around genuine concern for plot or story line. The readers are accompanied by workbooks, ditto masters, and testing materials; all are purchased at great cost to the school and lock teaching into the programmed agenda.

In the last decade teachers in American schools have begun to adopt an alternative to this approach from Australia and Great Britain. *Whole language* begins with the premise that students will learn to read and write the way they learn to speak and walk, by actually doing those things with the help and guidance of a competent adult. Thus, rather than reading basals, students read a wide range of "real" books and write about things in which they are interested. Teachers help them develop reading and writing skills while they are engaged in these high-interest activities.

At Hubbard Woods, as at Fratney Street, the entire language arts curriculum is based on the whole-language model. Every room is a "print-rich" environment, featuring samples of the children's writing and charts with words from songs, poems, or books that they want to share. In Ann Hardee's room the students are preparing for a daylong trip to the Pioneer Room, a replica of a settler's cabin, complete with fireplace for cooking, logs to be sawed, and materials for sewing, conducting lessons, and building furniture. As part of their preparation for the day, Ann and her students read books about pioneers, write their own books about early settlers for the classroom library, and listen to Ann read a chapter from a book about life on the frontier. Additionally, their spelling lists arise from this theme, their weaving in art class relates to pioneer survival skills, and they cook and can applesauce to eat while at the Pioneer Room.

Thus we see how the curriculum can be dealt with as a coherent whole once the teacher is free from the tyranny of getting through a text. Rather than drilling kids on word lists, teaching them phonics in isolation, or having them read generally dull and uninteresting texts, teachers using a whole-language approach connect reading and writing to students' interests and to the rest of the curriculum. The students will never forget these experiences, and they are learning academic skills in the context of use.

Additionally, when the curriculum is organized in this way, students themselves feel more powerful as learners. They see themselves as real learners and doers, not just as students reading a type of book (textbooks) that no one else outside of school reads. "We don't need those books over there," Jessica indicates the basals in Bill Elasky's room. "We have real books to read." Additionally, since so much of the curriculum is covered thematically, the students see the power of what they are learning as it helps them make sense of the world.

SEEING THE WORLD AS WHOLE

Once the textbooks are gone the teacher faces the question of how to organize the curriculum. As the push continues for more hours in specific content areas the curriculum becomes more disjointed. Students are expected to shift gears frequently, moving from Chaucer to fractions, from geodes to the Civil War. Even within each area the connections are loose, as students see subject matter as facts or skills to master, with no underlying theme or coherence.

To counter this tendency, teachers in our sample schools build their curriculum and teaching around themes that give the material internal coherence and meaning. These themes make things students are learning into tools for finding out about the world around them rather than just giving them the right answers for a quiz. To help them see the world, as high school social studies teacher John Duffy puts it, "as a coherent, well, at times maybe a not-so-coherent, whole. Something they can understand and not be mystified by. Something they can perhaps even control if they just get past seeing things as accidents piled up on each other and see them as the outcome of our daily actions."

For example, as we have seen at Central Park East, thematic teaching takes the form of a set of "essential questions," which guide inquiry in each area. For the entire year students and their teachers explore the material using questions that help them connect events and facts to one another. In all their work, in their exhibitions of what they have learned, in their discussion of what they are reading, students use the essential questions as a framework to hold the material together. Take the social studies/humanities curriculum as an example. During the year that the seventh/eighth-grade house is studying "Contemporary Political Issues with an Emphasis on United States History," the following is the list of essential questions that drives their work:

1. What is political power?
2. Who has it?
3. How did they get it?
4. How does power change hands?
5. What gives laws their power?
6. How do people respond to being deprived of power?

Teachers and students add additional questions to this list for each event or topic being explored. For example, when the topic was the 1988 election, the classes added the following questions: Does your vote count? How does one go about getting the agreement of the majority of a country? Are voting blocs really blocs? How does the media influence elections? How does one achieve political power? Is this the best way to choose a leader?

The power of these questions works when Ricky Harris's students take apart the issue of propaganda or David Smith's class sorts out the functions of powerlessness in *Of Mice and Men*. In each case students use the questions to interpret current events, sort through historical facts, or explore literature in order to better understand the world unfolding about them. The historical significance of the Jackson campaign for the presidency, its connections to the Civil Rights Act, poverty, Jim Crow laws, slavery, the Civil War, the Emancipation Proclamation, the personal toll of powerlessness as revealed in great literature, and even the tenets of the Constitution are not lost on these kids. Similarly, when they enter the next two-year house and begin their study of world cultures they will not be treated to the usual fare of twenty countries in fifty-two weeks featuring food and tourism. Rather, they will explore the literature, history, and culture of a few areas through the following questions: What is the relationship between culture and world view? How is political power achieved and maintained? What is "civilized" and what is "barbaric"? Who writes history, for whom, and why? How are cultures affected by imperialism? What happens when people of different cultures come in contact with one another?

Elementary teachers from time immemorial have used themes in their teaching. But often the themes form add-ons: snowmen for art in the winter, apples to count in the fall, songs about flowers and birds in the spring. At Fratney Street Elementary School we have seen that the entire curriculum is organized around themes. The themes themselves dictate what is studied; they provide points of departure for the curriculum.

For example, the first theme of the year, "Our Roots in the School and Community," utilized the historic Riverwest neighborhood where the school is located as a curricular resource and focus. Working together, the staff developed numerous ways to use the neighborhood around the school to teach academic skills. For reading and writing, students visited the neighborhood public library, wrote essays about the neighborhood focusing on its history and multiethnic roots (also covering social studies), and read stories about the various cultures in the city. For science, students drew maps of the nearby river, studied its ecosystem, and investigated animals in the area. For social studies, students developed oral histories of citizens in the area by interviewing parents and grandparents, read the papers to find out about current events, and explored types of work people did in the community. For math, students used graphs and charts to display housing types and population, and did surveys on how people used math in the area. For art, students visited local artisans and learned techniques, and for music, they recorded old songs that parents and grandparents remembered. In every activity, the very nature of the neighborhood emphasized the multiethnic nature of our culture and the many nonstereotypical jobs held and leadership roles played by women.

Not every teacher at Fratney completed all of these activities. Some teachers did very few, some did all of them and more. The point, however, is that by just utilizing the environment right around the school teachers immersed children in the curriculum in a very real, very connected way. In fact, many of the activities, such as writing oral histories or mapping the river, connect multiple subject matters. Just by using a theme rather than a textbook we can build a more connected curriculum.

In Marcia Burchby's classroom at Amesville the entire year is organized around themes. They are not all preplanned, as at Fratney; instead, she organizes them flexibly to meet the interests of the class as well as the curriculum of the district. For example, she used Peter Spier's book *People* to pique student interest in exploring other cultures; then the class embarked on the "Peace and People" theme. During a six-week span the classroom was host to speakers from fourteen different countries, and class activities were organized to take advantage of each one. Students read books and folktales, learned words from different languages, and wrote letters and sent pictures to six-year-olds in other nations. They held a style show, which they took around the school, featuring the dress of many nations. They prepared a mural for the hall depicting the countries they had learned about and sang songs from around the world that dealt with issues of brother/sisterhood (such as Raffi's "One Light, One Sun"). They prepared and cooked foods of different cultures, studied the housing types and occupations of people in other nations, and produced graphs depicting foreign transportation and distances between countries. A total reading, writing, art, music, science, social studies, and math curriculum revolved around their world travels.

Not all of Marcia's themes take up every subject area or are as extensive as that one. When an early cold snap and snowstorm hit in December, her kids took to the outdoors. "We might as well be physically out there," Marcia mused. "That's where their hearts and minds are anyway." Books by authors such as Ezra Jack Keats on snow and cold weather appeared, an experiment on how water changes from snow to water to ice took place, the kids sang snow songs, and they organized a snowball throwing contest so they could learn the concept of measuring distance. (The last event took a waiver of school rules, but satisfied that deep desire in all of us to play with a well-made snowball.)

"You can do so much when you concentrate on a theme or idea that holds the class together," Marcia explains. "If your goal is to teach children how to learn, how to put things together, how to really understand the world, I don't see why you wouldn't teach this way." Marcia's comment is precisely the point. If we want students to leave school able to make sense of a complex world and not content to settle for simplistic explanations, we need to bring them into that world directly. To assume that teaching them a fragmented curriculum will lead them to a unified sense of place and person is unrealistic. Instead, they will leave unsure of themselves, believing themselves incapable of careful consideration of complex questions, and they will be willing to defer judgment to "the experts." With only bits of information themselves, they will lack the confidence that democratic citizens require if they are to be able to make their own decisions, order their own lives.

But when schools tie learning together, pull in multiple perspectives on issues, show young people how to ask the right questions and how to find out the needed information, we gain the type of citizens our republic needs. Herb Rosenfeld describes this type of person when he talks about the hope CPESS nurtures for its graduates: "When they leave us we want our students to have real confidence in their ability to make decisions, to be able to find information, to understand what they read, to articulate ideas, to operate in the realm of ideas. What I mean is the ability to synthesize and to find resource materials, to know what it is they have to do to understand something . . . to have opinions and to be able to express those opinions and argue them with conviction." All of this is accomplished best by covering less, not more.

The Same, Not Different

One of the most permanent patterns of daily school life, one that is both explicitly and implicitly endorsed by the legislated-excellence movement, is the grouping of children for instruction according to ability. This pattern begins almost the day children enter kindergarten where they are sorted into reading groups with names like the "Robins," "Bluebirds," and "Crows."

The idea that students *should* be grouped by ability is so deeply a part of our belief system that it goes virtually unchallenged.[3] The traditional arguments for such patterns are that students learn best when segregated by ability and, further, that "low-ability" students will have a better self-image if they don't have to compete with high-ability students. Nothing could be further from the truth.

For years almost all the research on ability grouping and tracking has demonstrated that it does not deliver the goods as promised. In each of the following ways tracking hinders rather than helps children learn:

1. Children are organized by perceived academic ability, but such judgments are imprecise and often based on nonacademic characteristics such as cleanliness, family background, or the ability to communicate with adults.

2. No group of students benefits from grouping, and, in fact, students of average and lower abilities are negatively affected by ability grouping. Students placed in lower tracks actually develop lower self-esteem. Students in these tracks receive the least-inspired instruction, have lower career and educational aspirations, participate less in extracurricular activities, are alienated from school, and have higher drop-out rates.

3. Once in a track or ability group, students are labeled for

life. Since the major difference in how children are treated in tracks is the speed with which the curriculum is covered, children in lower tracks can never catch up.

Aside from the dismal academic record of ability grouping, it has a divisive social consequence as well. When children are segregated by ability groups, a social hierarchy develops. Kids in the "advanced" groups view themselves as better than their peers in lower groups. As Trevis Thompson, now a university student, recalls: "In high school I became aware that tracking divided the students socially. I began to notice that all the popular kids were taking the high level tracks while the less popular people were in the lower tracks. Most of us who were in the lower tracks didn't get to know those students who were in the higher tracks. In a way, though, I became an exception because of my involvement in track and field. I got to know a lot of the higher level students who ran track, but I was always embarrassed when they would find out I was in the lower level classes."[4] No matter how we disguise it, students know they have been segregated. When they carry these notions of superiority/inferiority into the world outside the school decidedly antidemocratic attitudes and actions develop.

Many teachers do not embrace tracking. Faced with overcrowded classrooms, however, they see ability grouping as one way to reduce the hectic nature of classroom life. Other teachers are literally forced to ability group due to school district practices. One teacher, opposed to ability grouping, reported that her school provided her second grade class of twenty-eight students with "eight top-group, twelve middle-group, and eight lower-group reading books," forcing her into ability grouping in reading. High school teachers, even in subjects not traditionally ability grouped, such as social studies, find that the nature of the school's daily schedule insures their classes are ability grouped.

Alternatives do exist, for either the entire school or individual classrooms. The curriculum doesn't have to be doled out differentially, and we are not stuck with creating segregated classes of students. Instead, we can have equality and excellence in our classrooms if we just choose to do so.

No More Bluejays and Bees

At Central Park East there are no academic tracks labeled college prep or vocational. There are instead just students, each and every one of them having equal access to the curriculum. Amazingly, this policy holds for students formerly segregated into special education classes. There are no separate, pull-out special education classes here. Rather, specialists come into the classrooms to work with all students, freeing the teachers' time to give individual attention to students who need it. Herb Rosenfeld tells the following story about how well this orientation works:

A lot of kids come to us who would not do well in the mainstream. . . . They have, you might call it, the eccentric qualities . . . that make it difficult for certain kinds of people to function in public schools. . . . I can think of kids that are now working on a level of brilliance who fall into that category. I can think of kids who might be out on the street who are functioning here. Their work isn't distinguished, but they are here.

Probably the best example for me is a kid who was a special ed kid. When we first moved into this building it was full of special education, there was a huge special ed program. We mainstreamed this kid into our program and he is one of the stars of our school. He is from a family where nobody has ever finished high school. It is a ghetto family, a welfare family; he is with his mother and life is difficult for her.

He was in my advisory when he first came in. I put him in my advisory because I wanted to sort of look after him. I remember the first meeting I had with him, his mother, and the guidance counselor from the special ed school. And that guidance counselor told him at least ten times in the course of our conference that he must keep in mind that there were certain things that were very difficult for him to do.

Now I have to tell you that it is only . . . what you might call the aging process that has made me into the kind of person who could sit and listen to that and not say what I felt either during or after to the woman herself. . . . Anything I said to her would have been very angry and very hostile and I know that would just . . . create animosity between us.

But I knew what to do with him. I knew that was going to be the last meeting that she was going to be at. I also pointed out to him that I disagreed with her. That I hadn't seen any shortcomings, quite the opposite. There was a great deal of evidence that he didn't have them but that he just needed the support to make it possible for him to succeed. And we keep things small enough, keep kids with us long enough, that kids like [this one] grow and blossom. I'll bet you couldn't pick him out of my class today. (I couldn't.)

At Thayer, when Littky hatched the idea of the team that became the Spectrum program, he claims he had only two guidelines for developing the project. "I wanted it to be a genuine team effort and it was to be open to every student regardless of ability. You know, unlike those special programs we have just for talented and gifted kids. This was to be our honors program for everyone." When word went out that the program was beginning in the 1988/89 school year, several interested students approached Littky. "They said, 'Hey, Doc, we want to do this but we aren't sure we can handle the work. Will it be hard?' And I said sure it will be hard, but we'll help 'em, we'll get them through it if they want to succeed. They were a couple of kids that hadn't done well in school, one in special education, and they were worried about being in class with the college prep kids. But they went in anyway, they trusted us, and they aren't labeled by ability group anymore, they are just in Spectrum."

Spectrum works for these kids, as Julie Gainsburg suggests:

I've got kids in classes that are supposed to be above their heads. One of the reasons I could justify putting them in there was the D block where I could give them extra help. I'm only teaching Algebra I and Algebra II, but there are really kids in there at all levels of math understanding. I've even got kids who were in special education last year who are in Algebra I now, and that's not easy. But at least I can see them all a lot and I can give them a lot of extra help and they are probably going to make it. And they work so hard because I think we are convincing them that they can succeed.

At Chauncey Elementary, Joyce, Joette, and Charlotte have eliminated the prime sorter and shuffler of students: reading groups. The reason for eliminating the groups was simple—the teachers saw what grouping did to their students' self-esteem and confidence. As Joyce and Joette put it in a piece they wrote about their program, "What happens in a traditional homogeneous group is degrading: once in a low reading group, always in a low reading group."[5] The manner in which they eliminated the grouping was pretty straightforward as well. It has to do with both how they organize reading and what they read. Joyce and Joette again describe the reading program:

> We meet with small groups of five readers while the rest of the class tackles work jobs, a variety of projects from writing to art or phonics worksheets. But we don't select the members of the reading group. We merely ring a small bell and the first five children who come up to the table are the reading group for that period. Depending on the work jobs that day, children may rush to the table in musical chairs fashion or leave a few seats empty. If they're really engaged at their desks, we have to "invite" them up. The result, in either case, is a good mix of children and abilities—one that's almost always heterogeneous.
>
> In the group we choral-read a book. . . . We introduce reading on day one and can say to the children, "Look, it's just the first day of school and you read a book all by yourself." For the children in our classes, many who come from homes without books, this must feel like an incredible accomplishment. But the real key is that all groups read the same books. We think that if the literature is good enough for one kid, it's good enough for others. Since they're all exposed to the same stories and same books, they share the spinoffs. For instance, if we read a little story about scary things at night, the children can talk about it on the rug, write about it in their journals, or help each other with phonics or grammar lessons that relate to the story. If we're reading an advanced book with quotes

in it, we'll teach the whole class about quotations. Before (when they used reading groups based on ability) only the "high readers" learned about quotes.[6]

By using high-interest material these teachers are able to draw all children, regardless of ability, into reading. In traditional ability-grouped classes the lower-group children get the least interesting materials, further reducing their incentive to learn. Not so in these rooms, as all children join in the experience of enjoying good literature. Further, all of these teachers report that by eliminating ability groups, the classroom becomes more cooperative, with children helping one another to read rather than racing competitively through workbooks. And, as Joyce Hanenberg puts it, "Children become risk takers. . . . Our kids aren't afraid to look at a book and try to read it. They might know only one or two words, but they'll pick it up and want to read it. . . . Just as we no longer mark books by color indicating reading level, this program builds self-esteem because it doesn't label children. And they don't label themselves either."

In each of these settings the antiacademic and antidemocratic practice of sorting kids for instruction is abandoned in favor of a classroom and school organization that is both equitable and excellent. What has happened has not lowered achievement or expectations for kids who find school easy; rather it has raised both for all kids. This change has involved more than just mixing up kids and carrying on business as usual. Instead, it arises from the careful practice of teachers like Dan Bisaccio, who argues that we need to "make the space for every child to succeed."

Throughout our discussion of classroom life and the curriculum, we have witnessed how teachers have altered the school day to make room for real experiences that lead to learning. This same orientation makes space in these classrooms for every student, regardless of ability, to succeed. For example, John Duffy undertakes all the enrichment activities usually reserved for high-achieving students with his lower-tracked U.S. history students. He argues that "those [enrichment activities] are the high-interest, meaningful things in the curriculum. These students deserve that experience as much as any other kid in the building." Another example is Eliot Wigginton, whose Foxfire program and its orientation toward the experience of his students opened him up to one of the most powerful relationships a teacher can have with a student. He describes a young man as one of the "sixth-period losers" who had taken him ginseng hunting, a traditional Appalachian experience, in his first year of teaching. After showing Wig how to find ginseng, the young man turned him loose on his own. He relates:

> I searched for what must have been an hour, feeling pretty foolish most of the time . . . until finally, beside a waist-high chunk of granite, I had it. I called, and within a moment, he was there. "I told you I wouldn't be far. I've been watching you. You've been looking good. Yep, this is it all right. Now you dig it up—see if you've learned anything. I'll stop you if you get into trouble."
>
> Carefully I eased the plant out without breaking the roots, and we saved it, top and all, for replanting. He slapped me on the back—"See, that wasn't so tough was it"—and he laughed. "Now let's find some more."
>
> . . . I've thought about that day many times since. Its most immediate effect, aside from the ache in my legs, was that I never again had a disciplinary problem in class with that boy (or his friends, whom he apparently talked to behind the scenes). . . . I had stumbled into a different kind of relationship of a much deeper quality. For one thing, our roles had been reversed and suddenly I was the pupil, he the teacher. I was amazed at the depth and quality of his knowledge about the woods. He knew far more on that score than I, and I could not help but respect him. He had his areas of knowledge and ignorance, and I had mine, and in that respect we were equal, each potentially able to share something with the other, to the enrichment of both.[7]

To this day, twenty-five years later, the Foxfire program admits all comers, regardless of the academic track they are on in Rabun County High School.

At Hubbard Woods the faculty and staff have taken a clear stand against ability grouping of their students. At the classroom level the cooperative and activity-based approach to learning make it possible to get away from ability grouping. Take Steven, an active, restless seven-year-old, who, because of his inability always to pay attention to what is happening in class might otherwise be a troublemaker, a student destined for the lower ability group. But in Ann Hardee's classroom, with its emphasis on active involvement in the material, manipulation of math objects, and teamwork Steven's energy is absorbed into the creative and exciting spirit of the room. Steven finds the space at Hubbard Woods to meet both his own agenda and that of the school.

So does Dexter, a student at Fratney Street who finds his creative energies absorbed into writing a book on free-style biking rather than in disrupting class. Or Jesse, a student in Marcia Burchby's class, who hasn't experienced a lot of school success until he becomes the class expert when they discuss growing plants. Jesse and his grandfather provide most of the family food during the summer and fall through cultivating a garden out of necessity, not pleasure.

In each case two ingredients lead to more equitable educational experiences. First, these experiences are developmentally appropriate. Rather than asking youngsters to remain seated all day and then punishing the ones who have the hardest time at this by placing them in the lowest groups, the teachers insure that all students are actively engaged with appropriate materials and information. Too often we ignore who children are in the rush to cover material. In these schools we start with the kids and make the materials fit them. As Charlotte Bond, the art teacher at Hubbard Woods, puts it, "I always start with leaves, because everyone succeeds at that."

Second, the curriculum in these classrooms is covered cooperatively. The goal is not to see who can get the highest grade, but rather what is the best product that the entire class can produce. In these classes there are multiple tasks to be performed, and they require the multiple talents children bring to school. Bill Elasky's kids soon see that with a project like the Math Maniacs "everyone has a piece, something he or she can add. So we draw on each other, and I draw on them, and we all learn and we come to see each other as colleagues, not competitors."

At the end of the Math Maniacs process, Bill's sixth graders gathered on the rug to talk about their experiences. Brad, a winsome blond, asks to be recognized. "All through school I've been watching my report card. And I know I've been behind by about two years and I know they have put me in a special class. But in this class I'm really learning, and I have almost caught up in one year. And I think Mr. Elasky and the other kids in this class right here have a lot to do with that." At this point Kim speaks up: "Brad, you're the reason we got a lot of stuff done; you're the smartest one in here about setting up those tables." Brad looks at his feet, considers this, and says, "Maybe I am, maybe I'm not as dumb as they have been telling me all along."

Use, Not Memory

The driving force behind the American school curriculum is not only the textbooks, but the standardized test as well. By one estimate, there are enough standardized tests given in the United States to insure that each child takes nearly three a year. Teacher-made tests and quizzes often mimic those tests in style and form, and become the primary way teachers evaluate what students learn. The reforms offered by the legislated-excellence movement calling for yet more tests and using standardized test scores as the only means of evaluation performance will only intensify and expand this habit.

As with the other legislative remedies for schooling, we cannot view testing in isolation. The call for a beefed-up curriculum, in more distinct areas, differentially parceled out, and measured to the smallest degree with standardized instruments, forms the current thinking. In this way we hope to insure that kids are learning, no matter how bad their teachers are.

One has to wonder why we believe that just because kids pass a standardized test they know something. No doubt they know how to take a test. No doubt they have retained in their memory some isolated fact or fragment that helped them outwit the test makers. Perhaps they have even been able to master the bits of disconnected information set out in lists such as Hirsch's *Cultural Literary* and its accompanying dictionary. But what, if anything, can they do with all this information?

A faulty assumption lies behind the movement to mandate more tests: the idea that what we memorize for a test will become useful to us in another setting. It doesn't take much to dismiss this supposition. Reflect for a moment on your own education. Yes, you memorized all types of lists and pieces of factual information with regard to, say, the physical sciences. But when the scandals hit the papers about the experiments at the University of Utah involving nuclear fusion, how much of the debate did you understand? Again, the problem is that we are concerned with *how much* we learn at the expense of *how* we learn.

PASSING ALL THE TESTS IN THE WORLD DOESN'T MEAN YOU CAN DO THIS STUFF

As with ability grouping and the organization of the curriculum, other ways to evaluate learning besides giving tests do exist. In fact, a test may be the weakest way to assess what a student has learned.

Central Park East students must "show off" what they know with an exhibition at the end of each unit of study. The exhibition may take any number of forms, such as an oral presentation, a publication, or a videotape, but it must be produced for a real audience and it must address both the habits of mind that run through the curriculum and the particular essential questions for the topic at hand.

At the start of each trimester students receive a list of potential exhibitions that they may perform. Their work as a group, including lectures, discussions, and problem-solving sessions, is designed to prepare them to perform the exhibition. They then pursue their exhibition in small groups, utilizing class resources, the library, the art room, computers, and community resources to prepare both group and individual products.

The list of possible exhibitions in any area is designed to foster inquiry and exploration rather than "correct" answers or memorization. A few examples will make this concept clear.

From the Division I (seventh/eighth-grade) science curriculum:

- Determine the heat content of at least five different foods in calories per gram. You may use the procedure outlined in *Nutrition: The Inside Story* and demonstrated in class. Describe your method, record your data in an organized way, and state your conclusions in a table. Compare your results with published information and account for any disparities. Record the questions which arose as you were doing the study. Investigate one of the questions either by library research or by experiment.
- Plan and carry out a study to determine the types of food advertised by TV commercials. Describe your method, record and organize your data, and keep a record of all questions which arose as you were doing this study. Investigate one of the questions further either by experiment or by library research.

From the Division I (seventh/eighth-grade) mathematics curriculum:

- Write a report that explains the chief contribution Babylonians made to geometry.
- Make a transit and map an area. Explain who uses them and how they are helpful.
- Write a formula that shows the relationship between the amount of degrees in a polygon and the number of sides it has.
- Make an abacus and write a report about its usefulness in terms of place value and computation.

From the Division II (ninth/tenth-grade) math/science curriculum:

- Build one of the following instruments: sextant and azimuth, Foucault Pendulum, or telescope. Design and perform some activity that uses the instrument. Write a careful and concise description of the activity and your findings. What essential question(s) does your activity address?

From the Division II (ninth/tenth-grade) humanities curriculum:

- Study the metaphors and dialect used in the book *Their Eyes Were Watching God*. Compare them to New York Urban dialect. How does one's use of metaphor show one's view of the world?
- How was religion used to achieve and maintain power both by the Maya and by the conquistadores? As part of your writing about the Mayas, include a discussion of theocracy.
- Jesse Jackson said, "For all Americans, voting is a matter of empowerment." Choose a group of Americans you think could be empowered by voting in a block (for example, black people, women, gay people, homeless people, farmers, or workers). Research the interests and needs of the group you have chosen and speculate on how voting in a block might empower them to solve their problem.

Of course, at the end of every list of possible exhibitions students are also offered the opportunity to "Develop a question of your own that you would like to pursue and discuss your idea with your teacher."

In all of the exhibitions the goals of the school are reflected: that students are able to find out things on their own, that the curriculum connects with who they are, that they go for depth rather than coverage. The old adage is that we get what we test for, so the CPESS faculty tests for what they want, not what the commercial test makers judge to be important to learn.

At Willowbrook High Richard Cargill sends his students on similar quests for information. Today we hear from students who have taken on a variety of projects in order to complete the English writing assignment. Terri starts with a report on a survey and study on the cost per ounce of soft drinks in various types of returnable and nonreturnable containers. Geoff and Kim detail their study of various ways to reduce water use in home toilets. Mark's study concerns the amount of recyclable paper thrown away by the school's main office; he has been surreptitiously removing it all and has brought it to display. Each of these reports and dozens of others are written up and submitted for publication to either the school newspaper or the Students for a Better Environment newsletter.

"When the kids do this writing, that's when I see what they are learning. And if we need to cover something again, I don't try and find it on a test, I find it when they are doing the work," Richard Cargill says about evaluation through actual use. "It's amazing that I get seniors who have taken all the tests, passed them, and the things they don't know. A kid in class wrote a letter to conservationists in Canada wishing them luck and wanting more information about their campaign to develop a sustainable development plan. And we had that letter typed for her because it always gives the kids a nice feeling to look at their work typed up, with letterhead and everything. So I gave it to her and asked her to read it over and make sure that was what she wanted to say and sign it. Well, she signed it below her name. And I said, "Well, that's an interesting place to sign it but most people sign it up here." She said, "Oh, I didn't know." A senior in high school and she had never had to sign a real letter before. Little things like that show you that passing all the tests in the world doesn't mean you can do this stuff after you leave school."

LEAVING A MARK THAT WILL FOLLOW THEM FOR THE REST OF THEIR LIVES

When asked how he grades the students' work, CPESS teacher Herb Rosenfeld laughs and says, "With great difficulty." Wherever students go they leave a mark, usually a letter from A to F in a teacher's gradebook that represents the teacher's evaluation of the student's work. But what do these letters represent? No one really seems to know, since grades are relatively idiosyncratic and work that earns a B from one teacher may be a D in another's eyes. Unfortunately, while grades tell students and parents little about what is being learned they do have the side effect of branding kids as "C students" or "A students." When we look at how students use the curriculum in real settings we discover a whole new way of thinking about methods of indicating student progress and learning. A new way of helping students leave a mark.

At Hubbard Woods and CPESS, students do not receive grades at all. Hubbard Woods teachers provide parents with a detailed narrative about how students are developing in curricular and social areas. Additionally, Katy Beck, for example, works out a contract with her fifth graders in which they list their strengths and weaknesses and set progress goals for the year. Parent/teacher/student conferences revolve around these goals and she regularly checks in with students, going over examples of ways in which they are or are not progressing. The students and their parents see their development in actual samples of the kids' work, not in lists of test scores or rows of letter grades.

At CPESS the faculty evaluates exhibitions as either competent or advanced. Students themselves choose what level to aim for, working with the faculty and basing their goal upon their interest in the subject, other tasks at school or home they are involved in, and the type of challenge they want to take on. Their work is evaluated as satisfactory, distinguished, or unsatisfactory regardless of level, and they must complete work at the satisfactory level before going on.[8]

These descriptions of student work are much richer than simple numbers or letters. They tell all interested parties exactly what students can do, in genuine situations, with the materials at hand. They also make it clear to all parties what the young person needs to learn next, what he or she is ready to go on to, what the next challenge should be.

An added dimension to these approaches is the portfolio. At CPESS, as mentioned earlier, every graduating senior must produce a portfolio of his/her work that demonstrates achievement in a wide range of areas. The portfolio is a mixture of written papers, test scores, aesthetic displays, testimonials, journals, everything that helps represent who the young person is at this moment in time. These materials are then compared to the school's goals for its graduates in determining whether the student deserves to be called an alumnus of the school.

Even when teachers work within schools that demand that grades be given, it is possible to create a genuine record of student accomplishment. As we saw earlier, Marcia Burchby, finding herself under fire from a district administrator because her students' test scores did not meet that administrator's demands, fought back by producing portfolios of work by her six-year-olds. To counter what she thought were phony results she gathered samples of each student's writing, math, and spelling as they were using the skills to complete class projects. Further, she kept extensive lists of books students chose to read during the day, particular reading skills they mastered with each book, and books the children took home to read to parents. These portfolios, which literally overflow with student's work, follow each of Marcia's students on to the next grade level, providing a much more complete picture of who the children are than the record kept in the school's cumulative file.

More public records of student achievement also exist. Eliot Wigginton's students can look back on the books they published and magazine articles they wrote. "No matter what anyone ever tries to tell me," Kelly remarks, "I will always know I can write. Because I wrote this article, it has my name on it, it's mine and it means more than any teacher's grade or school report card." Bill Elasky's kids won't be forgetting what they can do anytime soon either. Talking about the Math Maniacs project, Bill puts it this way:

There is so much behind that product that is learning and that is allowing people to go so much further the next time they do something. They have something now to look back on and reflect on. And not something just to look at and remember all the work they did or all the math they learned. But something that reminds them that they know how to find things out, how to do things, how to make a difference—that will follow them for the rest of their life.

But Do They Learn?

Any time it is suggested that there are alternatives to business as usual when it comes to the school curriculum, the same question is always asked: *But will they be learning the basics?* It is almost as if we believe that some teachers do not want their students to learn things like adding, spelling, reading, history, or science, so they devise new approaches to the curriculum. Actually, the opposite is true. The teachers and schools we have looked at are deeply concerned with the fact that so many kids learn so little in school. They share with other teachers a desire for their students to become better informed and better able to think more clearly after spending time in their classes. They care about this so much that they are pushing themselves to go beyond the traditional notions of curriculum in order to insure that their students will learn with depth, insight, and conviction.

Good intentions, of course, are not enough. It is only fair to ask for evidence that the students in these schools are learning. On this count, the evidence is very clear. If you only want to consider standardized tests as a measure of learning, in virtually every school and classroom we have visited these students score higher on such tests than their contemporaries or than what is expected of them. But let's go further. In addition to the tests, we have all the materials that are prepared and produced by students. Books, newspapers, speeches, models, experiments, reports—the list goes on and on. Compare this to what comes out of a more traditional approach to curriculum: a few tests, some worksheets, a book report or two. Which would you prefer your children to do?

More important, what would you prefer your fellow citizens, your neighbors, to do? In these schools we see all students engaged in comprehensive exploration of curricular materials in ways that help them connect what they learn to who they are and to the world around them. They are learning how to use what they learn so that they can understand and make a difference in the world. They see themselves as useful and important people who have learned that they have something to contribute to their communities and families. They know that what they have learned came about through extended effort, in concert with others, on topics that mattered. They have gained, in short, the ability to learn for themselves and for us.

All of this is best captured in the words of students themselves. Often I found myself wondering what a conversation among students from all these schools would be like if I could just get them together. Of course, that wasn't possible. But it was possible to collect their comments and put them together in the conversation they would have had, had they all been asked "What would you say you learned here?"

This has been a chance to work harder, not maybe just to work harder, but to be able to do some things myself and start working independently. I can offer ideas to the teachers, I can teach myself or learn by myself and go off on something, really study it. And they are going to encourage that, that I go on and study by myself. I think it's good and I think that all of the kids should have the chance at least to do that. Too many kids are just told to memorize and do something and put it on a test and they are not really taught to do it themselves. (Greg, Thayer Senior High)

In so many classes we are just memorizing the things the teachers want. In Mr. Cargill's class you learn something that can make a difference on your views, you know. I like learning and all but I think you should be practical about what they teach you. What Mr. Cargill teaches me, I'm going to remember forever, it will carry over in my life. (Kristin, Willowbrook High)

The subject matter of the school should be more than just what's in the books. I would say what we are learning is about participating in our democracy and what we can do in the process. How we can make a difference with what we know. (Daniel, Willowbrook High)

At the other school I attended we all were made to do homework. It was all just drill and repetition of what we had already done. It was easy, I didn't do much. Here the work is hard, I mean I really work at it, but I like it because it is important stuff. (Joe, CPESS)

In your classes [referring to her previous school] you learn, but you forget. You run from class to class and it is always something different and not connected. You might carry seven or eight books home every day, but I didn't read them, I just looked for the answer. Here we take the time to get to what is important. (Francine, CPESS)

In Mr. E's [Bill Elasky's] class we are doing real things instead of just working out of the book. That's good because the books are boring, but we learn real life stuff. We learn more because in the book it's just showing you how to do something, in our class we're doing it. (Brian, Amesville)

In the books we're just doing things we learned back in second grade. But we don't need teachers to teach us what we already know. Instead, like in this [Bill Elasky's] class, when we need help we get it. That way we are learning, really learning, all the subjects the way you really use them. We're learning how to do things so that they make sense. (Becky, Amesville)

Mr. E's [Bill Elasky's] way of teaching is the best way because we learn the real stuff, not the book stuff. Other teachers ought to teach this way too. I know the kids would be happier and learn more. I bet the teachers would be happier too. (Erin, Amesville)

CHAPTER 6

The School and the Community

You learn how to make a difference.

At the end of the school day Hubbard Woods teacher Katy Beck is sifting through a stack of packets for the mail that her fourth and fifth graders have put together. "You know," she thinks out loud, "I wish we weren't doing this. But it means so much to them I don't see that we can avoid it." "This" refers to the most recent class project, a letter-writing campaign promoting gun control. Katy's reluctance is not due to her fear of the issue, it's because the issue, tied to the shooting at the school in May 1988, just won't seem to go away. It rears its ugly head every time a similar shooting occurs at another school.

Most recently, killings in Stockton, California, set the class into action. "The kids came back [after the shooting] very angry that there were these guns all over and that kids were not safe going to school anywhere," Katy relates. "They just changed the focus from fear to action. We had a class meeting and discussed it two or three times that day and the class came up with the idea of writing letters to the President, governors, and others."

Initially, class members produced letters to George Bush. As other students heard of the project, they too wanted to add letters. To help younger students, the children from Katy's room took dictation and produced letters for those students who couldn't yet write.

"But we wanted to do something more," said Allison, the young woman who directed the project. "We learned that Bush was against gun control, so we thought we would write all of the governors too, and our representatives." Each received a nearly sixty-page packet filled with letters like this one from a student in Katy's room:

Dear President Bush:

I think that we should have handgun control laws because otherwise allot [sic] of people will die and there will be many more shootings like the ones in Cleveland and Hubbard Woods Schools. We want to protect the people of this country. Handgun control will be a step in that direction. We should have handgun control in honor of the people that have died because if there was handgun control they would not have died. Think of all the children that died.

Even worse think of all the children that are afraid to go to school now! All over the country children are afraid, afraid of madmen harming them. We have to stop this growing fear. Handgun control is the only way!

In this country you are supposed to have the right to make your own decisions and we want our decisions taken to Congress, not the N.R.A.'s. In this country you are supposed to have freedom and we want the freedom to go to school and feel safe.

If you look at and compare our number of gun associated deaths to Japan or England's you will find we have many more. How can we change that? What can we do? Handgun control is the only answer!

Sincerely,
(signed by the student)

Two other groups received packets from Katy Beck's kids. One was the local news media. "Every time there's a shooting they come and ask us if we're afraid. And they chase us down the street if we won't talk. And they show [the killer's] picture. We want them to stop and leave us alone." Robert sums up the class feeling as well as the message in their packets.

"And we felt other kids could help us," Steven adds. "The school said we had to raise our own stamp money and stuff so we are writing to other schools asking for their support." It's a strategy that paid off, as this letter, sent to the class from a middle school, points out:

Dear 4th and 5th grades of Hubbard Woods School:

We received your letter the 1st of March and I, at least, fully agree with your opinions on the gun ban. I am writing on behalf of the Student Council and the school to tell you of our plans. First, we are donating $25 to your school for stamps, envelopes, paper, and so on. Then, we are donating another $25 to Winnetka Citizens for Handgun Control.

We also have plans of our own. As you may know, some of the 8th graders are going on a trip to Washington, D.C. this weekend. We are now circulating petitions calling for a federal law to ban handguns. I will then personally deliver these petitions to Senator Simon, Senator Dixon, and Representative Porter's office, speaking to them if possible. I have already arranged an appointment with Senator Simon. If there is anything you want delivered, please get them to me by Friday.

Finally, classes are discussing handguns and we will be writing letters to Congress and the President. We thank you for your concern and are happy to help fight for handgun control.

Sincerely,
(signed by the Student Council President)

Of course, the outcome of all this was not the enactment of tougher handgun laws. But not even these kids, with all their enthusiasm and dedication, believed that would happen immediately. This issue is something they are committed to for the long haul, something they see as taking a great deal of time and energy, which they gladly give. From one of their letters: "I'm never going to stop fighting until it's finished, until the war over handguns is over, until we are all safe in our schools and homes."

And Katy Beck, when she thinks about it, sees it as a success as well. "What they are seeing is that they can make a difference. We've received some wonderful responses, and some horrible, awful ones as well. So they are learning that real changes can happen when they work together and can get a whole group of people doing something. . . . They see themselves making a difference in the world around them."

By doing "real things," kids learn that they can make a difference. Here we want to look at the ways the teachers engage their students with the stuff of the real world, how their classrooms reach well beyond the schoolhouse door. This engagement is yet another example of how well schools can work.

The legislated-excellence movement seems preoccupied with keeping all learning within the four walls of the school. By mandating more days and hours in school, more tests to take, and more texts to read, the opportunities to reach beyond the school diminish. As we saw earlier, some teachers are forced to abandon even an occasional field trip because it might interfere with the time a student spends in another subject matter.

A combination of fears leads to this unfortunate situation. First, we have a fear of losing control. If every minute of the teachers' and students' day isn't strictly controlled, someone might do something that an educational bureaucrat has not dictated. Time might be wasted, a page might go unturned. Second, there exists a fear of controversy. The assumption is that textbooks, sanitized as they are, are factual and thus noncontroversial. On the other hand, the real world is messy and multisided, and who knows who might be offended by something the kids do? Finally, there is a fear of children themselves. It seems that we are afraid of what they might do, given a chance, in the world outside the schoolroom. We put them in school for someone else to deal with for seven hours a day. We don't want to see them again until it's time for dinner. Maybe we fear that they may, once engaged with the world, ask difficult questions about the way things are (like the one's Katy Beck's kids are asking) and we would just rather not answer them.

If we are to grasp the attention of our children, if they are to develop the habits of heart and mind that will engage them as democratic citizens, we must overcome these fears. We need to see that less control, not more, is the key to real learning, that only when teachers and students are free to explore the world as it comes to them, not after it's prepackaged, are they able to understand the world in its complexity. We should understand that controversy is what life is made of, and that school is a wonderful place to learn to deal with it. It is precisely when our children ask hard questions that we know they are learning in school; perhaps they know more than we do, perhaps more than what makes us comfortable, but they are learning how to order the world around them. That is what good schooling is all about.

In the schools we are visiting the walls are pushed out to encompass the world around them in multiple ways. The community becomes the classroom, students carry out service requirements, the curriculum deals directly with life-after-school issues, and students are encouraged to engage in issue advocacy. While none of these operate exclusively of one another, and often operate in concert, we will look at them one at a time.

The Community as Classroom

It must be a Wednesday afternoon in Amesville, because there goes Marcia Burchby and her band of six-year-olds on yet another walk around the town. Today they are out doing an excavation, looking for whatever is down there in conjunction with their theme on dinosaurs. On other Wednesdays (Thursdays in case of rain) you can find them counting the number and types of trees, mapping the streets, surveying housing types, planting bulbs or a section of a garden, picking flowers, visiting sheep or horses, searching the gravel in neighborhood driveways for fossils (they find dozens), or, if you catch them at the end of their travels on a sunny spring day, just rolling down the hill in Marcia's backyard beside the school.

"I never thought about it, but I guess a lot of teachers don't take their kids outside. It is a real hassle, coats and mittens and all the rest in the winter, you know. But we go every week, and the kids look forward to it. It only seems natural; outside the room is where all the stuff we are learning about is anyway," Marcia explains.

Marcia's room is filled with the products of their trips. Models of the town and houses, sticks, leaves, flowers, trash, treasures, wool, horsehair, all woven into the fabric of the current theme. The room is the next best thing to being outside. But it is no replacement. "No matter how lousy the weather gets, I know we need to be outside doing things. That's when the kids learn best, when they see the academic material as having a use, as being useful to interpret and mold their world." And besides, where else other than the school driveway can you draw a full-scale dinosaur and compare it to the size of a school bus? (The dinosaur is followed up by a class letter to the principal warning her about the new addition to the school and telling her not to worry "because it's a plant eater, not a meat eater.")

While we all remember the big class trip we took at some transition point in school, few of us can point to using the community right around the school to our advantage. For the most part those field trips were more like rewards for getting to a certain point in school than genuine learning experiences. Separated from teachers by just a few physical feet, but by miles of tradition and bureaucracy, is a treasure trove of resources, both physical and human. All it takes is a belief that the curriculum is best covered by using real experiences to open up the students and teachers to a new world of learning. Yet few teachers take advantage of the world outside as a classroom. Allowing movies, books, and other artificial symbols to stand in, they foster a "look but don't touch" attitude in their students.

A wide variety of reasons exist for the reluctance to move outside the classroom in order to engage students in their learning. The most central one is, yet again, the bureaucratization and standardization of the school day and teachers' lives. Faced with time constraints, legal worries about liability, and textbooks to cover, many teachers find the path of least resistance to be just lecturing from the book.

Another way to examine this is to see that the traditional use of time outside the classroom has had the direct consequence of making such experiences seem like frills. Seldom are the yearly trips to the zoo or museum seen as tightly linked to the curriculum. Rather, they are scheduled to fit transportation availability or some similar need. The trip is viewed as a break, an unwanted occurrence, time away from learning. Soon all such time away from school is viewed in the same way, as a diversion from the work at hand rather than as a way to enhance it. Requests and plans to work in the community are then seen by administrators, staff, and students alike as avoidance rather than engagement.

It doesn't have to be that way. If, as with the teachers we are visiting, we see the community as a viable, daily part of the classroom, the vast space outside the school becomes a vital part of what goes on inside the school. This approach can only happen when several criteria that we can draw from Wigginton, Elasky, Beck, and all the rest are in place:

- The use of the community must be real, not contrived. It makes sense to produce a magazine full of historical interviews in Wigginton's English class in rural Georgia; it might not work in a chemistry class in a suburb. It makes sense for Bill Elasky and his kids to study the water quality of rural streams but not to bother with city sewage plants. (Though they did visit a treatment plant after they were well into their project.) In these and our other settings the use of community arises from the ongoing work in the classroom. Time outside is not seen as a "field trip"; instead it is just what needs to be done in order to carry out the task at hand.
- The world outside must be dealt with in all its complexity. Rather than just taking a piece of it, say attending a city council meeting to see what goes on, kids deal with an issue from start to finish. Bill Elasky's kids are at the council meeting because they need a variance for their nature study area. Dan Bisaccio's students meet with county commissioners because they want to organize informational hearings on a proposed toxic waste dump. Marcia's kids look for all the signs of seasonal change, not just leaves changing colors. Community actions and activities are not isolated into tidy job descriptions or seen as inde-

pendent events. Rather, the community is seen in all its diversity as a place to learn from and be involved in.

- All of these experiences must utilize the community at hand. The world right outside the schoolhouse door—not the city one hundred miles away, or the state capital, or the exotic animals in cages—is used in the classrooms we have seen. Indeed, why devote resources and energy to travel when the natural world of the students can provide some of the most educational experiences? David Lackey, a high school English teacher in Strongsville, Ohio, discovered this when he worked on a Foxfire-style project in his suburban classroom. The kids wrote not about rural elders, but about things that mattered in their lives: shopping malls, skateboards, domestic violence. The power in this is David's acknowledgment that part of the agenda "is to help kids value what and who they are, to develop a respect for, and commitment to the place where they live." Or as Dan Bisaccio puts it, "One of my own personal goals is to get kids to really appreciate what there is here."

The benefits of such an engagement with the community are numerous. We can see how these experiences enhance a hands-on, integrated approach. Putting students in another context and watching them operate in the world in which they are comfortable are situations that provide teachers with new ways to connect to and motivate their students. Leaving subject matter in its genuine setting lends credibility and rationale to the tasks at hand for students.

Of course, there are obstacles to utilizing the community as classroom, and the ways in which these schools have overcome these obstacles will be discussed in the next chapter. But they do find ways to insure that the walls between them and their community are not insurmountable. Every day the worlds of the classroom and the community flow back and forth, enriching the lives of students, helping them see that what they learn makes a difference. The community becomes the curriculum. Students learn that it is important to read, write, compute, understand science, sort out social studies concepts, and all the rest because this knowledge will make a difference in the world around them.

"We were returning from a walk and little Shauna just came up to me and gave me a big hug and said, 'Ms. Burchby, I love you,' " Marcia reflects on a recent trip. "But it wasn't me she loved, it was just that things were so good. We had found all sorts of signs of life on a beautiful spring day, and the kids were planning stories to write, books to read, things to draw, it was all just perfect. That's what she loved. And that's what we would miss if we stopped going out into the community for what we learn."

Making a Difference

Childhood is a time of paradox. On one hand we tell young people we want them to act like adults: take on adult manners, sit still and listen, in general to observe all the conventions of adulthood. On the other hand we seldom treat children like adults. They have little or no control over the institutions around them, and are not asked to take their own responsible actions. At school the most important decision the student council may ever be allowed to make is the theme for the prom. In their communities their opinions are seldom, if ever, solicited, even on issues of immediate importance to them such as parks or recreational facilities.

Some of this makes sense. Children are slowly coming into adulthood and should be forced to deal with the multiple responsibilities and jobs adults take on. In fact, rushing children to behave like adults in terms of dress, social behavior, athletics, and academics does grievous harm to them.[1]

However, when young people suddenly turn eighteen, we will expect all this to change. We expect kids, now adults, to vote, take public office, hold jobs, and be involved in the community. Yet the school will not have provided young people with any experience in these roles. This institution, the only common experience for our children, may have tried by exhortation to develop students into citizens but will have given them little direct experience with the role.

In the schools we are observing such a transition to active citizenship is facilitated in a number of ways. We have seen how young people develop a sense of the richness and responsibilities of community life by organizing the school as a community. In terms of the academics students learn we have seen how both the organization of the school day and the curriculum can facilitate learning so it can be utilized in the real world. Now we will consider how opening up the school to the world around it helps students develop the skills and commitment necessary to be involved and make a difference in the world.

"Memos fired off in cattail war," read the headline in the neighborhood paper. Indeed, what had started as a disagreement between teacher Richard Cargill and the Willowbrook High School administration over the draining of a cattail-supporting marsh on school grounds had escalated into a battle of memos, with Cargill, his students, and the teachers' union on one side and the school principal on the other. According to the school administration, the cattail area was a mosquito breeder and nuisance to people who got their feet wet going to football games. The area, they argued, could better be used for athletic fields. Cargill, however, hoped the area would become the cornerstone for the Willowbrook nature study area.

In the fall of 1986, all of his plans, and his teaching resource, were running out of the end of a drainage pipe which had been installed just prior to the school year. What the students had come to value as a wetland, the administration had seen as an eyesore. What perhaps no one had counted on was the commitment of Cargill's students, past and present, to maintaining their corner of the campus.

Cargill's former students flooded the principal's office with letters. Students who had graduated ten years earlier wrote, as did former students who now lived in other states. They wrote about what their visits to the wetland with Cargill and others meant to them, as well as their commitment to conservation that had been nurtured while at Willowbrook. As one young woman put it, writing from her university dorm room in a nearby state: "During my years at Willowbrook the cattail area was a beautiful, peaceful place to visit. Walking through such a pleasant, undisturbed place so close to campus was a treat. I think many students developed a new appreciation for nature by discovering such beauty right in Willowbrook's backyard." Current students joined the fray as well. They donned black armbands mourning the cattails and circulated petitions to have the offending drainage pipe removed. The student newspaper gave ongoing front-page coverage to the issue and a mural was painted depicting the struggle.

This story does have a happy ending. By the end of the school year the drainage pipe was gone and the site was designated as part of Willowbrook's nature study area. The area was cleaned up by student volunteers and local scouts planted trees in parts of the sanctuary. By the fall of 1987 the district administrators had joined the students in supporting a district-funded plan to develop the multihabitat nature study area. This was more than a happy ending; it was the beginning of Students for a Better Environment.

SBE is, as 1988/89 president Chris Curtis explains, "an outgrowth of Mr. Cargill's class. It started with the nature study area when a lot of kids wanted to stay involved. It gives us a chance to do more than just hear about this, we do it." The list of challenges taken on, and victories won, is impressive. Thanks to the efforts of these kids, a local real estate developer was halted in his efforts to drain a wetland, the local branch of a national grocery chain offers paper bags before plastic bags, the school itself recycles over twenty thousand pounds of paper a year, and its cafeteria no longer uses Styrofoam. Each victory is recorded with a deposit in the class sarcophagus: a piece of drainage tile, plastic shopping bags, a fast-food fish box (they led the area boycott of Icelandic fish products in support of campaigns to protect whales). The group's newsletter keeps members posted on the latest petition efforts to stop rainforest clear-cutting and the campaign to end the practice of serving veal in the school cafeteria.

All of this work follows the kids home, as Chris Curtis explains: "You can't turn around and go home, put the TV dinner in the oven, and throw it in the garbage and close your mind. It doesn't work."

* * *

For students at Thayer the experience of being engaged with the environment around them has led to similar efforts. Dennis Littky starts the story this way:

> It was a Friday afternoon and two kids come into my office and are really excited. They say, "Hey, Doc, you gotta see this." And they go around pulling down the shades in my office, and closing the door, and then they play the videotape. And it's a tape they made of the area in Winchester where the state wanted to put a toxic waste dump. And what they had on tape was all the natural beauty of the area as well as the fact that there were several springs in the area and several varieties of protected plants.

Of course, the students' work had not gone on by accident. In Dan Bisaccio's science classes students had first been alerted to the potential of the dump. Dan, when offered such a great opportunity to teach science, couldn't turn it down. "I was working on changing the kids' attitudes about science and school in general. The 'what's in it for me' sort of attitude. . . . So this issue put them to work on something that did affect them so they could say that it does make a difference as to whether or not you are going to, as in this case, let somebody come in and dump on you . . . [they] could also learn a lot more science, I believe by getting involved in a scientific endeavor."

The initial reaction of the community to the news of the dump was that it was only what could be expected. Outsiders saw Winchester as a poor town with apathetic people who would jump at the opportunity of having one or two more jobs and an increase in tax revenues. How wrong those outsiders were.

"The kids were really excited about the issue," relates Dan. "At first I don't think that they really believed they could make a difference. But they were willing to try." Several of Dan's classes moved into action almost immediately, and Dan describes their work:

> One group quickly became involved with looking at some of the plants and animals in the area, and they found some endangered species which right away began to cast doubt on whether or not this was an area that was suitable. . . . Another group actually

took a perk test and found the soil was glacial sand and that even with the liners [in the dump] there would be a contamination problem. . . . And then another group took a selectman and actually rented a video camera and filmed a spring on the site that is part of the area's aquifer. . . . The fourth group organized a hearing on the dump here at school. They invited proponents and opponents and key people who were leading both campaigns. . . . The kids had been doing a lot of homework and reading about what was going on and they asked some really good questions.

Those questions were asked in front of a packed gymnasium, much to the surprise of the state officials who attended. Those questions caught the attention of community members who began to ask hard questions of their own. Those questions ultimately insured that no dump was to be dumped on the residents of Winchester.

No one asked the kids at Thayer or Willowbrook to be crusaders. Nor did they ask Katy Beck's kids to work on gun control, or Bill Elasky's kids to work on water quality. Each of these advocacy actions arose as a result of the students' own logical extensions of the work they were doing at school.

David Jones, coordinator of petition drives for SBE, talks about what he learned from working with Richard Cargill. "You learn how to make a difference so you have control over what goes on around you . . . and you change, you become a different person, because you are more aware of the world around you." His sentiments are echoed again and again by other students who work with Cargill. "I think that even though there are a lot of things wrong with the world I can go to this class and get inspired because we can change things, we love the power." "I think I understand now what kind of people we are makes a difference in what goes on." "I've taken four years of honors English and all it is is papers and it's monotonous. I don't think I'm getting anything out of it . . . but with this class, I've already started to do something about it and I know I will do something about it in the future." "Five years from now you are not going to be able to remember the book you read for a term paper. But you will remember this class." "And I think it's about time we learn something in school that you can make a difference about. I just wish it was earlier, not when I'm a senior."

Clearly, pushing the curriculum outside of the school walls, can lead to students taking an active interest in the world around them. A general set of guidelines that make such efforts both successful in terms of results and educative in terms of the school's academic mission operates here:

- Each of the efforts noted arose from student interest. This is not to say that the teachers were not sympathetic or didn't model action in their own way. (During one of Cargill's classes a student mentioned that her dentist's office has a severed gorilla paw displayed as an ashtray. "Give me that guy's name," Richard requested, "I'm going to give him a call.") However, the student advocacy projects were chosen, researched, and designed by the students themselves. At SBE meetings Cargill sits in the back of the room and seldom speaks. And when Bill Elasky tried to suggest a project of his own design the students turned him down flat. In each instance the impetus for student work comes from the students themselves, preventing both an imposition of the teacher's agenda and the flagging of student interest.

- Each project is feasible, and this is where the teachers often step in to help. It is easy for young people to expect too much of themselves, to take on more than they can accomplish. For example, when Bill Elasky's students began to explore potential issues to investigate in their community, the first issue they came upon was the high rate of unemployment in southeastern Ohio. This issue has bedeviled politicians, policymakers, educators, and social workers in the area for decades and it was unlikely that Bill's twelve-year-old students would soon solve it. Bill counseled patience and taking another look at their possibilities, which soon paid off in the water-quality survey. The survey was also a major undertaking, but it was a project that would lead to a definite product and had a foreseeable end to it. Bill frames it this way: "I don't want them to be cynics, I want them to see the payoff of their actions." Of course, how

far off the payoff is and how much uncertainty students can
live with changes with the age and maturity of the kids. If the
goal is to make a difference it needs to be a difference kids can
see as directly related to their actions.

- Each project involves real action. How many times do teachers
  have their students send a letter to the governor, senator, or
  president, the response to which is a nicely autographed picture
  for the room? What kids learn from these activities is that letter
  writing is futile. It doesn't make a difference, unless you need
  something to fill up your picture frames. The types of issues
  that Cargill's students take on, for example, have a definite
  target accompanied by real action—a petition, picket, or other
  type of campaign. As Cargill's students pointed out again and
  again, it only makes sense to do yourself what you are asking
  of others.

- Each of these projects carries with it a very definite academic
  agenda. Bill Elasky carefully correlates all the course objectives
  to his students' work as they write letters, produce radio spots,
  edit and develop books, perform scientific tests, and on and on.
  Richard Cargill's students have to undertake extensive research
  projects on any issue they are going to petition and present
  their findings in written and oral form so SBE members can
  decide whether or not to pursue the issue. The academic mission is not left to chance.

The combination in each of the projects of an academic as well
as social mission insures a quality learning experience.

A Place to Serve

Besides organized group involvement, we take on tasks as individuals in our communities. So do kids who are fortunate enough
to attend these schools without walls.

If the mission of public education is to make democracy possible,
then a spirit of public service, of commitment to the community,
must be part of the school's mission. A number of recent reports

have called for just such a mission, usually to be met by a few hours of public service after school. At Central Park East Secondary School the commitment to community is taken seriously, as demonstrated by the "community service requirement."

One morning a week every student at CPESS can be found somewhere other than inside the school. You might find students in an elementary school, hospital, nursing home, museum, community newspaper, just about anywhere in Harlem. They may be working with a small group of children, sharing stories with an elder, moving hospital equipment or transferring patients, writing a story, answering the phone, conducting tours, or sorting the mail. They are carrying out one of the central parts of their educational experience at CPESS—the community/school service requirement.

Every CPESS student spends two and a half to three hours a week at community service. The purpose of the program is clearly stated in school materials: "CPESS believes that all of its students are capable of contributing service/work on a more adult level. Our students need to recognize that they are able to contribute to the community now, not at some far-off time in the future. All young people should have the opportunity to work with a variety of adults in many different settings in addition to their families and school staff. To achieve these goals, CPESS requires all students to participate in the Community/School Service Program."

Naomi Danzig and Mara Gross oversee the program, which places nearly four hundred students yearly in daily volunteer work positions throughout the Harlem area. For seventh graders just entering the school, an extensive orientation to community service is provided, and most of their placements are in elementary schools as classroom aides. As students move through the school their placement options increase; the past year nearly fifty such options were available. Each student undertakes two placements a year. Naomi describes the placement procedure:

What Mara and I do with the choices [of students] is based on our knowledge of the student. We try to make as good a match as possible between their choice and how they have performed in the past. . . . There is almost nothing that demands tremendous skills. I mean, those students who want to work in office settings have developed the skills to work there, but basically it is on the student's own—what they bring with them as human beings: their competence, their maturity, their thoroughness, their likability, and how they meet with and get along with the adult who is the placement supervisor. The experience really is designed to give them an opportunity to be in a different kind of setting and a different kind of role. Not student, not child, but helper or assistant. Beyond the school and beyond their parents.

After being placed the students travel in pairs to their service sites and must provide their own introductions to their supervisors. Throughout the placement, it is the student's responsibility to arrive on time.

When CPESS students enter the Senior Institute, the community school service requirement continues and is expanded into an internship experience. Here students are allowed to develop one placement throughout both years if they see fit. As part of their senior exhibition they are required to provide two items from their community service endeavors: first, an essay that either provides an in-depth assessment of what he/she gained in terms of skill or knowledge from one of the job experiences, discusses a particular issue or problem that relates to several job experiences, or outlines an alternative way the work could be organized; and second, a formal written resume of his/her work and employment experiences.

Getting a job is not what the community/school service program is all about. Naomi, with the program since its inception, explains that job skills were part of the original idea. "Debbie [Meier, school principal] and I were riding over to the school board office when she turned to me and said that she would like people to graduate from this school with a marketable skill. . . . [But I thought] there were other experiences that were valuable to the growth and development of young people, and unless you wanted to have a trade or technical school there was no way in which you could guarantee each and every student would have a marketable skill when he or she left—nor was that necessarily desirable because that would put the focus on our school somewhere else."

Instead, community/school service was developed. Focusing on who these young people are and how they can be valuable members of the community around them, it gives them the space to see what they can be. CPESS students find out that who they are is valuable to the world around them. Success story after success story walks out of the building every morning to contribute to the community. One indicator of this success is the number of requests the school gets for help. Classroom teachers call asking for aides because they know the help they get will be more valuable than that they get from undergraduates and master's degree students at the nearby colleges. Community groups, understaffed and with few funds, call and request help just to keep themselves going. Hospitals and nursing homes welcome CPESS students with open arms as they rapidly become the best friends of infants waiting to see doctors or elders with time on their hands.

Just as important are the things the students learn about the community. They find resources, both human and physical, all around them that they didn't know even existed. "We try and find places that are culturally relevant to our kids and will also allow them to see adults as role models in many different settings," Naomi on placements. "It's very important to try and find those positive places because the media would have you to believe that East Harlem and Harlem is devoid of this and that is not true." Indeed, the area is a wealth of cultural, civic, social, and educational resources, most of which students are not aware of until they go to work with them.

Of course, the real payoff is what the students learn about themselves. Mara Gross talks about one student's experience:

Another student is working at Mt. Sinai [Hospital], he does maintenance. . . . And this is a young man that some said could not rise to academic challenges. But last year he was part of an evaluation team on some of the kids in the hospital. He worked alongside of the psychologists and they cross-checked observations of kids with his observations, so his opinions were taken into account. He knew he was helping those children get well.

Similar stories are repeated over and over; students who felt they couldn't write suddenly have a byline in the community newspaper; students nervous about speaking in public conduct tours for children in a museum; a child whose mother is gone and who saw her brother commit suicide learns to make physical and emotional contact with others through working at the school for the blind.

Students at CPESS tell stories about how they feel important, valuable, and worthwhile, because of their community/school experience. Johnnie talks about his work with senior citizens at a local center: "I enjoy being with seniors; they make me feel good. I like to hear what they have to say. They remind me of my grandparents." Ife talks about working with preschoolers: "You have to watch out for them, help them play and not get hurt. And they are so happy I'm there." And Kelly reacts to her work in the hospital: "Without me, those [patients] wouldn't have anyone to talk to, just to listen to them. And without them I wouldn't have learned how important I am."

Mara sums it up this way: "This is an opportunity for them [CPESS students] to be in a place where they make decisions and they also see that they get to follow up on the outcome of the decisions and choices they have made. Whether it is solving a conflict between two [elementary school] kids or answering the phone, they are making choices about what they are seeing, what they are doing. And they value that and see it as important. . . . Just the other day I was listening to some of our students talk about community service and I remember one of them saying, 'My job is helping others, what could be better.' "

Preparing for Reality

Preparation for community life goes well beyond developing an ethos of service. Our students will become parents, wage earners, consumers—a multitude of roles that adults play every day. But where are young people to learn about these roles? Historically, an argument has been made that the family would handle all of a child's education beyond reading and writing. We know, of course, that

that is no longer possible as family structure changes and as children no longer apprentice for jobs at a parent's side. We might even make the argument that this form of education is not always desirable, that it can be parochial as it is limited to the experience of the parent or guardian. It seems clear, however, that when young people leave school they are expected to fill a wide variety of roles for which many of them are totally unprepared.

Again, the legislated-excellence movement says little about these roles. Because it is concerned primarily with academic learning, interest in students as productive community members is limited to recommendations for an occasional physical education or home economics course. The struggle for space within the curriculum and school day leads to this myopic view of schooling. By the time the day is filled with more hours in the academic core it seems almost impossible to conceive of doing anything else. Besides, there are vocational and technical schools to deal with job training for kids not destined for college.

The faculty at Thayer have decided to challenge the conventional ways of thinking about preparing students for the world after school. Rather than seeing their mission as primarily vocational, preparing kids for either college or a job, they see their work as primarily civic, preparing kids to make a contribution to the world around them. They believe the best way to do this is to engage students in exploring that world while they are in school, not only with an eye toward the curriculum or services, but with a focus on who they will become as members of the community.

One piece of this preparation is the apprenticeship program. Dennis Littky explains its origin: "The more I talked to students, the clearer it became that all the students' needs could not be met within the existing school. Thayer lacked the staff, the materials, and the money to provide the broad range of courses and experiences the students needed. . . . So the teachers and I began looking outside the school and into the community for help. That triggered the apprenticeship program."

Unlike traditional work/study programs, where students spend half a day at a job site instead of going to school, the apprenticeship program is an integral part of the school day. Once a student selects an apprenticeship with a business or school, he/she has to go through a rigorous application process complete with resume and interview. During the apprenticeship each student keeps a daily journal, which is checked by English teachers for grammar, content, and creativity. Students are also required to prepare a semester project utilizing the knowledge and skills gained on the job; the project can take the form of an in-depth paper, public presentation, or other demonstration.

The apprenticeship program is not so much job training as it is academic enrichment through real work in the community. Dennis discusses how this enhances the academic program:

> One student was really floundering in school. His grades were bad and so was his attitude about school. . . . When his advisor learned he was interested in autobody work, he suggested the student contact the owner of the autobody shop in Winchester and see if he could organize an apprenticeship with him. Excited, the boy immediately called the body shop and the owner agreed to serve as his site supervisor.
>
> The site supervisor let the student watch all phases of the business and then gave him small jobs to do. Eventually, he loaded him with books and pamphlets about autobody work, which the boy devoured, and sent him to an out-of-town workshop. One day a car was brought in that had been severely damaged in an accident. The owner told the boy to take a section of the car and do the repair work. And he did. Another time, the owner of the body shop said he was swamped with work and was getting farther behind and desperately needed help. So he asked the student to do a couple of major repair jobs on his own, figuring that even if they had to be done over again he would still be farther ahead. Much to his delight, the jobs were completed perfectly. That semester, the student made the honor roll for the first time. There are dozens and dozens of stories like these, students on the brink of dropping out or bored by school, who were turned on and turned around by an apprenticeship. Of course, though, not all apprenticeships are wildly successful; sometimes students are fired [itself a good learning experience], and sometimes the experience just adds another dimension to a

student's curriculum, but doesn't cause any bells or whistles to go off.

Because the faculty at Thayer knows that life after school is not just a job, they have developed a mandatory class for all seniors called, appropriately, "Life After Thayer," or LAT. Dennis Littky discusses the origins of the class: "One of the most important things I learned from my first meetings with students was that very few Thayer students knew what they were going to do upon graduation, and many hadn't even thought about it. Enter a new course—'Life After Thayer.'"

The LAT classes meet once a week, about ten students (segregated by gender to make it easier to talk about sex and dating, etc.), with a teacher for an hour. The primary function of the course is to expose seniors to career opportunities, study social issues they might encounter as adults or are encountering now, and teach practical life skills like apartment hunting, budgeting, managing bank accounts, and going to interviews. More important, points out Littky, "It creates a safe environment for students to talk about serious, pressing or personal concerns."

Don Weisberger has had an LAT class for the past six years. He organized the current course syllabus, which focuses on five different areas: who are you?; where are you going?; specifics of life after Thayer; the here and now; and responsibility. This last section really sums up the course for Don: "Responsibility is a very important issue that doesn't get dealt with a lot because we don't think about it—kids or adults. So the class raises this question directly: what is your responsibility to yourself, your peers, and your community?"

What students do, not what they know, is the most accurate measure of their success in schools. But we leave so much of it to chance. We seem to assume that because we have in some way marshaled their obedience and attention, or at least passivity, that the kids we send forth will continue to function within given social norms. At Thayer the clear intention is that if something is central to our mission, we will not leave it to chance. Front and center in the school's mission statement is the goal that "all our students choose a place in life rather than being forced into one." Accomplishment of this goal is one of the reasons for both the LAT class and the apprenticeship program. As Don puts it, Thayer intends that should "kids leave with a better sense of who they are, how they fit into society as a whole, how they can better work with people as individuals . . . [that] they leave here with a strong sense of who they are and what their options are, what they can be."

True Neighborhood Schools

The image of American schools as a vital part of our neighborhoods and communities is deeply ingrained in our national psyche. Paintings and photographs of American towns and cities frequently feature the school and/or church in the center. When we return to our hometowns, a visit to the old school to pay homage is a mandatory ritual. The closing of schools is fought tooth and nail by neighborhood groups who fear not only a decline in property values but also a loss of something almost spiritual in terms of the community's self-image.

In recent years, the notion of neighborhood schools has been perverted by bigotry and racism. Disguised as attempts to preserve neighborhoods, campaigns have been launched to keep minorities out of some schools because those students are not geographically part of the community. This closed, exclusive notion of the neighborhood school belies what the schoolhouse can and should mean in the life of the community. The vision of the school as one of the centers of community life is a vision that schools that work share. This vision includes the entire community as a vital part of the classroom, has kids actively working to improve life in their hometowns and neighborhoods, and acknowledges the school's role in helping young people make careful and informed choices about their future. This vision of public schooling is fundamental to democratic community life.

The outcomes of acting on this vision are clear. First, kids *want* to learn in these settings, so they learn even more, about both the world around them and themselves. Second, students don't have to guess how to use what they are learning; they see it in use all the time. Finally, they come to value who they are, what their community is, and their role within it. This vision is, as one of Bill Elasky's students put it, "the best way to learn about stuff, about all the subjects, and about me. More people should teach like Mr. Elasky. If they all got us doing stuff outside instead of just sitting inside this place and listening, we might all do better."

It's a Tuesday at Willowbrook High, and in Richard Cargill's room there is quite a commotion. Surrounded by representatives of the local media, Chris, David, and Kristin are sending off the first thousand-pound load of paper collected at the school to the recycling center. They proudly display the recycling cart they built that makes its rounds every other evening after school to collect paper from each room. It's a big moment for them in their effort to bring the environmental issues home to the school.

After the short ceremony (to be repeated nearly twenty-five times as the students recycle nearly twenty-five thousand pounds of paper), we are off for a tour of the nature study area.

"These are the infamous cattails," Chris pronounces as we begin our walk. "Hard to believe the school wanted the little area for more sports fields when they have all that space." He waves in the direction of the nearby football field.

We wander down the paths the students have created and lined with wood chips. Chris points out each variety of habitat, discusses the types of flora and fauna likely to be found there. And he discusses the long-range plans for observation decks and interpretive guides.

"It's really changed my whole way of seeing the world," allows Kristin. "I'm more aware and less afraid."

Less afraid? Afraid of what?

"I don't know . . . I've never written official letters and things like that and I was scared at first. I thought they would come to school and write nasty letters and stuff. But they didn't, in fact, they didn't answer at all. So we kept pushing them and we finally won. I mean, I think they are afraid of us . . . [and] I've learned not to be afraid to speak up. And I've learned to change myself, not to throw litter all over the place because I'm too lazy to pick it up."

As we return to the school we cut across the large paved parking lot and head for the back entrance. Just short of the door we stop at a big green trash barrel. There all three students start emptying their pockets—Dave from his varsity letter jacket, Kristin from her suede designer coat, and Chris from his beat-up blue jean jacket—which have slowly filled during our walk with the litter these young people refused to pass by.

PART THREE

Getting There

I n telling the story of these schools my goal was not to propose some grandiose scheme for restructuring all of public education. Such grand designs are usually ignored. They seem unfeasible, and too utopian because they ignore how difficult it is to change a school.

I did not intend to foster more armchair critics of the public schools either. We have enough of those, and most of them, as I've tried to point out, are ill-informed and downright unhelpful. Instead, my aim has been to examine some positive models of what schooling can be in every community and to encourage people to use these models locally however they see fit. My frame of reference was the school my children attend, the school where my wife teaches, and the schools in the neighborhoods nearby. What could I learn about schools that work that could be replicated in the school next door?

The schools discussed in this book raise a series of central questions for the schools we know so well in our hometowns and neighborhoods. Are they genuine communities of learners? Are kids actively engaged in the life of the school and in what they are learning? Does the curriculum hang together as a unified whole? Do students have genuine experiences in the community? Possibly you see a great number of these things happening in your school, or perhaps you see very few. Regardless, the question with which we are ultimately left is how did the schools we have visited get to where *they* are and what can we learn from them?

The last section of this book deals with how democratic school reform came about and how it continues to evolve in these schools. We'll look at how they are organized so that innovation and change are nurtured rather than blocked. In the Appendix there is a listing of sources for people who want to take the next steps in democratizing their school.

There is a temptation among school reformers to fantasize about the future of schooling. Painting rosy pictures of the schools of the future, they seldom talk about the hard work of getting from here to there. It's as if they only need to wish it for it to come true. But people involved in the day-to-day work of educating and raising children know that such fantasies just aren't possible. They know that schools are very much driven by tradition, that they often respond slowly if at all to calls for change, and that grandiose, one-size-fits-all reforms seldom have an impact on the daily lives of kids in schools. Joette Weber put it this way: "You know, I hear about all the things the state legislature is supposedly doing to make schools better. But when it gets right down to it, when I close my door, it's just me and my little guys. All that stuff doesn't have much effect. It doesn't help me at all. I haven't noticed one bit of positive difference from all the noise and money spent by those guys." This refrain sounds strangely familiar from state to state.

What is possible in restructuring schools is change on a more local scale. The basic building block of the school system in the United States is the local school. If genuine, democratic school reform is to occur, it must begin at this most fundamental level, proceeding school by school, district by district.

Of course, this is the most frustrating way to think about school reform. We all long for the grand stroke that will turn schools around and suddenly solve all our problems. But as quickly as that stroke could be carried out, it could be undone. Lasting change will take a deep commitment to the daily work of making schools the component of democratic life that they were intended to be. This last section is addressed to those committed to the long haul. This last look at our schools is offered to those teachers, parents, administrators, community members, and everyone concerned with change in order to help you begin to think about change in your own schools.

Remember, nothing here is offered as a blueprint or recipe. None of the schools we have visited would ever claim that to bring about reform others should follow their lead precisely. Rather, these schools are models, examples of what is possible, visions that help us think in new ways about the organization and mission of public schools. We should learn from their work and borrow whatever seems relevant. But we should always remember that we work in local schools, which take their contours and individual personalities from the world immediately around them. While they all serve the vital national function of preparing democratic citizens, they each do it in a decidedly individual way.

To those who would say that the changes described in the book are not possible on a larger scale, this would be a good place to stop reading. However, I see no reason to believe that our schools cannot, through genuine structural changes, become centers of democratic renewal. Given the changes we have recently witnessed in Eastern Europe it seems to me that cynicism is passé. If people can go so far as to change the world, there is no reason why we cannot change our schools.

CHAPTER 7

Creating the Schools
Our Children Deserve

You don't just jump start these things.

Bob Peterson, the program coordinator and resource room teacher at Fratney, is sitting in his room on a bitterly cold February morning. He is the person largely credited with bringing the parents, teachers and community members into the coalition that fought for and won the new Fratney School. It's a role that he's uneasy with. You sense at times he'd rather just teach kids, but he fills his role with grace and humility. This morning he is talking about some of the struggles the school has faced, chief among them trying to start an entirely new program in a new (to them) building with a new faculty in all grades K/4 (four-year-old kindergarten) to five.

> We wanted to start smaller. You know, with a core of teachers and just a few things that would be different. That way we could build the unity a little easier, bring people into the vision more slowly. I think for the sake of just logistics and program development, and then also for the sake of staff development, that makes a lot of sense. But under the pressure of a big-city school system that is facing classroom shortages we didn't have that

luxury. We are surviving it, but it could have been a lot easier. You don't just jump start these things, you know.

This sentiment is echoed repeatedly by educators in each school—take your time, do it carefully, build from the ground floor up. This message was clear in Joette Weber's claim that "we are as democratic as we stand to be." Wigginton gives the same advice when he counsels teachers to start with that one piece of the curriculum they are most familiar and apply the Foxfire approach to it. Dick Streedain means the same thing when he says that in any school change only comes after "a period of losing your identity, where the goal is just to get through the chaos and mature, then move on to the real issues." Dennis Littky, often asked for advice, offers that "I don't give advice . . . you have to take the time to make your own mistakes."

What can get lost in all this caution is the desire to do anything at all. But what these teachers are trying to express is that school reform, especially reforms that focus on helping young people become active and engaged citizens, takes a level of commitment and an allocation of time that we often aren't willing to give to our schools. Yet in order for our fondest dreams for public education to come true, in order to recapture the democratic promise of public schooling, it is precisely this type of commitment that we must now make. The shot-in-the-arm, one-size-fits-all approach of the legislated-excellence movement is a dead end leading not to genuine school improvement but to alibis for adults who should know better. In those schools and classrooms where the genuine, far-reaching, and fundamental changes are going on, the hope for a more democratic future is nurtured.

A Noble Quest

Throughout my visits and travels, as I sat and talked with teachers, administrators, parents, and students, it became clear to me that each of these schools and classrooms is driven by a vision. David Smith of Central Park East put it best when he said, "It is . . . a

Don Quixote kind of feeling, as if we are on a noble quest almost. Maybe it's an impossible dream but what a grand dream it is. And that creates a sense of people wanting to work together, supporting each other."

There is a great deal in the school reform literature today supporting the notion that schools with a clear mission statement will be more successful than those that are unclear about their tasks. What the schools in this book in particular have done is to elevate their mission statements to the level of a vision that everyone is beholden to. This vision is not limited to what kids learn about academics *in* school, but designed to encompass what sort of people they will be when they *leave* school.

Listen to just a few samples from these schools, taken not from documents filled with high-sounding educational jargon, but from the mouths of teachers and administrators who work daily with kids. In each case all I had to do was to ask each individual to talk about what he or she hoped students learned at his or her school.

Real confidence in their ability to make decisions, to find information, to understand what they read, to articulate ideas, to operate in the realm of ideas. What I mean is the ability to synthesize and to find resource materials, to know what it is that they have to do to understand something . . . to have opinions and to be able to express those opinions and argue them in terms of what we call habits of mind—finding appropriate evidence, looking for the connectedness, figuring out who might care, questioning what if something were not true. (Herb Rosenfeld, Central Park East)

For the most part I really want them over the course of time to become more responsible for themselves and directing themselves. If they can think critically and they can question and develop their own thoughts about things, that's really learning. That's the bottom line for learning: being able to know what it is you want to know, to be able to investigate it and to evaluate it on your own terms, to take ownership, to be empowered in the kinds of things that one is learning about because that's what life is. In reality, the people who do that, the people who decide for themselves where they are going, are empowered and have responsibility and are the leaders of our society. And I want the kids to know that that is something that has got to be developed. Here at Fratney we really want children to leave perceiving that they can develop those kinds of thinking skills and hopefully be the leaders in Milwaukee as they grow older. (Rita Tenorio, Fratney)

When it all works, I like the kid to really be an inquisitive learner. To be somebody who is excited about reading a book or learning something or seeing something. A person who is strong enough to stand up and speak for what he or she wants. A person—whether they make a decision to go into the army or college or a job—who is continuing to learn and to grow. Somebody who understands him or herself and understands learning. That's what's important. (Dennis Littky, Thayer)

These few voices speak for the rest. The vision they set out, one of engaging kids in school so they will become participating members of their community, responsible for their own learning, and willing to work for a better world, was shared by all the educators with whom I spoke. This ideal gave rise to development of a school climate based on community, to a commitment to change the school experience from passivity to activity, to develop curricula that connect with kids, and to open the school doors to the world outside. The way in which this vision came to be a central part of all these teachers do illustrates the first step in meaningful democratic school reform.

LEADERSHIP

There is no getting around the fact that in the schools we have visited there has been a person or persons who began the process of developing a school vision. Most often it was the principal, but it didn't have to be. But this individual or group of individuals was always able to lead democratically by sharing and developing the vision of what the school could be.

It's important at the outset not to confuse charisma with leadership. Too much is made of claims that it takes a superman or woman to really help a school or staff grow and change. In fact, many of the leaders we have seen are not charismatic at all. They aren't flashy personalities who attract a cult following. Rather, they are people who care so deeply about the school, about the kids and adults within it, that they became school leaders through their demonstrated dedication to the task at hand. They are the people who lead by example. This is what democratic leadership means.

At Thayer, Dennis Littky took on the task of developing a vision for the school. He came to the school with one: "I knew that I wanted the kids to be good thinkers, to use their minds, to like school. I wanted the atmosphere to be good. I knew I wanted the relationship between teachers and kids to be good, I wanted us not to be fighting but to work together. So there was all that stuff I knew." His task was not to lead by forcing all his vision on the teachers. Rather, his vision, while very clear, was broad enough to accommodate many things. His leadership helped the staff mold the vision into something they could all share.

"It starts with strong leadership; without it little or no restructuring will take place," says Littky, describing his own approach to making school change possible. "The leader, typically the principal, prepares the climate for change. He or she looks at the big picture, and then works with the staff, students, administration, community and school board on aiming toward a common vision. But by no means does he or she call all the shots or impose his will on everyone else. Restructuring is a process that involves everyone. The more people who are involved in coming up with creative solutions to problems, the more good ideas there will be to work with."

For the entire summer before school and through his first year at Thayer, Littky made good on his commitment to share the vision. Meetings with students, parents, and faculty were not devoted to the mundane parts of school administration—locker assignments, schedules, and bus routes. Rather, the focus was on what people wanted the school to be. Everyone was encouraged to imagine the school he or she wanted, to dream about what could happen with their kids, in their town, at their school.

A school philosophy emerged from that process, culminating in a statement about what the Thayer community would provide for its students. Teachers refer to this document, and Dennis reads it to anyone who will listen.

Building this schoolwide philosophy was the first step for each school. In some cases it was a process of setting out a philosophy and then starting a school to put it into place, for example at Central Park East and Fratney. In other settings it means constantly referring to the historical vision that the school has attempted to uphold, such as at Hubbard Woods. In yet other settings it means creating a schoolwide vision for a school in transition, as at Thayer. In a more limited arena, it means that small groups of teachers, or an individual teacher, first developed a vision of what the classroom could become and then moved toward that. A vision of what young people will be like, of how they will be different because they spent time with these teachers, lies behind the successes of these schools and classrooms.

Further, in every case as many members of the school community as possible (if not all) are encouraged to share in the vision. This is clearly no easy task. But it is possible when we direct our attention to what we want young people to *be* like when they leave school, rather than being preoccupied with what they will be able to *do* while they are in school. Here it is easier to find a common ground, based in democratic traditions, traditions that demand that as citizens and neighbors we pay close attention to the common good, be able to think carefully about and act on issues of public concern, and be tolerant of divergent or minority points of view. What these attributes of democratic citizenship mean for children of different ages and in various communities is best established by the local school community. But they do provide for any school a place to start in thinking through how to become a place that makes a mark on the lives of young people. The next step is to put them into practice.

Theory into Practice

The most eloquent mission statement is only words on a piece of paper. Its strength arises from day-to-day practices within the school. Remembering Bob Peterson's admonition that we not see this as "jump starting," we should ask: How did the vision each school held get turned into practice?

Each school had to overcome numerous barriers to reform through the collective work of all the faculty. Dennis Littky explains, "The more responsibility given out, the more responsibility assumed. Everyone has a stake in the process, so everyone wants to see it through. That's the theory, anyway. The reality is not nearly as slick as all that—less like a supercharged locomotive and more like an ornery mule. The reality is that it takes incredible patience, persistence, stamina and hard work. It also takes guts and a good sense of humor."

Putting vision into practice means making space for the types of interactions these schools value. It means challenging some of the most sacred myths about public schooling. For decades Americans have believed that big equals better, that coverage equals knowledge, that schools should work like factories, both administratively and pedagogically. We have accepted virtually without question the way schools currently look and operate. It's as if schools in their structure and form but not their output are sacred and beyond question. Throughout this book all of these assumptions have been challenged. We have looked at schools that do well for their students by refusing to do business as usual, that instead have altered the very nature of schooling in order to meet their broader vision. Rather than change their vision to fit the current structures of schooling, they have changed the structures to accommodate their vision. In each case, teachers, administrators, and parents have decided what they wanted for their kids and then built a school to match that dream. For virtually every school and teacher that meant beginning with issues of size, moving on to issues of time, and then turning to the issue of governance. These are the places where any community needs to begin in rethinking schools.

MAKING IT SMALLER

Each school started by making itself smaller—that is, making itself *seem* smaller. The reason was simple—to give teachers more contact with students and with one another. For each child to connect with the school, he/she must have extensive contact with the people in it. If curricular changes are to be made, staff must be small enough to meet and make changes readily. Debbie Meier, principal at Central Park East, puts it this way: "The school must be small enough so that everyone *can* know everyone else, and respond easily to needed changes. Teachers, kids and families who do not share a common geographic, ideological or historic community, need optimum face-to-face contact over many years to build a strong school-based community with a coherent common set of understanding."

These schools have used a variety of strategies to reduce their size. At the elementary level, Hubbard Woods' multiaged grouping insures that students come in contact with only three or four, as opposed to six or seven, teachers during their grade-school years. At Fratney, clusters of classes at different grade levels (for example, a class each from the kindergarten, second and fifth grades) form houses that work together on projects and assist one another in classroom work. At all the elementary schools the classrooms are self-contained, so that kids are not shuffled from class to class for various subjects. (Departmentalization is an unfortunate but growing trend as elementary schools try to cover more content and look more like high schools.)

Other strategies could be adopted by any school regardless of size. For example, a large elementary school could organize itself into teaching teams, with a group of teachers taking a group of students through several years of schooling, say four teachers who work with eighty to one hundred students for grades one through three, or even kindergarten through sixth grade. Multiaged grouping in classrooms could also be used in any school, allowing children two years to really get to know a teacher and teachers two years to watch each child progress.

At the secondary level, grades seven through twelve, the need to reduce school size is even greater. Large, impersonal mega-schools (some containing more than five thousand students) cannot engender the sense of community and commitment for all students that we have seen in our sample schools. Further, genuine educational change in these settings is next to impossible given the logistical difficulty of just getting the staff together. Strategies for reducing school size at the secondary level are simple and easily undertaken. First, the concept of advisory reduces school size by putting students in close contact with a single faculty member. Second, teaching teams across disciplines that work with students create smaller units within the school. Third, a great number of nonteaching staff (such as specialists, counselors, psychologists, and assistant principals) can be reassigned to teaching, thus reducing class size. These three steps can begin to break down even the largest schools into more genuine teaching and learning communities. Such smaller schools are possible tomorrow, if we have the courage to demand them and the imagination to make them happen.

Debbie Meier, a veteran of the New York City school scene, argues that an even broader restructuring in terms of size could go on in the schools.

[Smaller schools] appear impossible because we're visually thinking of our big buildings and huge staffs. Just as the Empire State Building contains hundreds of companies, so could all our big school buildings contain many schools. They could contain schools with different age groups and varying styles and ways of organizing. Small schools may share some facilities such as the gym, labs, auditorium, and occasional personnel. They might hire a building manager to coordinate, as does the Empire State Building. But the educational life of each school would remain distinct and independent. Simple changes that would be impossible to make in a mega-school can be decided around the table one afternoon and implemented the very next day in a small school.

Regardless of current size, any school can get smaller, get closer to its students, and make more rapid movement toward its vision for students. This is the first step in building schools that work.

TAKING OUR TIME

The tyranny of the clock was often the second battle fought in order to develop schools of commitment and excellence. Our current concept of time in schools comes from an earlier era when we were trying to make schools look like factories. If we reject that metaphor, if we substitute the metaphor of the school as community where future democratic citizens and not merely workers are nurtured, school time requires a radical restructuring.

While this pressure is felt most accurately at the secondary level, time pressures come to bear on elementary teachers as well. Faced with state requirements for the number of minutes to be spent on a given subject, frequent interruptions for special classes or announcements, and only having children for one year, elementary teachers feel rushed into covering the mandated curriculum, with little time to do much else. However, just a few simple changes reduce a great deal of this pressure in the schools we've visited. For example, by forgoing departmentalization, teachers can control their own daily schedule, including recess. Multiaged grouping keeps kids and teachers together for more time. Principals allow teachers to cover the content flexibly, without requiring a set number of minutes per subject per day. Even more fundamental, at Hubbard Woods for example, much of the special help students receive in math and reading forms pull-in as opposed to pull-out programs. Rather than take a few students *out* of the classroom for help, thus creating scheduling and organization problems, the resource teacher comes into the room and works with the teacher and students. In this way all the students get more contact with their teacher and the entire group sees itself as part of everything that goes on in the class. The goal is to keep the entire class as intact as possible throughout the day.

For secondary school teachers the clock is perhaps the most personal enemy. Meeting on a frenzied schedule of as many as eight class periods of forty-five to fifty minutes a day with twenty to thirty students in each, it's not surprising that many teachers resort to lectures and workbooks. "I often can't remember what jokes or stories I told what class," lamented an English teacher in Georgia.

"After seeing nearly 180 students the entire day often seems like just one big blur." In survey after survey of secondary teachers the frustration of not having enough time with their students surfaces.

As we have seen, time is not an intractable problem. At Thayer the first step in dealing with time was to cut the number of periods in the day and expand those that were left to a full hour. After that came the teaming strategy that spawned programs like Spectrum, in which a team of teachers had an expanded amount of time with one group of students. Central Park East Secondary School has taken this same approach, using fewer class periods, more time, and teams of teachers.

An additional and often overlooked time problem is one having to do with lack of time for teachers to work together as a team. In many of today's schools it is almost as if someone designed the school day with the express objective of keeping teachers apart. Responsible for children throughout the day, with only twenty to thirty minutes for lunch and smaller breaks scattered during the rest of the day, most teachers seldom have opportunities to talk with their colleagues during the day. For that reason it is hard for them to view the school as an entire unit, to plan multidisciplinary units, or to work on issues of school climate. As with other working people, teachers need time structured into their days to work on their work.

Making this change isn't an impossible task. At Hubbard Woods the entire staff shares a seventy-five-minute lunch period brought about through creative use of aides and parent volunteer time. During this time, the faculty meets, teams of teachers work on the curriculum, and collaborative projects are planned. At Thayer the schedule is arranged so that all teachers on a team share the same planning period. CPESS house staffs have one morning a week free to work together while their students are involved in community service. Just as we need to take time to know our students, we need to insure that there is time available for teachers to know one another.

Time, like size, is fundamental to rethinking our schools. Why we currently believe, or *act* as if we believe, that racing students from class to class, shifting gears from Chaucer to quadratic equations to the War of 1812, will provide a quality learning experience for young people is hard to understand. Furthermore, why we ever believed that teachers work at their optimum level while they face seven to eight large classes a day in rapid succession is just as confusing. As a logical reaction to these constraints, teachers lecture and drill their way through the text as opposed to taking the project-centered approach we have seen in places like Thayer, CPESS, and Foxfire.

The clock should be learning's servant, not its master. We should take whatever time is necessary to insure that students ask the right questions and search out the important answers. Part of making time available has to do with cutting back on what is taught at all levels. So many times I have heard teachers complain about the futility of trying to teach everything there is in the third-grade science, seventh-grade health, or eleventh-grade American history text. (Quick, how many of you got beyond World War II in your American history class?) It gets harder all the time as textbook publishers, for fear of offending someone, never remove chapters from revised texts but rather add another chapter for every new topic or decade.

In each school we have visited, the faculty has deliberately cut back on the amount they try to teach. Part of this comes from rejecting the texts as syllabi and seeing them as resources instead. The faculty then decides what skills, abilities, and information children do need to acquire in order to become thoughtful, participating and wise citizens. This approach frees teachers from the demon of coverage and opens up space for genuine teaching and learning. It is futile to try to teach everything, even everything of importance. But teachers who have their eyes set on a vision can choose what is really important, do those things well, and realize that schooling is only that part of education that prepares them for yet more learning.

MAKING DECISIONS

The mention of Foxfire earlier reminds us that not every teacher we visited worked in a school that radically altered the use of time or its size. The teachers in Athens County, the Chicago suburbs, and rural Georgia all work within schools that choose to accept the status quo to a certain degree. Yet they are still able to radically alter the way life goes on inside their classrooms for one simple reason—they're in control. This is the third thing that must be changed if we are to have the schools our children deserve. The power of decision making about the things that really matter—curriculum, school organization, the budget, the evaluation and treatment of students— must be moved from the statehouse and central office to the schoolhouse and classroom.

Debbie Meier speaks for virtually every educator with whom I met: "[Faculties need] the maximum freedom over their own budget, curriculum, staffing, examination and assessment procedure. Only the most parsimonious general rules should be imposed—rules that prevent racial segregation, creaming off 'easy-to-teach' students, political, religious or racial bias, and assume basic safety standards. Fancy proposals are irrelevant without dramatic changes in where and how power is legitimately exercised."

We saw this happening when Joette Weber and Eliot Wigginton talked about having the freedom to cover course objectives in their own way. Bill Elasky is free to indicate the multiple ways his students' projects, chosen by the kids themselves and not taken from a text, covered the district course of study. John Duffy has the space to engage students in case studies as opposed to textbook interpretations in order to cover the central and recurring issues in U.S. history. In each of these classrooms the teacher was given the freedom to choose what to study, how to study it, and the pace at which to deal with it. This freedom may have been hard-earned by the individual teacher, coming from the respect due to the outstanding work of his or her students. Or it may just be a product of benign neglect, as the teacher is left alone by a school administration. The result is pretty much the same: a classroom that is alive with a genuine spirit of inquiry, discovery, and community.

Of course, the danger in such class-by-class autonomy is that the school itself may become fragmented. Students, as they go from teacher to teacher, may receive mixed messages about school and learning. On one hand I believe the fears of such mixed messages are exaggerated, perpetuated by those who want to enforce the status quo under the guise of continuity. On the other these fears do suggest the need to explore the issues set out in this book on a schoolwide basis.

At Hubbard Woods, Fratney, Thayer, and CPESS, the power to make decisions about administration of the schools is vested in the staff, and often in the community as well, as with Fratney's site-based management team. At each school, teachers and administrators together decide how time will be used, what the curriculum will be, and how to evaluate children. Further, the staff presides over a variety of other issues that we haven't examined—school budgets, interviewing and hiring new staff, school decor, lunchroom and additional duty policies—all the things that make a school run smoothly.

This decision making is time consuming, but teachers don't have to be entirely bogged down in administrative details. At Thayer, Littky turns his staff loose to explore how to team-teach and make learning more active while he makes sure the detail work gets done behind the scenes. "My job is to question everything we do, to make sure it is good for our kids, fits our mission. If it does, then I need to get out of the way and promote that work in any way that I can." Debbie Meier at CPESS operates in a similar vein, always sharing new resources and ideas with the staff, taking time to sit in on classes, raising questions about what everyone is doing, but not burdening teachers with the trivia of parking, where the copying machine goes, or fixing the lights.

Earlier we saw how Dick Streedain at Hubbard Woods makes sure teachers solve the real issues the school faces by the way he organizes faculty meetings. A teacher volunteers to facilitate the meeting and leads the staff in brainstorming issues for the agenda. Then the staff prioritizes the list and works through as many items as it can during the allotted time. "We really get to what is important to the school this way," Streedain claims. "In the winter someone always wants to talk about snowball throwing. It goes on the list, but it's a low priority, after, say, the math program or how to integrate art into each theme. So we never get to it and by spring the snow is gone and it's not an issue anymore. Everybody is happy and we don't waste time on nonissues."

In each case the reform insures that the important decisions get made by the people who are most capable of making them—the faculty. Decisions that genuinely affect the mission of the school, that reflect on the shared vision under which the school operates, are the ones that the staff, not an outsider, decides. These decisions vary from school to school; an issue at Thayer may not be one at CPESS, so there is no reason to generate a list of items with which every teacher must grapple. But the one constant that runs through all of these schools is that decision making is school- and classroom-based.

Control of the structure of size, time, and governance may not seem like the most exciting concept in a school. But to me it is the key that unlocks the doors, making it possible for teachers to achieve the democratic visions they have for their classrooms. Edwina Branch, who teaches math/science at CPESS, points out how crucial changing the structures of time, size, and governance is: "If you were to ask me to use exhibitions instead of standardized tests, integrate the math/science curriculum, and really get to know all my students in a typical high school with 8 periods and nearly two hundred students a day, I'd just laugh at you. It's the structure at CPESS, the way we do things every day, that makes all these things possible. And that makes it possible for me to really connect with my students."

To foster and nurture these close relationships with students we need to make the space, in terms of size, time, and decision making, for teachers to realize the vision they have for their charges. "Teachers," argues Debbie Meier, "will not have a major impact on the way kids use their minds until they come to know how their students' minds work." Such wisdom comes only when we create the structures that facilitate it. In Meier's words:

> [Teachers] cannot help young people make sense of things if they do not know what is not sensible to them, if they do not have the time to answer their questions. They cannot improve a student's writing if there isn't time to read it, reflect on it, and then meet occasionally with the students about his or her work.

They cannot find ways to connect new ideas with old ones if they have no control over the curriculum or pacing. Nor can they influence the values and aspirations of young people if they cannot shape the tone and value system of their classroom and school. To do this they need the power to reorganize the school, the curriculum, the use of time and the allotment of resources at the school level.

Roadblocks

So what stops us? Why don't we see these changes happening all over the country? Why will you have to search for a school that is making these things happen in your community? There is no easy answer to these questions. We face a multitude of roadblocks to rethinking schools in order to prepare students for democratic citizenship. What follows is a sampling of the problems teachers and administrators shared with me as we talked about their hopes for their schools. The task is for each school, each community, to knock down as many of these obstacles it can to enable teachers and schools to be the places of caring, respect, and commitment that we hope they will be.

IN THE SCHOOL

The first set of challenges for educators and parents to overcome are those found within each school. Before teachers can get serious about developing a curriculum for democratic life they need to have the time and space to discover what such a curriculum means. They can't do that when they are literally papered over with bureaucratic demands.

In recent years the number of forms and paperwork teachers deal with daily has exploded. Most of this is due to recent calls for more accountability on the part of teachers. But the fault for translating these calls into reams of paperwork, with little or no demonstrable effect on student learning, lies solely with local districts. For example, in one Ohio school the district adopted over three hundred language arts objectives for students in grades K–12 and then four different categories of remediation for any student not achieving the objectives. That system means, for example, that a fourth-grade teacher who has twenty-five students and twenty of these language arts objectives to cover, with four remediation strategies, has twenty-five hundred separate bits of information to record, in just *one* subject area!

Another mountain of paperwork awaits any teacher who tries anything out of the norm in schools. A simple field trip requires notes from parents, completed transportation forms in triplicate, leave requests, and on and on. If a school values the work of its teachers, it could demonstrate it by asking how we can help make valuable extracurricular activities possible. How about making hands-on, experiential, community-based teaching as easy bureaucratically as it is to lecture and have kids do workbook pages?

The second problem each school needs to overcome is the sad misdirection of funds. One teacher lamented that the only repairs she'd requested over the summer concerned her curtains and a table—neither was fixed. Another pointed out that by December 6 all of the markers, a valuable tool in illustrating class-made books, were used up. Teacher after teacher shared stories of digging deep in his or her pockets to facilitate projects and activities. It doesn't have to be this way. While schools do need more money (and such money is easily available with just a little trimming in the military budget, for example), there are better ways to use funds that are currently available. For example, instead of spending thousands of dollars on bright, shiny new textbooks, money could be spent on real books and resources for kids. This expenditure is allowed by law in most states. Or rather than purchase stacks of workbooks that kids fill out and throw away, teachers could use funds to purchase consumable materials that the kids and teachers decide how to use. All this takes is some careful and creative budgeting and the will to do what is best for the kids.

Finally, inside each school there must be an unwritten rule that the time teachers and students spend together is sacred. Interruptions, such as announcements, assemblies, fund drives, and all the rest, should be eliminated during the day. While this point may sound almost trivial, it's important to recognize what such interruptions do to a teacher and his/her students. I cannot count the number of times a magical moment in a classroom was shattered by the dreaded "attention teachers" crashing in through a P.A. Imagine if you will what would happen if those same teachers just barged into the school administrator's office? Clearly, such interruptions show that we don't value teachers or their work. This simple fact demeans much of what goes on in school, and such useless interruptions should come to a halt tomorrow.

IN THE DISTRICTS

One step up from the school level, at the level of district office, similar changes need to occur. Most of these changes involve actually enabling change. So much of what comes out of central offices, especially at the middle level of school administration (for example, assistant superintendents and supervisors), seems to have no real purpose but to stifle and limit teachers. A simple example is the push for more and more standardized tests. Virtually every school district in the United States administers more standardized tests than are required by law. The reason, as far as I can see, is to give some educational bureaucrat some way to exercise power. Pointing to minute gains or losses on a test printout, administrators give orders to teach more of x, y, or z. Of course, x, y, or z may have no relation to the curriculum or program, but no matter; if tests test it we need to teach it.

As a counter to this bureaucratization of schooling we need to ask three questions about every central office initiative. First, how will this help kids learn? Second, how will this help teachers teach? Third, what does this cost (testing programs are very expensive) and how else could the resources be utilized? If satisfactory answers to each of these questions are not readily and clearly available, then these "educators" ought to be put to work doing something more valuable.

Another abuse of school district administrators is the standardization of how teachers are to teach. A great deal of this book has dealt with the way in which teachers cover content and how they select that content. Not a single teacher I spoke with objected to broad school district guidelines in terms of what students should learn. However, what many of them cited as hobbling their efforts were district curricula that mandated both what and how they were to teach. As one teacher put it, "Why bother with me? They've lined everything out that is to be taught, when it is to be taught, and how to do it. Why don't they just put it on TV and I'll go do something that uses my brain?"

This trend, often referred to as "teacherproofing," is not new. It has been with us since the turn of the century when we populated schools with women teachers who were believed only to be suited to take orders from male administrators. Based on the assumption that teachers are not very bright, the process of teacherproofing (stipulating virtually everything that goes on in a class) was meant to insure that teachers were just conduits for a factual curriculum. You would think we were beyond that today, but obviously we are not, as districts mandate, often in response to statehouse demands, more and more of what teachers are to do.

We cannot justifiably expect teachers to treat students with more respect than that which they themselves receive. In moving beyond a legislated-excellence curriculum, in embracing a classroom orientation that trusts students to undertake and complete complex tasks, we are saying that we trust the developing abilities and sensitivities of our students. Teachers can only do this when they themselves feel trusted and valued. The equation is really quite simple. A teacher who is told to produce particular test scores using preselected material is unlikely to allow his or her charges to spend time exploring essential questions or engaging in learning experiences outside the classroom. Further, the entire framework of community collapses in such settings as the denial of equal community-member status to teachers results in teachers unable or unwilling to build community in their rooms.

The appropriate role for a school district office is to help teachers and the community set realistic general goals for students and then help teachers as they work to reach these goals. Further, the function of such offices should be to insure that all available resources are put into classrooms with kids. This means reassigning administrative positions into classroom teaching positions and reallocating expenditures from testing manuals to quality materials. Finally, it means acting as an active promoter of the types of restructuring we have discussed here as opposed to enforcing the status quo.

IN THE COMMUNITY

We are a nation that loves to complain about schools, yet wants to *do* very little to help. If we are to have schools of commitment and community, democratic schools, schools that work, we need to make sure our communities stand behind us. First and foremost we have to insure that the funds are there to make good schools happen, and this means changing national spending priorities as well as providing sufficient local funds.

We can do other, more immediate things in our neighborhoods and communities to help support schooling for democratic citizenship. First, parents need to look for programs and teachers like the ones in this book and become their advocates. That means telling school boards that these are the types of programs that are valuable and should be supported. It also means letting teachers know that their efforts are valued and appreciated.

Second, parents should be better consumers of their children's educational experiences. Ask questions about what the mission of the school is, and how the worksheet, standardized test, or project fits with that mission. Look beyond the simple answers so often given by educational bureaucrats or politicians about a percentage point rise on a test score and ask what kids are really learning. Take a day off work and go back to school with your child. Think about which experiences kids are having in schools that will enable them to be good thinkers, decision makers, neighbors, and community members. The ways in which kids are treated daily in schools will be reflected in the ways they live their lives outside of school.

Third, communities need to be more receptive to welcoming students to their daily events. Rather than viewing the school day as a welcome respite from young people, community and governmental agencies, businesses, and civic organizations should seek out any opportunity to open their doors to schoolchildren. When young people can work side by side with adults, making adult decisions, doing adult jobs, kids and the community win. Young people gain an opportunity to feel powerful, and to see that they do make a difference. The community taps a valuable resource, one that will become more valuable in the future. There is so much that can and needs to be done, as well as so much that can be learned, in our own backyards today. Underuse of these resources continues to be one of the biggest educational wastes of the day.

IN THE STATEHOUSE

Having watched the performance of our state legislatures, I am not optimistic that much can be done in this area. With mindless abandon and in a seeming rush to get elected, legislators mandate one quick fix after another that does little but hurt schools. Driven by a myopic concern with standardized test scores and possessing little understanding of life inside schools, the states, charged with control of public education, seem destined to continue making the same mistakes of overregulation.

After over a decade of trying to mandate reform and failing, one would hope that legislative bodies would get the hint. And some have. North Carolina, for example, is freeing schools from the state regulatory process and California is allowing schools to choose multiple ways to reach state educational goals. In Chicago a bold new experiment in local control of schools is under way. We need every state to back off, decide on general goals for schools to reach, and then allow each school to figure out how to get there.

The new accountability movement reflected in the legislated-excellence drive is anything but genuine accountability. How can we believe that a teacher who is told how to teach, what to teach, how long to teach it, and how to test it can be held genuinely accountable for the outcome? It's like telling a physician how to diagnose, what treatment must be given, when it is to be given, and then holding him/her responsible if the patient dies. Instead of using this straitjacket approach to schooling, legislatures could better direct their attention to enabling schools to promote excellence rather than attempting to force them to. Two simple things are called for.

First, set clear state goals for public schools that are reasonably related to the schools' missions. Goals such as guaranteeing every student a job will not work. Employment is a function of a healthy economy, not diplomas. Goals that establish reading levels, graduation rates, and public service are feasible. These goals should be widely debated and publicized and become the hallmark of each state's schools.

Second, get out of the way. While ensuring that students will not be discriminated against, or put in physical danger, legislatures should remove many, if not all, regulations placed on how schools operate. The amount of time spent on subject matter areas, staffing, and length of day, for example, should be left up to the local school district. If, and only if, a district proves itself unable to handle this responsibility, the state should step in. Short of that, schools should be encouraged to make their own way in designing the types of experiences that enrich the lives of our children.

Classroom by Classroom, School by School

"One of the problems we face," comments Bill Elasky, thinking out loud with a group of colleagues, "is that too many people want a big, exciting change tomorrow. It just doesn't happen that way." In every case discussed in this book school change was, and continues to be, a difficult, slow, and time-consuming process. It is not a job for one-shot consultants, part-time politicians, or commission report writers. The task before us is too important to be taken lightly or without care. It is the single most vital task before us today if we care about the future of the republic.

The restructuring of size, time, and governance is where any effort to rethink schools must begin. But they are just beginnings. These changes only lay the groundwork for slow but steady work required to bring about the types of schools and classrooms we have visited. These changes make it possible to create democratic classrooms for democratic lives.

The time has long since passed to begin these efforts. We have too willingly suffered the unsuccessful grand designs of educational experts. We have been too quick to trade our hopes for schools that would foster democratic citizenship for a few more points on standardized tests. We have been too anxious to make teachers and administrators into scapegoats for school problems rather than help them create the schools our republic and, most important, our children deserve.

In the end we are talking about our children. All of the reforms in the world will not matter if they do not affect the day-to-day lives of kids in school. The legislated-excellence movement, for all its sound and fury, will have little impact on our kids and their classrooms. We shouldn't be surprised, given that most of the legislated-excellence reforms have more to do with adults than with children. For example, a great deal has been made recently of school choice programs that allow parents to choose which school their child will attend. But when such programs are not accompanied by allowing schools to take a variety of approaches to teaching and learning, they seem primarily designed to soothe parental fears about where children will go to school and who their classmates will be. The rush to mandate more and more content for kids to cover, most of which adults don't know, is another reform that isn't child-centered. I would suggest that our attraction to books pointing out what Americans don't know and blaming this ignorance on schools is primarily a response to adult ignorance. Our own lack of knowledge about history, science, world cultures, and so on is harder to deal with than, say, making kids study more. We can, and should, do better than this.

We can, for a start, see that all of our schools are genuine communities, with a shared vision of the kind of human being a young person will be when he/she leaves the school doors. These communities should engender the habits of heart and mind that are required of democratic citizens, habits of compassion, careful reflection, tolerance, mutuality, service, and commitment that are only learned through experience, not exhortation.

We can see that teachers and students have enough time together to engage in genuine educational experiences, experiences that cut across artificial distinctions of subject matter area and engage students in doing real things. We can make time to create students who think reasonably, are able to find and generate information, and who can learn along with us as we grapple with the problems and prospects of modern life.

We can insure that our young people have the chance to make a difference in their communities today, not in some never-arriving future. We can give them a chance not only to make a difference, but a chance to practice (and perhaps fail at) participatory citizenship. We shouldn't worry about failure; we should welcome it, as school is precisely the place to fail safely and learn from such failure.

Utopian? I think not. To those who say we should be more realistic or practical there is but one response: What is so realistic about assuming that schools as they are (or adding on more of the same) will generate the attributes needed for democratic citizenship in our young people? No, it is not utopian to work for schools that do well by all of our young people, our communities, and ourselves. It is visionary, by sharing the dream that all of us can be educated to be the thoughtful citizens a strong democracy needs.

After all my visits, two images stay with me that sum up the message these schools had to share. The first is a general impression, one that I took away from every school and classroom, of how happy people were to be in these places. These were joyful, exciting places where interesting and often unexpected things happened all the time. Herb Rosenfeld, when talking about CPESS, summed up what seems to be the case at every school: "Everybody here loves being here; every adult here *wants* to be here; every kid here *wants* to be here; there is not a single person who would like to be someplace else. That by itself is outstanding."

The second image comes from the day Bill Elasky took his sixth graders (the Water Chemists) to the middle school for seventh-grade orientation. The kids have been given the grand tour of the building, shown the new textbooks they would inherit, and had heard all about their new responsibilities in the more "grown-up" world of middle school. After the tour and talks were over, the teacher escorting the group asked if the youngsters had any questions. Immediately a hand went up and the student, Mike, was recognized.

"First I want to thank you for the tour of the school. It looks very interesting," said Mike, who knew a great deal about public speaking. Bill's class practices a lot, and Mike had also been part of a team of students who, on their own initiative, spoke before the governor of Ohio's commission on education reform advocating more teaching like Bill's. "But I was wondering, when will we get to do projects and stuff?"

Taken aback at first, the teacher responded, "What kind of projects do you mean?"

At that, Mike launched into a long explanation of the work of the Water Chemists and what the class was learning from it.

"Oh, well, that does sound interesting," was the polite response. "But you have to understand that here at the middle school you have more than one teacher every day. And since we change classes a lot there just isn't time in the schedule to do those types of projects."

"Well, then," replied Mike, asking the question we should all be asking all the time, "why don't you just change the schedule?"

Indeed, why don't we? Why don't we start tomorrow to make our schools the democratic communities they all could be? And while we're at it, let's make sure that the school we know best, the school down the street, becomes a place from which we can expect the neighbors we need if democratic community is ever to be possible.

Epilogue

Summer 1991

By the early months of 1990 I felt I had learned enough about the educators in this book to begin telling their stories. Of course, in the meantime, life has gone on for these teachers, administrators, parents, and students. I have done my best to stay in touch with them while writing this book—dropping in for visits, making phone calls, meeting at conferences. With some of these educators I have continued relationships that cover nearly a decade. With others I have built relationships while working on this project that I hope will last for decades to come.

A few things have changed in these schools since the manuscript first went to the publisher. As might be expected, each of these changes has broadened and deepened the work described in these pages. In every school, in each classroom, the changes made reflect more clearly the agenda of developing citizens prepared to work for democracy in our communities and neighborhoods. In spite of the fact that the official school reform agenda keeps repeating the shopworn calls for more tests, these educators continue their work often unnoticed, but always appreciated by the children and parents they serve.

It's not possible in these few remaining pages to be exhaustive in recounting all that has gone on in these schools since early 1990. But from the vantage point of the summer vacation of 1991, we can look back on the highlights of the past year or so.

You'll still find Bill Elasky, Mick Cummings, and Marcia Burchby teaching at Amesville Elementary. Every year the kids in Bill's class continue to tackle a major project designed to accomplish something worthwhile in the community while integrating the sixth grade curriculum. During the 1989–90 school year Bill's kids took on the task of designing and building a pond/marsh wildlife study area for the school district. It took several tries before they found a suitable spot, but when they located one on the district's high school grounds, the class immediately went to work on soil testing, plant and animal inventories, fund raising, designing boardwalks and fences, and more. This summer, after two years of work, Bill and his kids are putting the final touches on this project that will benefit every student in the community.

Mick Cummings entertained all of Amesville with another of his famous spring rocket launches this year. He added a more detailed look at the physics of rocketry and flight to his curriculum. Though most people are astounded by the daunting task of teaching physics to fourth and fifth graders, Mick just takes it in stride. "Because we are *doing* physics, not just talking about it, I can teach them almost anything."

Marcia has moved to teaching kindergarten, giving her a chance to empower even the youngest learners in the school. Outside of her classroom she has recently begun a project to get books into the hands of every child in the school, called "Amesville Rolling Books." Marcia has used book club memberships to stock a low-cost bookstore on wheels for the school. Open every Wednesday at lunch, the rolling bookstore offers books of every kind at every level, often for a dollar or less. In this school where nearly 40% of the students qualify for free lunches, the bookstore has sold or given away over 2,000 books in its first year. In recognition of her work, the Appalachian reading council presented her with its 1991 Literacy Award.

In the fall of 1989 a major renovation project was completed at Amesville, bringing teachers from both buildings under one roof. When you enter the refurbished building you are greeted by a chart on which anyone can note accomplishments of any student, teacher, or parent. When each sheet is full, it is removed and placed on a hall wall which, by the end of the year, was papered over with glowing comments about kids and their work. These lists add to the wonderful array of student art work, projects, and displays that fill every hall in the building.

Much of this increased activity is due to the work of the staff over the past year to develop and put into place a school mission statement that emphasizes active, participatory learning. This statement calls for the climate of the school to be "child-centered . . . one that encourages ownership, pride, cooperation, creativity, and risk-taking." Of course, putting this mission into practice is harder than just saying it. But to that end the school and district have begun to work out a partnership agreement with neighboring Ohio University's College of Education, focusing on efforts to develop a deeper sense of the school as a community. At the same time that all of these advances are taking place, the voters in the district defeated a school tax levy by a vote of 2 to 1. Faced with a $300,000 operating deficit, administrators are planning cuts, but none that will change the direction the school has taken.

On the other side of Athens County, Joyce Hanenberg, Joette Weber, and Charlotte Newman are continuing their efforts at Chauncey Elementary. Charlotte has moved to fourth grade and there continues to build her curriculum around the interests of her students, not the demands of the textbooks. Joyce now teaches in the Reading Lab, where she can share her love of reading with every child in the school.

Joette still spends two years with her charges. This year they finished second grade with a group and so next year will move over to pick up a new group of first graders. Joette now teaches half time; the other half of her day is taken by Betty Mason, a former Chauncey teacher who has returned to teaching after three years in

Europe. The reason for Joette's move to half time has just celebrated her first birthday.

In Milwaukee, Fratney Elementary continues to thrive in spite of the political chaos that surrounds the city's schools. This year has seen the resignation of Superintendent Robert Peterkin and the move of Assistant Superintendent Deborah McGriff to the helm of the Detroit City Schools. Both were Fratney supporters who cut through much of the bureaucratic red tape that impeded Fratney's early days. But Fratney's success as a school will probably insure its survival. Requests to enroll at Fratney are up, as is student attendance. And Fratney continues to draw the attention of the press and parents as a school that works, reflected in both the quality of its graduates and its connection to the community.

However, Fratney does have its critics among the school system's administration. Perhaps the strongest attack on the school was prompted by the lower than average (but somewhat higher than expected) test scores for students on the district-wide reading tests. Of course, such scores came as no surprise, since students of lower socio-economic class status often do poorly on such tests. Further, since Fratney practices the whole language approach to reading and writing, the students are not accustomed to the type of testing the district uses.

The staff has begun to attack this challenge on two fronts, first by just teaching kids what is not-so-lovingly called "reading-test reading." Recognizing that kids will, for the short tun, frequently be facing such tests, teachers are showing kids how the tests work, how to understand the questions asked, and the proper way to fill in the test forms. On the second front, the staff is researching and developing alternative ways to measure reading success that are consistent with their approach to teaching reading. While they hold little hope that the entire district will soon change its approach to testing, they feel confident they will find more accurate ways to report to parents what their kids are learning.

As mentioned, parental and community involvement and support remains high for Fratney. The community mobilized again this past year to demand long overdue playground improvements. Dozens of parents fought city hall with petitions, pickets, and protests, and now Fratney's children have a safer, more appropriate place to play. What's unfortunate is that parents and teachers have to work so hard for what schools should willingly grant to every child.

Another of the highlights of the past year was an individual award that reflects the quality of work throughout the building. Kindergarten teacher Rita Tenorio was named Wisconsin Elementary Teacher of the Year for 1990–91. Showing devotion to the community in which she works, Rita calls the award "ours," not "mine." "This just reflects the quality of the school, of our community," she claims. "I can only do what I do because we have created a place where good work is possible, as opposed to being unlikely."

At Hubbard Woods Elementary School, Dick Streedain describes the year's agenda: "[It] has been to find ways to become less self-absorbed, to really see how we are connected with the city, to realize that this is part of our world." This began with the parents' interest in the reforms going on in Chicago's public schools. A series of panels and discussions about the changes in the city led to the decision to find one urban school that would become a "partner" with Hubbard Woods. "What we wanted to do was [find] a way to really get to know the city school culture," says Streedain. "We felt the only way to do that was to get to know one school really well."

That school turned out to be Hendricks Academy, a school that serves predominately black children on the city's tough South Side. Throughout the year the principals of both schools (Streedain and Ann Hines of Hendricks) have met to share their work and common concerns. More recently, groups of teachers from each school have met for meals and have visited one another's classrooms. Next on the agenda are student and parent exchanges. Streedain isn't sure where this effort will take him and his staff, students, and parents. But he does know, as he is anxious to point out, that "while there is a lot to be said for finding out about the rain forests, we need to be more aware of what's going on right here in our community—including the city."

Of course, no year goes by at Hubbard Woods without some

sort of celebration. This year it was the celebration of the 75th anniversary of the school. The week-long party featured returning teachers (several over 85 years old) sharing the oral history of the school, as well as visits from past students. In fact, several former students flew in from California just to spend a few days visiting. It's not just a school, it's a community.

John Duffy and Richard Cargill still teach in public high schools in Illinois. (Duffy moved in 1991 to Hinnsdale.) They continue to create classrooms where young people are encouraged to ask good questions, think carefully about what they hear or read, and act on behalf of what they believe. Unfortunately, they work in schools so large that school-wide movement toward the type of engagement students experience in their classrooms seems unlikely. That is not to say that there are not many other good teachers in the schools where they work. But it is still surprising to find such excellence in settings which are clearly not conducive to excellent teaching.

Eliot Wigginton has spent the year celebrating the 25th anniversary of Foxfire. The year was marked by two new books produced by students, *A Foxfire Christmas* and *Foxfire: 25 Years*. The anniversary has also led to a major fundraising program to expand Foxfire's work both locally and nationally. Of course, the magazine continues to appear quarterly and the awards Wigginton earns continue to come in (most notable recent additions are Georgia's Teacher of the Year and a MacArthur Foundation Fellowship—the so-called genius award).

Locally, Foxfire has begun an attempt to turn back to its roots, so to speak. Under the guidance of a former student, a local Foxfire alumni group has been established. After several meetings an agenda has yet to be established, but the momentum is building for finding ways to use Foxfire and its resources to improve the quality of life in Clayton County. Additionally, a local elementary school has become the first school nationally to implement the Foxfire approach to teaching on a school-wide basis. This project, part of the Foxfire Teacher Outreach program, offers yet another opportunity to find ways to make schools work for the good of their communities.

Next year will be a year of changes for Wig as he attempts to go from teaching to teaching about teaching. He will move home to Athens, Georgia, where he will join the Faculty of Education at the University of Georgia, and teach courses for future teachers. His projects will include working with an elementary school that wants to become a Foxfire demonstration school and teaching a ninth grade English class at a local high school. Both schools are his alma maters, the high school having given him, as he puts it, "the opportunity, which I had to accept, of repeating the ninth grade." The program is a one-year commitment that could extend to three years if all goes well. Back in the mountains, George Reynolds and Mike Cook (along with a replacement for Wig) will continue to help young people see the strengths of their own roots and the significance of what they can add to their community.

Dennis Littky continues to brighten and enliven the halls of Thayer Junior and Senior High School in Winchester, NH. He has just finished his tenth year as principal and shows no sign of leaving any time soon. Having survived the one attempt to oust him years ago by a few people taken aback by his relaxed style of leadership and living, he and his staff enjoy widespread support in the community. (Littky's successful struggle to keep his job is best told in the recently released book by Susan Kammeraad-Campbell called, simply, *Teacher*.)

Of course, Thayer's success is not simply the work of a charismatic leader. It is, rather, the product of continued day-to-day efforts of the staff to insure that Thayer graduates are, when all is said and done, young people who will make a difference in the world. To that end, in the time since we last visited Thayer, they have expanded their efforts to give kids real experiences and to make sure every student is connected to the school and its mission.

Dan Bisaccio and his students pulled off one of their most exciting genuine experiences this past year. After several months of studying the environmental importance of the tropical rain forests and the threat to their survival, Dan and his students decided to study the situation first hand. It took some intensive fund-raising, but the trip to Costa Rica was both awe-inspiring and educational for Dan and the team of students who went with him. As a way of paying back the community for its support, the students now share their travels and their research with elementary school students through a slide presentation they have prepared.

Throughout the building now you will also find every teacher on a team, similar to the Spectrum program started five years ago. At each grade level, seven through twelve, a team of teachers works with one group of students for the first four periods of every school day (the last two periods of the day are left open for electives). Unlike the Spectrum program, each team incorporates only one grade level instead of two. However, all of the other features of that early experiment remain in place. Teachers have control of how to best use the morning's four hour block, groups are not organized by ability, and all special education students are mainstreamed into a team setting with a special education teacher to provide support services. The school now looks like what the staff had hoped it would when they first wrote their school mission statement nearly nine years ago. It's been a lot of work, difficult at times, but today, as Littky puts it, "structurally we're beautiful."

Of course, the work of the teachers at Thayer has not gone unnoticed. Through their association with the Coalition of Essential Schools and a variety of media reports on their work, a great deal of attention has focused on Thayer. The staff is thus besieged, by numerous requests for in-service and workshop sessions, many of which they must turn down because these visits interfere with their own teaching. To solve this problem, Littky has secured a grant to produce a series of videotapes on Thayer, featuring teachers at their daily work. These tapes will then be available for cable network broadcast and for loan to other schools and teachers. Further, printed materials will also be available, as will the Thayer staff for phone consultations.

"The real beauty of this plan," Dennis enthusiastically points out, "is that it features teachers at their work. People can see it, not just talk about it. It makes teachers the trainers."

At Central Park East Secondary School, the Spring of 1991 was a time of celebration. On June 21 the first graduating class gathered to present to family, friends, and teachers the products of their six years at CPESS. As we saw earlier, "finishing" at CPESS does not mean merely amassing credits toward a diploma. Rather, each student presents a portfolio of his or her work in fifteen separate areas to a faculty committee (see chapter Five for a full description of these areas), making public presentations of their work in seven of the fields.

Over eighty percent of the senior class finished all their requirements for graduation on time, and virtually all of these graduates are headed for college. The list of institutions that are lucky enough to be receiving these graduates is impressive, including Brown, Smith, Spellman, Virginia Tech, Syracuse, and Cornell. For those who did not finish their work "on time," the good news is that the traditional concepts of school time do not apply here. Instead, students may stay on at CPESS through the summer and into the following year while they finish their work.

The real measure of the success of CPESS is not university attendance, however. It is instead the deep and lasting impression that the teachers and staff have made on their students. A few stories best illustrate this.

Remember the student Herb Rosenfeld described in chapter Four, the young man who was labeled as a special education student, who was told he couldn't learn and that he would never go to college? He is enrolling at Syracuse, the first kid in his family to go to college. It wasn't easy for him, or his teachers. But the CPESS community was supportive enough to make it happen.

Or how about the student who, as part of his work in the Senior Institute, took on organizing a city-wide youth coalition against apartheid in South Africa? When Nelson Mandela visited the United States in 1990, this student found himself on the New York City reception committee. Not only that, he was invited to speak with Mandela at New York's Riverside Church.

Stories like these could be told over and over about the kids who graduate from CPESS. And to make sure that these stories continue to be told, a special birthday party was held in conjunction with the 1991 graduation. In honor of Principal Deborah Meier's 60th birthday, a fund-raising celebration was held in which hundreds of those touched by the work of Debbie and the CPESS educators donated to a fund to help students after they leave CPESS. Whether it be college or trade, kids at CPESS will never be abandoned when they venture forth into the larger world outside the school.

APPENDIX:

Resources for Change

None of the teachers, administrators, or parents we have visited would say that they have gone it alone. Many of them, in fact, know one another and share ideas, insights, and strategies. Just as important, they have read widely, visited other schools, made use of a multitude of resources. To help you think about restructuring your school the following lists of sources and resources are offered as a place to start.

This resource section is divided into three parts: first, a list of organizations that support teachers and schools that are working to restructure; second, books and resources that are tied to particular teaching approaches discussed in the book; finally, the addresses of the schools and teachers you've met in this book, all of whom would be glad to help you in your work and to hear about additional ideas you might have.

ORGANIZATIONS FOR CHANGE

The Institute for Democracy in Education
McCracken Hall
Ohio University
Athens, OH 45701
614-593-4531

Started by the teachers we met in Athens County, Ohio, the institute now has members around the country and in Canada. IDE publishes a journal written and edited by teachers (*Democracy and Education*), holds conferences, offers workshops, and provides resources to teachers. Individuals and/or schools may join the institute or just subscribe to its publications.

The Coalition of Essential Schools
Box 1938
Brown University
Providence, RI 02912
401-863-3384

Begun by Ted Sizer to assist secondary schools in putting into practice the ideas he developed in *Horace's Compromise*, the coalition counts among its members Central Park East and Thayer. Schools may get involved with the coalition through pledging to embrace a "less is more" philosophy.

The Foxfire Teacher Outreach
c/o Hilton Smith
Rabun Gap, GA 30568
404-746-5318

An attempt to reach and support individual teachers who are interested in the Foxfire principles as set out in Wigginton's *Sometimes a Shining Moment*. The outreach effort works through networks that operate from Washington State to New York to Georgia. The outreach effort also publishes a journal, *Hands On*, which chronicles the classroom efforts of teachers involved in experiential learning.

The Center for Collaborative Education
1573 Madison Avenue
New York, NY 10029
212-860-8935

Begun with a donation from Debbie Meier's MacArthur award, the center is located in the same building as Central Park East. The center helps other schools learn from the work at CPESS as well as other progressive efforts in New York City. Additionally, the center is coordinating research projects at several schools on alternatives to standardized testing.

Educators for Social Responsibility
23 Garden Street
Cambridge, MA 02138
617-492-1764

ESR is devoted to developing new approaches to education to meet the demands of the nuclear age. It publishes curricular materials, sponsors workshops, and publishes a journal dealing with issues of participation, decision making, and conflict resolution. It works with both individual teachers and entire schools.

RESOURCES FOR CHANGE

BOOKS ABOUT EDUCATION IN GENERAL THAT DEAL WITH PROGRESSIVE SCHOOL CHANGE

Each of these titles is easily accessible to school people and laymen alike. Together, they offer a broad view of what our schools could become.

Robert Bullough. *The Forgotten Dream of American Public Education*. Ames, Iowa: Iowa State University Press, 1988.

John Dewey. *Experience and Education*. New York: Macmillan, 1938.

John Goodlad and Robert Anderson. *The Non-Graded Elementary School*. Rev. ed. New York: Teachers College Press, 1987.

Sara Lawrence Lightfoot. *The Good High School*. New York: Basic Books, 1983.

Mary Ann Raywid, Charles Tesconi, and Don Warren. *Pride and Promise: Schools of Promise for All the People*. Wesburg, N.Y.: American Educational Studies Association, 1984.

Ted Sizer. *Horace's Compromise*. Boston: Houghton Mifflin, 1984.

BOOKS ABOUT TEACHING IN GENERAL

The works address progressive, democratic approaches to classroom teaching. They are a valuable addition to any educator or parent's library.

Lucy Calkins. *Lessons from a Child*. Portsmouth, N.H.: Heinemann Educational Books, 1983.

Herbert Kohl. *Growing Minds*. New York: Harper & Row, 1984.

Eliot Wigginton. *Sometimes a Shining Moment*. Garden City, N.Y.: Doubleday, 1985.

RESOURCES FOR TEACHING WITH PARTICULAR STRATEGIES

To help teachers who are working on particular changes, several sources are offered in each of the areas below. Only books are listed; a wide variety of articles in each of these areas is available in educational and popular journals.

Whole Language Approaches to Reading and Writing

Judith Newman, ed. *Whole Language: Theory in Use*. Portsmouth, N.H.: Heinemann, 1985.

Donald Graves. *Writing: Teachers and Children at Work*. Portsmouth, N.H.: Heinemann, 1983.

Regie Routman. *Transitions: From Literature to Literacy.* Portsmouth, N.H. Heinemann, 1988.

Nancie Atwell. *In the Middle: Writing, Reading, and Learning with Adolescents.* Portsmouth, N.H.: Boynton/Cook, 1987.
(Note: The entire Heinemann/Boynton-Cook catalogue is excellent in this area.)

Brian Cambourne. *The Whole Story.* New York: Scholastic, 1988.

Developmentally Appropriate Approaches to Early-grades Education

Sue Bredekamp, ed. *Developmentally Appropriate Practice in Early Childhood Programs Serving Children Birth through Age 8.* Washington, D.C.: National Association for the Education of Young Children, 1988.

Cooperative Learning

Robert Slavin. *Cooperative Learning: Theory, Research, and Practice.* Englewood Cliffs, N.J.: Prentice-Hall, 1990.

David Johnson, *Circles of Learning.* Alexandria, Va.: Association for Supervision and Curriculum Development, 1984.

Elizabeth Cohen. *Designing Groupwork.* New York: Teachers College Press, 1986.

Alternatives to Standardized Testing

Kenneth S. Goodman, et al., eds. *The Whole Language Evaluation Book.* Portsmouth, N.H.: Heinemann, 1989.

Sidney Simon and James Bellanca, eds. *Degrading the Grading Myths.* Alexandria, Va.: Association for Supervision and Curriculum Development, 1976.

Fred Newman and Don Archbald. *Beyond Standardized Testing.* Reston, Va.: National Association of Secondary School Principals. 1988.

Journals for Teachers

Each of the following journals and newsletters is directed toward teachers; most are written by classroom teachers as well.

Democracy and Education. Published quarterly by the Institute for Democracy and Education. See IDE's address under "Organizations."

Hands On. Published quarterly by the Foxfire Teacher Outreach. See address under "Organizations."

Rethinking Schools. Published by teachers in the Milwaukee area, the newspaper format journal explores issues of general interest as well as covering local education issues. Contact: 1001 East Keefe Avenue, Milwaukee, WI 53212.

Fairtest Examiner. Focusing mainly on issues of testing reform, this newsletter is an invaluable source on the limits and alternatives to standardized testing. Contact: National Center for Fair and Open Testing, Box 1272, Harvard Square Station, Cambridge, MA 02238.

THE SCHOOLS

Fratney Street Elementary School
3255 North Fratney Street
Milwaukee, WI 53212
Phone: 414-264-4840

Hubbard Woods Elementary School
1110 Chatfield Road
Winnetka, IL 60093
Phone: 708-446-0920

Thayer Junior/Senior High School
43 Parker Street
Winchester, NH 03470
Phone: 603-239-4381

Central Park East Secondary School
1573 Madison Avenue
New York, NY 10029
Phone: 212-860-8935

THE TEACHERS

ATHENS COUNTY, OHIO

Bill Elasky
Marcia Burchby
Mick Cummings
c/o Amesville Elementary School
Amesville, OH 45711
School Phone: 614-448-2501

Joette Weber
Joyce Hanenberg
Charlotte Newman
Chauncey Elementary School
Chauncey, OH 45701
School Phone: 614-797-2323

ILLINOIS

John Duffy
604 South Gunderson Avenue
Oak Park, IL 60304

Richard Cargill
Willowbrook High School
1250 Ardmore
Villa Park, IL 60181

GEORGIA

Eliot Wigginton
Foxfire
Rabun Gap, GA 30568
Phone: 404-746-5318

Notes

Introduction

1. See, for example, National Commission on Excellence in Education, *A Nation At Risk* (Washington, D.C.: Federal Government Printing Office, 1983); Twentieth Century Fund, *Making the Grade* (New York: Twentieth Century Fund, 1983); National Science Foundation, *Educating Americans for the 21st Century* (Washington, D.C.: National Science Foundation, 1983); or Education Commission of the States, *Action for Excellence* (Denver: Education Commission of the States, 1983).
2. Cited in *Education Week*, 4 October 1989, p. 12.
3. Harold Howe, "Remarks on Equity and Excellence in Education," *Harvard Educational Review*, November 1987, p. 201.
4. Quotes in the text, unless otherwise noted, come from interviews with the author.

Chapter 1

1. Since this writing all of the classrooms at Amesville have been gathered under one roof in a renovated building. The displays continue to grace the hallway outside Marcia's classroom.
2. By one estimate an elementary school student will bring home over one thousand worksheets a year in language arts alone.
3. Themes from following years included: "I Respect Myself and My

275

World," "We Care About Each Other," "We Learn the Stories of the World," and "We Made a Difference on the Planet Earth."
4.   On standardized tests the median score is the score above and below which exactly half of the test takers fall. The mean score is the average score for all test takers.

Chapter 2

1.   E. Wigginton, *Sometimes a Shining Moment* (New York: Doubleday, 1985), p. 31.
2.   *Ibid.*, p. 38.
3.   J. Puckett, *Foxfire Reconsidered* (Champaign, Ill.: University of Illinois Press, 1989), p. 94.
4.   Wigginton, *Shining Moment*, p. 37.
5.   Puckett, *Foxfire Reconsidered*, p. 90.
6.   L. G. Page and E. Wigginton, eds., *Aunt Eire: A Foxfire Portrait*, (New York: E. P. Dutton, 1983), pp. 205–206.
7.   Wigginton, *Shining Moment*,, p. 39.
8.   Since this was first written, Iceland has bowed to international pressures and announced a halt to its whaling practices. Cargill's students celebrated the victory as another example of how they make a difference.
9.   A wide range of literature on the factory model of schooling is available. Among the best are D. Tyack and E. Hansot, *Managers of Virtue* (New York: Basic Books, 1982); J. Spring, *Educating the Worker-Citizen* (New York: Longman, 1980); D. Tyack, *The One Best System* (Cambridge: Harvard University Press, 1974); and E. Stevens and G. Wood, *Justice, Ideology, and Education* (New York: Random House, 1987), chapters 6 and 9.

Chapter 3

1.   R. Louv, *Childhood's Future* (Boston: Houghton Mifflin, 1990), p. 337.
2.   I take the concept of communities of memory and hope from the work of Bellah et al., *Habits of the Heart* (New York: Harper & Row, 1985).

Chapter 4

1.   This particular term comes from J. Goodlad in *A Place Called School* (New York: McGraw Hill, 1983). Information on the nature of life in classrooms for the rest of this section comes from Goodlad; also from

Boyer, *High School* (New York: Harper & Row, 1983) and T. Sizer, *Horace's Compromise* (Boston: Houghton Mifflin, 1984).

2. Cuban, *How Teachers Taught* (New York: Longman, 1984), provides an excellent survey of the history of classroom teaching.

3. This pattern is so typical that even a slight deviation from it, the moving of the teacher's desk to one side of the front of the room, was cause for Tracy Kidder to proclaim the teacher he was observing as innovative, See *Among Schoolchildren* (Boston: Houghton Mifflin, 1989), p. 13.

4. Taken from W. B. Lauderdale, *Progressive Education: Lessons from Three Schools* (Bloomington, Ind.: Phi Delta Kappa, 1981), p. 12.

5. R. V. Bullough provides an excellent examination of this reality in chapter 5 of *The Forgotten Dream of American Public Education* (Ames, Iowa: Iowa State University Press, 1988).

6. Boyer, *High School*, p. 16.

7. As I was finishing this book, a story that clearly exemplified the danger of the emphasis on testing was shared with me by a high school teacher in the county where I live. This teacher, inspired by the work of Bill Elasky and others, had his ninth-grade government class deal with current events in order to learn how government worked. In particular, the class focused on the environment and organized proposals to the school board on buying recycled paper, a recycling drive with the county health department, and voter information materials on environmental legislation among numerous other informational and public speaking activities. Everyone—students, parents, and administrators—judged the year a success, with students being more involved in this class than ever before. However, when the students took the standardized state-mandated civics test (including all important questions like the name of the state bird) less than half of the ninth graders passed it. In response, the district is considering changing the curriculum in ways that would eliminate this teacher's projects. Once again the legislated-excellence movement defines a skill, this time citizenship, as a test-taking behavior rather than the ability to actually do something.

8. I am indebted to my friend, Barbara Hays, a teacher of the Developmentally Handicapped at Amesville, Ohio, for this analogy. Her classroom itself is one of the best examples around of the classroom as laboratory.

9. As we will see throughout this discussion of successful school practices, none of them operate in isolation. The building of cooperative groups in the classroom certainly also promotes the sense of community covered in this chapter, just as the nature of the curriculum, discussed in chapter 6, affects the type of classroom work we are discussing here.

10. Wigginton, "Foxfire Grows Up," *Harvard Educational Review* no. 1 (February 1989): 27.

11. It is almost impossible to even list just the best sources in this area. The most recent summary of theory, research, and practice (including an excellent bibliography) is Robert E. Slavin, *Cooperative Learning* (Englewood Cliffs, N.J.: Prentice-Hall, 1990).

Chapter 5

1. See, for example J. D. Hirsch, *Cultural Literacy* (Boston: Houghton Mifflin Co., 1987), Chester Finn and Diane Ravitch, *What Our 17-Year-Olds Know*. (New York: Harper & Row, 1987).

2. For a more detailed description of whole language see the works listed under "Whole Language" in the "Resources for Change" section of the Appendix.

3. Data on tracking and ability grouping come from the most definitive study on this subject to date: J. Oakes, *Keeping Track: How American Schools Structure Inequality* (New Haven, Conn.: Yale University Press, 1985).

4. T. Thompson, "Sneaking Into Class," *Democracy and Education* 4, no. 1. (Fall 1989): 34.

5. J. Hanenberg and J. Weber with Ellen Gerl, "No More Bluejays and Bees," *Democracy and Education* 4, no. 1 (Fall 1989): 28.

6. *Ibid.*, pp. 27–28.

7. Wigginton, *Sometimes a Shining Moment* (Garden City, N.Y.: Doubleday, 1985), pp. 71–72.

8. Of course, there is always the question of how colleges deal with transcripts that do not use grades. CPESS has not found this to be a problem, because of the extensive explanations sent with each student's work.

Chapter 6

1. David Elkind is the foremost chronicler of the dangerous travail of hurrying our children. See his three works: *Miseducation* (New York: Knopf, 1987); *The Hurried Child* (Reading, Mass.: Addison-Wesley, 1981); and *All Grown Up and Noplace to Go* (Reading, Mass.: Addison-Wesley, 1984).

Index

⓪ SIGNET **MENTOR**

FOR YOUR REFERENCE SHELF

(0451)

☐ **NEW AMERICAN DESK ENCYCLOPEDIA.** The comprehensive, one-volume paperback guide that combines information on all major fields of knowledge with up-to-date coverage of the contemporary world scene. With over 14,000 entries. Perfect for home, school, and office. (158180—$7.99)

☐ **SLANG AND EUPHEMISM by Richard A. Spears.** From slang terminology describing various bodily functions and sexual acts to the centuries-old cant of thieves and prostitutes to the language of the modern drug culture, here are 13,500 entries and 30,000 definitions of all the words and expressions so carefully omitted from standard dictionaries and polite conversation. (165543—$6.99)

☐ **THE LIVELY ART OF WRITING by Lucile Vaughan Payne.** An essential guide to one of today's most necessary skills. It illumines the uses—and misuses—of words, sentences, paragraphs, and themes, and provides expertly designed exercises to insure thorough understanding. (627121—$4.99)

☐ **THE BASIC BOOK OF SYNONYMS AND ANTONYMS by Laurence Urdang.** Expand your vocabulary while adding variety to your writing with thousands of the most commonly used words in the English language. Alphabetically arranged for quick and easy use, this indispensable guide includes sample sentences for each word. (161947—$4.99)

Prices slightly higher in Canada.

Buy them at your local bookstore or use this convenient coupon for ordering.

NEW AMERICAN LIBRARY
P.O. Box 999, Dept. #17109
Bergenfield, New Jersey 07621

Please send me the books I have checked above.
I am enclosing $_____ (please add $2.00 to cover postage and handling).
Send check or money order (no cash or C.O.D.'s) or charge by Mastercard or VISA (with a $15.00 minimum). Prices and numbers are subject to change without notice.

Card # _____ Exp. Date _____
Signature _____
Name _____
Address _____
City _____ State _____ Zip Code _____

For faster service when ordering by credit card call **1-800-253-6476**

Allow a minimum of 4-6 weeks for delivery. This offer is subject to change without notice